COALDUST TO STARDUST
PEAKPUBLISH

Jackie Toaduff is the son of a coal miner born in County Durham in the 1930s. He worked down the pit for over twelve years whilst at the same time making a name for himself as a tap and clog dancer. He became British Clog-Dancing Champion, making 17 solo appearances at the Royal Albert Hall, his dancing admired by the Prima Ballerina, Margot Fonteyn. He danced with the likes of Hollywood star, Ginger Rogers and Princess Margaret (and then back to work down the pit the next day).

He and his partner, Roy, enjoyed considerable success onstage and were asked by the War Office to headline several shows abroad for the Combined Services as well as headlining shows in theatres, cabaret and on the QE2.

Jackie has been credited with making clog dancing a spectacle and taking it worldwide. "Jackie demonstrated clog dancing routines at the Royal Ballet Schools (Senior & Junior) and one outcome of these visits was a French ballet, "La Fille Mal Gardee", incorporating some of the elements of the North country garland and the clog dance steps.

More recently, and several generations later, the North-East style of clog-dancing, which Jackie introduced to the Royal Ballet, has manifested itself, with all Jackie's rhythmical skill and vitality too, in the movie 'Billy Elliott'.

Acknowledgements

My grateful thanks to Nora Sutton whose help, encouragement and incredible patience made this book possible. I am deeply indebted to her. I thank Nora for spurring me on to finish the book when I thought I was unable to carry on, without her I would not have done it.

Also I thank my friend and manager Colin Edwardes for the use of his diaries, photo albums, scrap books and programmes he had kept from day one of our meeting, many moons ago.

To Margaret O' Brien, Ava Astaire and Cunard QE 2 Captain Bob Arnott who wrote reviews for my book.

To Mike Cheadle for his time and patience in helping me set up the format and to my dear and loving friends too many to mention individually who believed in me and urged me on to write my memoirs.

Thanks also to Stuart Hammond, Joan and Gordon Hampshire and Samantha Jones for listening to my words, my doubts and fears when writing my book, and to Mike Hennessey and Elaine Blaire for introducing me to my publishers.

COALDUST
TO
STARDUST

JACKIE TOADUFF

peakpublish

Peakpublish
An imprint of Peak Platform
Hassop Station
Bakewell
Derbyshire
DE45 1NW

First published by Peakpublish 2010

Printed in England

A CIP catalogue record for this book is available from the
British Library

ISBN: 978-1-907219- 08-5 (Hbk)
ISBN: 978-1-907219 -14-6 (Pbk)
www.peakplatform.com

I dedicate this book to my stage partners,
Colin Edwardes and Roy,
for all the wonderful times we shared
and who took me from Black and
White into glorious Technicolor.

Contents

1

First Steps

"Twins, Mrs. Toaduff. Yes, you're definitely going to have twins."

That was the last thing she wanted to hear. Sarah and Tom Toaduff already had three sons, Billy, Ronnie and Tommy, and the thought of two more babies on the way was the most devastating news to them. Life wasn't easy in the coal-mining town of Stanley, County Durham in the early 1930s. Tom was a coal-face worker at the Billy Pit in Stanley; he was an extremely hard-working man, even though he suffered with his chest almost continuously and endured back problems. Both of these ailments were commonplace among the miners there because they often had to work in coal seams which were only fourteen inches high. To help make ends meet, Sarah took in laundry, as well as knitting for the neighbours and making mats and woollen rugs for them out of cuttings of old socks and jumpers.

Her younger sister Ellen had married John Pattinson Kirk, a local businessman who was moderately well-off. When Ellen and John saw how distressed Sarah was at the thought of two more mouths to feed, they came to the rescue and offered to take the twins at birth and bring them up as their own. However, on 17th of May 1933, the doctor's words were proved wrong, as I was the only baby - just me -

no twin brother or sister. Apparently, my mother had a very difficult time bringing me into the world and nearly died in the process. This caused her to change her mind about keeping me. She told Ellen that she hadn't the heart to give her baby boy away after all but said that she would like to name him John Pattinson, after Ellen's husband. Incidentally, it was little wonder that twins had been diagnosed because, by all accounts, I was a very large baby and a great kicker in the womb. My mother was often heard to remark later in life that I could dance long before I was born.

Like many of the people in our neighbourhood, my parents were no strangers to sadness. One of my mother's brothers was murdered but the crime was never solved. A short time before my birth, there was a pit explosion in Stanley, which took the lives of many miners, including my mother's fifteen-year-old brother, who was burnt to death. Ironically, another of her brothers, who hitherto had never had a day's absence from the pit, did not go to work that morning as he had severe toothache and thus avoided being killed.

I clearly remember that this pit disaster was the main talking point among the locals for years. They used to say that 20,000 people turned out to attend the miners' funerals, which lasted for three days. They never tired of reminding each other that 168 men were killed in the Burns Pit disaster — exactly the same number, they used to say, as dots on a set of dominoes and almost every family in South Moor, the district of Stanley where I lived, lost one or more relatives.

There were other explosions later, of course, and if the hooting of the pit-buzzer sounded during a shift, the first reaction was an uncanny and uneasy silence, as it usually meant that there had been an accident or a death at the colliery. Mining was certainly a hazardous, underpaid occupation in those days.

As a child, I can still remember my father coming in from work and stripping down to climb into the bath. There were cuts and bruises all over his arms and back. More often than not, he would have been working in a wet seam, so his shirt and shorts had to be dried in front of the coal-fire, ready to wear the next morning.

There wasn't much money around in South Moor but there was certainly a strong community spirit there. Apart from the odd argument in the back street, which rarely developed into anything serious, people generally got on well together. They hardly ever locked their doors, and it was common practice for neighbours to run in and out of each other's houses, asking if they could borrow half a cup of sugar, half a glass of milk or even a crust of bread. One neighbour who stands out in my memory used to turn up at our house every Friday without fail, because she knew that we ate fish and chips on that day; she always asked the same question - could she please have the fish skins for her tea.

My mother's infectious sense of humour and bubbly personality ensured that she had a wide circle of friends. She could certainly tell a joke as professionally as any comedian on the stage or radio; I'm sure that, had she been a young woman today, she would be performing on television. All the kids loved her too. I used to bring home all my playmates to listen to her sing songs in what she called her 'foreign' languages; she didn't know any foreign words of course but she used to sing those strange sounds with such confidence that we all thought they were foreign. She'd enthral us all with songs in French, German, Spanish, Zulu and even Red Indian. Everyone thought she was unbelievably clever and I was always so proud of her.

Nevertheless, we all knew never to cross her. She could put people in their place at the drop of a hat. Her temper was famous in our house and more often than not, I was at the receiving end of it. How I remember those good hidings! On one occasion when I was about five years old, she was wall-papering, when an ice-cream seller came into our street with his horse and cart.

I ran in and asked, "Ma, can I have an ice-cream?"

"No," she replied. "I'm busy. Can't you see that?"

"Please, ma," I begged.

"No," she said firmly. "I've no money." This was probably true.

3

"I could ask Nora Duffy for you, if you like..."

She interrupted me, shouting, "Jackie, go, just go!"

And I honestly thought she meant that I could ask Nora.

I went round to Nora's house; she said she didn't have much money to spare but she could lend my mother two shillings. By the time the money was in my hand, the ice-cream cart had gone from our street but I met a pal of mine, Alfie Taylor, who said, "He'll be a long way off now, Jackie, but don't worry. I'll walk with you down to Bove's ice-cream shop, if you like."

"Would you like an ice cream as well, Alfie?" I asked when we were in the shop.

"Oh, yes," he said.

The pair of us were walking back home, enjoying our ice-cream cones, when we noticed that the local fruit shop had a window full of delicious-looking strawberries. As I still had some money left, I couldn't resist going into the shop and buying a punnet.

When I arrived home, the back door was open and I walked in unnoticed, carrying my strawberries. At that moment, I heard Nora's voice coming from the other room: "Well, I did think it was very strange, you borrowing money, Sarah, but I thought you must have run out of wall-paper or maybe some wall-paper paste."

"Well, I hadn't," my mother said, "and when that lad comes back here, he's going to get such a bloody good hiding, he'll wish he'd never been born."

I crept quietly into the bathroom, sat on the floor and, out of sheer terror, started cramming the strawberries into my mouth, leaving the stalks scattered all over the floor.

When my father came home from work, I heard my mother saying, "Have you seen our Jackie out there?"

"No, I haven't," replied my father. "Why?"

Then, from my hiding place, I listened while she told him the whole tale.

When I was finally discovered, still trembling in the midst of discarded strawberry stalks, I owned up to my crime. As I began telling her that I'd not only bought myself an ice-cream but one for Alfie as well and then, on top of that, the strawberries, I could see her face growing redder and redder. I'll never forget the punishment that followed.

Ours was a district where children could wander into other people's houses in the neighbouring streets and usually be made welcome. One of the houses where I liked to make myself at home was Mrs. Armstrong's. Her daughter Sylvia was having private tap-dancing lessons from a man called Jocka Richardson. Nobody seemed to mind me, a mere five-year old lad, going in and sitting down, watching the lessons, but I was fascinated and looked on in amazement with my mouth shut tight so that I could take it all in without being noticed.

I'm not sure how old Jocka would be at that time, but I remember him as a small, slim man in a flat cap, smoking and tap-dancing at the same time; I can still hear the sound he made with those brown, shiny tap-shoes. To this day, no dancer has impressed me more.

After watching each lesson, I'd spend the rest of the week trying to copy Jocka's style and his sound. I had no tap-shoes of course so this meant that I had to tap harder to make the same sound. The noise used to drive my mother crazy. "Will you stop that, our Jackie!" she'd shout at me. "You'll wear the bloody oilcloth out."

But I couldn't stop, so I'd go outside and continue in the back yard. Pat Boyle was another tap-dancing girl in our street and she used to practise in her back yard as well. One day, while I was standing at her gate watching her, I asked, "Can I try your taps on, Pat, to see if I can dance?"

"Okay," she said, "you can try them. Only for a minute, mind."

And, although those shoes were slightly too big for me, that was it. It was the first time I'd ever worn tap-shoes and I was hooked. How I loved the sound that they made and I knew that all I wanted in life was my very own pair.

One day, when I was in Mrs. Armstrong's house, watching the weekly dance lesson, Sylvia was having great problems trying to master a particularly intricate step. However hard she tried, she just couldn't grasp it.

"Come on, lass," Jocka said. "It's a bit tricky but not too difficult. I bet even little Jackie here could do it."

"Yes, I can," I piped up. "At least, I think I can," and I promptly stood up and performed.

"Who taught you that?" asked an amazed Jocka.

"You did, Jocka," I replied. "I've been watching you." He was really taken by surprise and, at the end of the lesson with Sylvia, he walked home with me. He called to see my mother to tell her that I was a natural dancer and he suggested that I should become one of his pupils.

"No, thank you very much," my mother said. "We don't want any dancers in this house. He's a lad and when he's old enough, he's going down the pit just like his father. Dancing is for lasses; lads don't dance."

"I'm no lass," Jocka said, "and I dance - and haven't you ever heard of Fred Astaire?"

"Of course I have," she retorted, "but he's not from around here. His father didn't work as a pit-man."

So that was it. I wasn't to dance. My mother was adamant.

I went to watch Sylvia's lesson the following week and Jocka said, "I'll still teach you some steps, but don't tell your ma, okay? Just keep it quiet."

In next to no time, I was happily tap-dancing to the tune of I'll be your Sweetheart and I could sing it too.

One day, I went round to Mrs. Armstrong's as usual but Sylvia was sitting at the table reading a book and there was no sign of Jocka.

Puzzled, I asked, "Where's Jocka, Mrs. Armstrong?"

"I'm afraid Jocka won't ever be coming back, pet," said Sylvia's mother in hushed tones.

"Not coming? Why?"

"He's dead, I'm sorry to say."

"Dead?" I just couldn't take it in. I was stunned because I had really liked and admired Jocka. With tears streaming down my face, I ran home and sat miserably on our cold, grey front step.

That night in bed, I also realised that Jocka's death probably meant the shattering of my own secret dream. I just didn't know of any other dance teachers in our area.

2

Gotta Sing, Gotta Dance!

In the 1930s, holidays were unheard of in our area of South Moor, but we did have this once-a-year day trip to the seaside for all the children and their families. As we stepped on to the buses, every child was given a paper bag containing a few pennies, a small bar of chocolate, two or three sweets and perhaps an apple. We'd set off for South Shields or Whitley Bay – always a favourite of mine with its Spanish City fairground, but the outing I recall most vividly was the day we all went to Redcar.

As we were driving along the promenade, gazing at Redcar's glorious stretch of beach, I spotted a poster advertising the 'Leon Dodd Show with Children's Talent Contest'. That was it! I couldn't think of anything I wanted to do that day other than get off the bus and enter the contest.

It seemed ages before the buses stopped but when they finally drew to a halt and all the families had found spots on the sand, I was off. I started running down the beach in the direction of Leon Dodd's stage, without so much as a word to my folks or anyone. It was a long way off but nothing was going to stop me performing.

In no time at all, I was on that stage, singing *I'll Be Your Sweetheart* at the top of my voice and following it with a fast waltz tap-danced to the same tune.

"What did you say your name was, sonny?"

"Jackie Toaduff," I answered.

I was told I had won that heat and now had to sit down on one of the deck chairs, as I would be appearing in another heat during the next performance "in fifteen minutes' time, folks." Collecting boxes were then passed round the people who had been watching on the sands.

I can't remember exactly how many times I had to repeat my act that day but it was quite a few. After each performance, Leon would ask my name and announce that I had won. Finally, after winning several heats, I was declared the over-all winner and my prize was a blow-football game, which was to be presented to me on stage, after one more chorus of *I'll Be Your Sweetheart.*

As I was coming to the end of my final performance of this song, however, my heart sank. My mother and father had arrived on the scene and were now approaching me, looking absolutely livid. No sooner had I stepped down from the stage, clutching my prize close to my chest, than my mother grabbed me firmly by the arm and started shouting at me, telling me that I'd completely ruined everybody's outing as they had to spend the whole day looking for me.

"But look, ma, I've won…" I began.

In one fell swoop, she snatched the game from me and hit me on the head with it.

"Eh, don't do that, missus," Leon Dodd protested. "Your lad's a very talented young man."

"Oh, he is, is he?" she replied. "And I suppose you think you're bloody talented as well, keeping him here like this. Good God, he's only six. You should be locked up," and she threw the blow-football box at him.

"Oh, don't be mad," another lady joined in. "If he was my son, I'd put him in a glass case."

"Well, I'm thinking of putting him in a bloody cage," my mother retorted as she dragged me off in tears, leaving my broken game behind.

When I got back to our crowd, everybody started telling me what a bad lad I'd been, going off without telling anyone. So for the rest of the day I was down in the dumps because I was in the black books of all and sundry. It was only on the bus journey home that attention was diverted from my disgraceful behaviour, when I was saved by Mrs. Boyle. Always a cheery soul, she soon put everyone in jovial mood with her well-known comic songs. She opened with:

> Oh, the driver's got the wind up,
> Oh, the driver's got the wind up,
> Oh, the driver's got the wind up
> But he cannot put the wind up me

and soon my misdeeds were forgotten. It was the end of a very eventful day!

In 1939, war was declared and many of the young men in our neighbourhood, including my eighteen-year brother Billy, were sent their calling-up papers. Billy was drafted to the Royal Marines. All the children were convinced that Stanley was an important part of the war because, in a very short time, we started to hear the air-raid sirens during most nights. There was an air-raid shelter in our garden but I can honestly say I don't remember any of us ever using it. Whenever the warning siren sounded, we'd wrap up in warm clothes and stand outside in the dark, fascinated by the searchlights criss-crossing in the sky. Sometimes, when a plane zoomed overhead, my father would say quite knowledgeably, "Oh yes, that one's a Jerry, all right. I can tell by the noise the engine's making."

And all along the street, people used to stand on their doorsteps, calling to each other in the dark.

"Oh look, they've got a plane in the searchlight," I remember someone once shouting. "They'll be bombing Newcastle and Consett tonight, you'll see. They're getting closer to us all the time."

It was quite scary and even though I was just a child, I hated those air-raid sirens. It was always a relief to hear the sound of the all-clear.

But for most of the time in the early part of the war, life went on as usual for me, going to school, playing in the street with friends and getting into minor scrapes – all part and parcel of every young boy's life in those days. Even though I no longer had the benefit of Jocka's tuition, this did not prevent me from performing. Joe Platten, my best school pal and most enthusiastic supporter at that time, used to organise impromptu concerts in neighbouring backyards, with a makeshift stage in front of the coal-house and an audience of cheering boys and girls who sat on the steps.

There were two adults from that period who stand out clearly in my memory. The first was Grandma Savage. In truth, the Savages were no relations of mine. My own grandparents were dead and buried long before I'd been born, so Grandma and Grand-dad Savage became my 'adopted' grandparents and they played an important part in my early life. If I'd been their own grandchild, they couldn't have loved me more. Looking back, I seemed to have spent more time with them than I did with my parents. When I was five, they bought me my first birthday cake – iced in a peachy-orange colour, with my name and number 5 on it and five candles. I also remember the time when my older brother Ronnie became seriously ill with spinal meningitis and was taken to hospital. The bedroom that I had always slept in with my brothers Ronnie and Tommy had to be fumigated and sealed, so I stayed with Grandma Savage and her family for several weeks.

Coming home from school one day when I was eight, I was met by Grandma Savage, who was walking from our house with the local midwife. She smiled and told me that there was a big surprise waiting for me at home. "You've got a new baby sister," she said.

I hadn't even known that my mother had been pregnant, but I raced home and was greeted by a strong smell of Dettol.

"Go out and play for a little while, Jackie," I was told, "and when your ma's feeling a bit better, we may let you see the baby."

We were all overjoyed, but no one was as happy as my mother. She was over the moon, as she'd often been heard to remark that she'd love to have a little girl. There was no question of this baby being unwanted. It became clear that my sister, who had been christened Norma, was rapidly becoming the apple of my mother's eye and I realised that my nose was being well and truly pushed out – not that it had ever been in very much in the first place!

The other grown-up I remember with great affection was one who had a tremendous influence on me both at that time and later. Her name was Mrs. Allison, known to everyone as 'Tiny'. She was only just over five feet tall with platinum blonde hair and she looked for all the world like the famous ice-skating movie star, Sonja Henie. Tiny was a dance teacher and she used to put on live Sunday night concerts with her troupe 'Tiny Allison and her Tiny Tots' at the Arcadia Cinema. One Sunday night, I was lucky enough to go to one of these performances and was spellbound from beginning to end. Tiny was an incredibly talented dancer and I was dazzled by the lights, the costumes, the music and, of course, by the troupe of dancing children.

Just by chance, I spotted her walking up the street a couple of days after the show; I can see her now, in a blue rain-cloak with a hood falling at the collar. Tiny was a brisk walker but I was determined to talk to her so I was almost running to keep up.

"Hello, Tiny," I said, "I saw you on Sunday night at the Arcadia. I think you're a smashing dancer."

"Do you think so? That's nice of you to say so."

"I can dance, you know," I said breathlessly, "and I can sing too."

"Can you? Well, that's good, pet," she said, still walking fast. "Have you got a dance teacher?"

"Jocka Richardson," I answered, "but he's dead now."

"Oh yes, I knew Jocka. He was an excellent dancer."

"Where do you live, Tiny?"

She told me.

I said, "I'd love to join your dancing class, only my mother wouldn't let me," and I proceeded to tell Tiny the whole tale about my secret lessons.

"Oh, that's a shame," she sympathised, just as we were reaching her house. "Why don't you come and see me and my troupe at the Arcadia in a fortnight? I'm sure you'll enjoy the show. It's going to be very good."

On the way home, I felt really pleased with myself that I'd actually spoken to Tiny Allison. I kept thinking about the coming show and fervently hoping that I could not just be in the audience but also be performing on the stage!

The next day, I just couldn't help myself. I went round to Tiny's house and knocked on her door. It was Tiny's mother who answered.

"Is Tiny in?" I asked.

"Yes," replied her mother. "What do you want her for?"

"Well," I said, "I want to sing for her and dance as well."

She called to Tiny, "There's a little lad here who wants you."

Tiny came to the door, and smiled as she recognised me. Then she led me into her front room. "Well, what do you want to sing for me?"

"*When They Sound the Last All-clear,*" I answered and started to sing.

"Stop just a minute," she said with a broad smile on her face. She walked out of the room and I could hear her saying to her mother, "Just come and hear this little lad singing."

"Start again, pet," said Tiny, and I sang it through to the end this time.

"And what else do you know?"

I sang *Rosa Day*, a popular song of the day and I did my waltz tap at the same time as singing.

"That's grand," Tiny said, "and I'd love to put you in one of my concerts but I can't - not without your mother's permission. Why don't you go home and ask her if she'll let you join the troupe? I'd give anything to have you in it."

I ran home and breathlessly blurted out where I'd been.

"Oh, bloody hell," said my mother, "he's been at it again. No, you can't join the troupe. Tap-dancing's only for little lasses. Everybody will be laughing at you."

"No, they wouldn't, ma. Honest, they wouldn't."

"Don't be so daft, you silly lad. You can't join a dance school. You should have been a little girl, you should."

The next day, I called round to Tiny's house again. Her pianist, Joyce Stone, the local MP's daughter, happened to be there, so this time I sang my songs with Joyce at the piano. It sounded wonderful to me because I'd never sung with a piano backing before.

"You can go on stage a week on Sunday, if you like," smiled Tiny. "Was everything all right with your ma, then?"

"No, she won't let me but please, Tiny, please put me on. My mother won't find out because she never goes out on a Sunday night. The neighbours come in and they play cards for pennies all night, so she'll not know anything about it."

Tiny, her mother and Joyce seemed to be as keen as I was to get me on that show. They went into the kitchen to have a chat about me and then Tiny came back

"Okay," she said, "you can go on if you're sure that your mother won't find out."

"She won't, honest," I said. "She never goes out."

On the Sunday night of the concert, I slipped out of our house, knowing full well that I was safe because the 'card school' was already in full progress. Where my stage clothes came from I don't recall, but I do remember that I wore a white blouse and blue velvet shorts and some tap shoes that Tiny had brought me from somewhere.

Tommy Mounter was the compère and when he announced me, he told the audience that I was making my very first appearance on the stage. I walked on and sang *Rosa Day*, dancing it in the new way that Tiny had quickly taught me in her front room. I came off with the applause ringing in my ears, and then I was sent back on to sing *When They Sound the Last All-clear*. I sang it through and at the end, quite unrehearsed, I shouted to the audience, "Come on, all join in now!" and the whole cinema sang with me.

"Good lad," they all called out, clapping as hard as they could at the end. Then Tiny made me go back on stage and take a bow. The audience was still applauding when I walked back on and so, to everyone's amusement, I sang the song again. As I walked off for the last time, I'd never felt happier in my life. Standing in the wings was Tiny, who put her arms round me and said, "Ah, that was lovely, Jackie, really lovely."

When I arrived home, I slipped quietly upstairs. The card game was still in progress and nobody had any idea that I had been on the stage and a hit too. Nobody, that is, until the next day, when some of

15

the neighbours came to tell my mother how good I'd been the night before.

"Our Jackie was in no show last night," my mother said.

"Yes, he was. He was great. Why, weren't you there, Sarah?"

"No, I tell you he was here in bed all last night."

"No, he was definitely at the Arcadia."

"Well, what did he sing then? What did he wear?"

When I came home from school that day, all hell broke loose. I was met at the door with a crack across the head, as my mother launched into a scathing attack on my disobedience and naughtiness.

"And don't you ever," (wallop) "ever," (wallop) "ever do that again," (wallop, wallop, wallop) she shouted finally and then sent me outside.

I must add at this stage that my mother wasn't a bad mother – just the opposite, but the fact that she couldn't make me see her point of view about dancing really infuriated her.

I ran down the street sobbing and knocked on Grandma Savage's door. Through my tears, I told her all about appearing on stage. She listened quietly and then, seeing how terrified I was about going home, she put her coat on.

"Come on, Jackie. I'll talk to your ma," she said.

"Wait for me," joined in Grand-dad Savage. "I'm coming with you."

Once inside our house, Grandma Savage set about calming my mother.

"Look, Sarah, don't stop him," she pleaded. "I think you're wrong to do this. You ought to let him join that dancing troupe.

16

Everybody's been saying how good he was. If it makes the lad happy, let him do it. Go on, tell him it's okay."

"I'm not paying for any lessons," said my mother stubbornly. "I just can't afford any."

At this point, Grand-dad Savage settled the matter. "Well, we'll pay for the lad's lessons," he said firmly. So that was it. My mother gave in and I was able to join the Tiny Allison dance classes.

When my brother Billy came home on leave, he made me my first pair of taps from some aluminium he'd found. He cut the toe-taps to size and made some for the heels as well. I remember that he put two farthings in each heel to make a jingle sound. I couldn't wait to try them on so, as soon as they were finished, I ran into the back yard and tried a couple of steps on the cement. Magic, simply magic! Now I had the shoes and the dance teacher. I was the proudest lad in Stanley as I walked to Tiny's dance class with my new shoes in a small case, which I still own to this day.

At that first lesson, I think I was the only lad in the class with about sixty girls. Joe Platten, who came along with me for moral support, sat at the back of the hall and watched. We all seemed to get on well together, although I didn't have much time for socialising – I was too busy learning steps from everyone. I remember that there was another lad, Brian Kennedy, who joined just after me with his sister Dorothy, who was an excellent dancer. Brian's cousin, Lucy Kennedy was also in the troupe. She was billed in Tiny's show as 'Stanley's Vera Lynn'. Eventually, I had billing too, as 'The Entertainer – Jackie Toaduff'; later, I was variously billed as 'Jackie Toaduff - the Great Entertainer' or 'Stanley's Wonder Boy' or 'Stanley's Very Own Fred Astaire'.

When I wasn't at school, my life now started to revolve round dancing and singing. I loved performing so much that I wanted to be in everything. Tiny had to tell me laughingly, "You can't be on the stage all the time, Jackie, you know." When she was with her friends, she'd smile and say, "I sometimes think that Jackie would do anything I asked him to on stage. In fact, if I told him to break his neck while performing, he'd try to do it!"

17

For some of the shows, Lucy Kennedy and I were billed as 'The Singing Sweethearts, Jackie and Lucy'. Tiny taught me the harmony of *Let the Rest of the World Go By* so that I could sing with Lucy. The only drawback was that, at first, I was very shy about holding Lucy's hand on stage. I even blushed just to look at her.

"Listen, Jackie," Tiny coaxed, "you're supposed to be sweethearts. You've got to look as though you're in love with her."

But every time I looked at Lucy, I wanted to laugh because I was so embarrassed.

The first night we performed that song, Tiny was in the wings, miming to me to put my arm around Lucy but I couldn't bring myself to do it.

"Go on, put your arm round her," Tiny was mouthing.

In the end, I thought I had better do it because I knew that Tiny would be really annoyed with me if I didn't, so I pulled Lucy towards me and very awkwardly put my arm round her. How the audience laughed and cheered! Then Lucy and I laughed too and we had to start the song all over again, much to the amusement of everyone - except Tiny, of course, as it wasn't considered very professional to laugh at yourself on stage.

Gradually, I started being referred to as 'Happy Jackie Toaduff' and happy I truly was now that I was a featured pupil in Tiny's group of young entertainers. There were plenty of concerts, one nearly every other week, with titles like *Salute the Soldier*, *Wings for Victory* or some other patriotic theme. As I became better known, I was invited to take part in other people's variety shows too, which I thought was marvellous, especially if my name was up there in print on the posters.

It took my mother quite some time before she made up her mind to see me perform on the stage. When she eventually did, she didn't give me one word of praise or encouragement although, according to Grandma Savage, she brushed away a few tears from her eyes while

I was performing my solo turns. All my mother said to me, however, was, "It was a good show. I don't know where Tiny gets all her patience from, teaching you kids."

In those early days, I loved going to the cinema and, of all the films I saw, musicals were my favourite. Those Fred Astaire-Ginger Rogers films fascinated me and, once outside the cinema, I would tap-dance my way home, imitating their complicated routines. I also loved movies starring Ruby Keeler and the Busby Berkeley Spectaculars, and all those glamorous stars - Betty Grable, Alice Faye, Marlene Dietrich, June Allyson, Margaret O'Brien and the Andrews Sisters. Little did I know then that I, a coal-miner's son from a little pit town in the north east of England would one day not only meet my idols but, in many cases, become close friends with them and live in their Hollywood mansions – but more about that later.

3

Going Down, Coming Up

I was really happy when one of my school pals, Ronnie Brunskill, moved into our street with his parents, two brothers and little sister Joyce. In a way, Ronnie became my passport to freedom in the evenings as I'd always been petrified of the dark, but being with Ronnie meant that I had no fears any more. We often used to play in the streets at night and we always went carol singing at Christmas. Ronnie didn't have much of a singing voice but I used to make up for the pair of us. We were enthusiastic but we weren't always welcome.

"Go away," some people would yell from inside their houses or, "you're too early," or even, "run off or we'll send the dogs after you."

We'd always shout back, "Merry Christmas, Scrooges! Merry Christmas, humbugs!" and laugh all the way to the next house to try our luck.

One year, Ronnie's father took Ronnie and me for a week's holiday in the country. I was excited because it was my first week away from my home town. We stayed with Ronnie's Aunt Mary and Uncle Jack Richardson in Castle Bolton, next door to Tom Mecker's farm near Ripon. Ronnie and I lost no time at all in getting to know the local girls, including Tom's daughter Mary and her friend.

One day, the four of us were larking about in the fields when we were spotted by Mary's dad, who bawled out, "keep off my daughter, you two young buggers," and he started chasing after us, brandishing a big stick. "I'll kill the pair of you."

"Run for your life, Jackie," shouted Ronnie. "He's got a gun." We'd never moved so fast – just like a couple of Olympic champions.

"Jump over that wall," Ronnie called. We did and promptly landed in a muddy pigsty full of pigs grunting and grovelling all around us. What a mess we were in! We were convinced that Ronnie's Aunt Mary would be really furious but, fortunately for us, she couldn't stop laughing as we got out of our stinking clothes and into the bath.

When we were fifteen years old, both Ronnie and I left school. He was a couple of months older than I was and started work at the Louisa Colliery at the Easter break and I started at the same place in the summer. I left school on the Friday and went to the colliery with Ronnie at four o'clock on the following Monday morning. We were what was called surface miners, working on the long conveyor belts, where the tubs of coal that came up to the surface from the pit were tipped over. The coals would come tumbling noisily down on to the belts and it was our job to pick out all the stones. Then we had to throw these stones down a shoot and into the wagons below us.

It might sound an easy job but, at the end of every shift, our hands would be cut and bleeding. We were supposed to wear gloves but I could never get used to them as they always seemed to be a size too big for me and I couldn't grip the stones. If we missed the shoot, the stones would accumulate on the ground all around us and after a while we'd have to stop the conveyor in order to shovel them up. I have to admit that I found that work very hard as I was only a skinny little lad, weighing no more than eight stones. Sometimes, I used to wonder just how much more difficult the work would be when I eventually had to go down the mine - for down I'd surely have to go, just like my father and brothers before me. There wasn't much choice for me. It was either the pit or National Service in the army for two years.

The war was over by this time and shows were few and far between, so I left Tiny's troupe and gave up my singing and dancing in public. After what seemed a very short time as a surface worker, I was asked to go for six weeks' training in order to prepare for working below. There I was taught all about the pits and instructed in the dangers I might have to face as a pitman. If truth be told, I was dreading the day I eventually had to go down. The only consolation was that the pay was better.

When that day came, I didn't even have my pal Ronnie with me for company as he'd just been promoted to another job on the surface, so I started on my own. My mother woke me at half past three. "Jackie, come on. Get up," she called. "I've made you some tea." She'd made up my 'bait' as well – strawberry-jam sandwiches without butter - I hated butter - and a bottle of water. The sandwiches were put in a tin container because it was common knowledge that the rats down the pit would get at them if they were wrapped just in paper.

As I write this, I can still re-live the emotions running through my mind on that morning. I still had not got over my fear of being alone in the dark and now, here I was, having to walk about a mile down to the pit, not only in the dark but past the cemetery as well.

"Don't be so daft," my parents said, when I confessed my fears to them. "You're a man now. What the hell is there to be frightened of? Who do you think is going to touch you, anyway? Nobody! The dead can't harm you. Just walk in the middle of the road."

"I'll watch you down to the bottom of the street," my mother said after I'd drunk my tea, "and when you get to the main road, you'll hear plenty of other men walking."

She was right. I could hear the footsteps of others walking in front of and behind me in the dark. Nevertheless, that first day I ran like the wind past the graveyard; in fact, I can't remember a single occasion when I didn't run.

When I reported for work, I was fitted out with a helmet, a hard-hatted lamp-cap, which had the light fixed to the front and I carried a battery behind me. They also gave me a safety lamp, which I was told I had to keep with me at all times for two reasons – first, in case the one on my cap failed and secondly, to detect gas. I was instructed to sit and wait at the cage-top until somebody was ready to accompany me down to the pit. As I watched the miners entering the cage, I can honestly say I couldn't have been more frightened if I'd been on my way to the gas chamber or the electric chair. To a man, they all seemed to have sad faces, as they moved in slowly and silently, about eight at a time. The cage closed with a slam. A bar pushed against it and down they hurtled out of sight. A few minutes later, another eight would descend.

"Oh, my God, it's going to be my turn next," I thought to myself and I started shaking like a leaf.

"Come on, Jackie lad, let's be having you," a jocular voice called out. "You'll soon get used to this routine. Do you know, I took a trainee down with me last week and he fainted at the bottom. He was a real softy, he was."

If I'd dared, I'd have burst into tears there and then but I just gritted my teeth and braced myself. The cage door closed noisily and down I dropped, almost as fast as lightning. I felt as though my stomach was coming up into my mouth.

"Now that didn't hurt, did it?" I was asked. "Are you okay?"

"Oh, yes, I'm fine," I lied.

"Who've we got here then?" the man at the bottom of the shaft asked. "It's not Jackie Toaduff, is it? I didn't think we'd ever see you down a pit, lad. I thought you'd have been in one of those London shows by now."

I was quite taken aback when I looked round me. There were electric lights, which I hadn't expected, and it was much more spacious than I'd imagined. The other miners were all very friendly and helpful. My first job was right there at the pit bottom, coupling the empty tubs together, ready for them to be taken to the pit-face where they would be filled and sent up to the surface.

Looking back, I find it hard to believe that I actually worked down the pit for eleven years. I didn't particularly like the job but it wasn't all doom and gloom and sometimes I think it held me in good stead in later years. I had some great companions down there, very sociable and humorous, always ready for a laugh. I often think back and have a little chuckle at some of the things we did.

One of the funniest characters I met there was 'Jinx' Harrison. He used to tell us all kinds of tales, most of which he'd probably made up. But one that was definitely true was about the Sunday morning he'd taken his dog for a walk. As they were strolling past the ash tips, the dog uncovered the body of a naked woman. At first, Jinx thought it was a tailor's dummy but, on taking a closer look, he realised it was a human corpse. He made great haste to the local police station to report his find.

"Now, Mr. Harrison, think carefully. Was it you or was it the dog that saw the body first?" he was asked by the police officer on duty.

"The dog found it first. He was scratching at some cardboard boxes."

"What's your dog's name - and could I please see his licence?"

"Oh, I'm afraid he hasn't got a dog licence."

"Well that's hard lines," the police officer replied. "I'm afraid I'm going to have to fine you for that." And he did!

In 1949, after I'd been working for about a year, I met Tiny Allison on the main road.

"Hello, Jackie," she said. "How are you doing? Everybody in the class still talks about you and how good you were and I really miss you in the shows. Do you do any dancing these days?"

"Only for my own amusement," I admitted, "and only if nobody else is around," I added truthfully.

Tiny then told me that the English Folk Dance and Song Society had been advertising in the northern newspapers for clog-dancers to take part in the Northumberland and Durham Clog-Dancing Championships. "I'm entering the senior championships," she went on. "You'd be marvellous at clogging, Jackie. Why don't you join me? You could go into the junior section. It's much more intricate and interesting than tap-dancing. Why don't you give it a try, just for the fun of it? It's in three weeks' time at Hexham. Go on, you could do it. You never know, you might even win a cup."

Tiny could see that I was keen. "We'll have to work fast but I'll teach you a few steps," she went on. "A man in Sunderland is making some clogs for me. Shall I ask him to make some for you too?"

"All right," I replied, "I'll have a go."

Here was a new challenge and, as it turned out, one that I thoroughly enjoyed. The clog steps that I had to learn came to me quite easily and I loved the rhythm.

Clog dancing, I am told, originated in Lancashire but it soon became a popular dance in the North East of England. In my home town of Stanley we had two quite famous cloggers, Harry Robinson and Jack Burrell who became a world Champion in 1906, moved into theatre and travelled extensively with his dancing and eventually worked in Vaudeville in the USA. He found life more exciting in the states than our own mining towns and moved to America. In the late 20s he opened a dance academy in Pontiac, Michigan, teaching all aspects of dance, including the now more popular, American tap dancing. Charlie Chaplin and Stan Laurel, of Laurel and Hardy fame, were also famous clog dancers before they became comedians. Charlie and Stan were both part of a troupe of clog dancers called,

'The 8 Lancashire lads'. What a fantastic sound they must have made. Well they also moved to the USA and we know what became of Charlie and Stan. Harry on the other hand didn't want to travel to America even though he kept in contact with Burrell who tried to coax him over the pond. How fortunate for me he didn't go, for many years later when I became a well known dance champion, Harry became a big friend and fan of mine and even taught me some of his dancing steps, most of which I have passed on to other dancers. Harry often told me of the time he entered a clog dance contest in Chester-Le-Street. The prize was a piglet. He won the prize but the condition was that he had to do an encore with the young piglet tucked underneath his arm - much to the amusement of the crowd. It was hilarious, he said, until he couldn't hold it any longer and it fell, and the poor little thing broke a leg. He sold it to a local butcher who gave him 10 shillings for it. He loved that day and incident so much he used to repeat the story to me on a regular basis. Even so, we always laughed about it. He was the first person, I think, who gave me the tile of the lad with the lightening feet.

Clog dancing seemed to fade out around the first world war and was overtaken by American tap dance and the musical song and dance films of the likes of Ruby Keeler, followed on later by Fed Astaire and Ginger Rogers. Had it not been for the likes of Harry Robinson, clog dancing would have been lost forever. Harry had a dancing school in Stanley and among his pupils was Tiny Allinson, who taught me the art many years later.

In later years, I met Harry, who by then had become a fan of mine. He was a tall, smartly dressed man in his late 70s. I remember that he was kind enough to teach me some of the special steps that he had devised.

At the time of the 1949 Championships, Tiny herself had not practised clog-dancing for many years but, after a refresher course with Harry and three weeks' strenuous practice helping me, she entered the competition and became the 1949 Senior Northumberland and Durham Champion, the first woman ever to do so. And guess what? I won the Junior Contest! In fact, I went on to win it in 1950 too and, in 1951, I won both the Junior and Senior events on the same day, beating my own teacher and very good friend, Tiny.

It has been said by many that I did more than my fair share in reviving the popularity of clog-dancing and that I was the inspiration for many future dancers. The media gave me a tremendous amount of positive publicity. Whether it was because I was a coal miner or whether it was that I danced faster than anyone else - I was known in clogging circles as 'the boy with the lightning feet' - I don't know. It could possibly have been that I found it fun and smiled a lot while I danced, while other dancers seemed to have permanently serious expressions on their faces and danced stiffly, full of concentration.

It was in Hexham in 1949 at that first clog-dancing contest that I had the great privilege of meeting Peter Kennedy, the son of Douglas and Helen Kennedy, directors of the English Folk Dance and Song Society. Peter has played a very important part in my story, as I always feel that I was his discovery. He encouraged me to do more clogging and, through his efforts, I took part in *BBC Children's Hour* and *Barn Dance* on radio, and received my first fee for dancing – two guineas plus expenses.

The lads at the pit were always quite excited for me whenever they read my name in the *Radio Times*. I began to be in great demand, being asked to take part as a soloist in many dance festivals. It was great fun and my photograph started appearing in the newspapers on a regular basis.

One day, Peter asked me how I would feel about a three-week tour of Denmark

"That would be marvellous Peter," I said, "but I have to work at the pit and I wouldn't be able to get the time off."

"Well, leave that side of things to me," Peter replied. "Have you got a passport?"

"No, of course I haven't," I smiled.

"Well that's the first thing we have to get sorted out." Without more ado, he rang the passport office there and then. "The name is Toaduff – no, Toaduff - T-O-A-D-U-F-F – no, TOAD, like a frog that hops. That's right, and UFF as in 'plum duff'. Yes, you've got it."

I soon had my passport and Peter had arranged with the colliery manager for me to have time off to allow me to tour with the English team of dancers to Denmark. There was much excitement in our village of South Moor because flying to Denmark in those days was almost like venturing into unknown territory. All the other members of the team were from the south of England, mainly London, and they all seemed to be university students or graduates.

"You know, Peter, I don't think I should be in this team," I confided. "I'm sure I'm not good enough. I'm going to be like a fish out of water and I can't speak any Danish."

"Well, I wouldn't worry about that," said Peter. "You'll be fine. We'll all help you out."

I was speaking to Peter recently and he recalled that, strange though it may seem, the Danes found my accent and way of speaking the easiest to understand – and I was an instant hit with my clog-dancing. He also reminded me that, in one of the last towns we visited, I didn't want to leave because all the local girls had taken a great fancy to me – my first groupies, I suppose!

A short while later, I received a letter from Douglas Kennedy in London, thanking me for my successful contribution to the Danish trip and inviting me to take part in the annual Festival of Dance at the Royal Albert Hall in London.

"What an honour that will be for you," my colliery manager said as he gave me permission to take part in it.

It was my first ever trip to London and everyone seemed to fear for my safety. "Don't talk to strangers," I was warned and "If you get lost and have to ask directions, make sure you only ask a policeman," and "Always remember that there are some very funny people living in London, so you've always got to have your wits about you." It was enough to put me off going but of course I was young and it didn't!

The Royal Albert Hall was far grander than I had expected. When I entered that arena for the very first time, nothing had prepared me for such an experience. It was vast. It was quite a long walk from the stage entrance to the centre of the arena where I had to perform my solo clog-dance, accompanied by my friends Peter Kennedy and Peter Swann, who played the fiddles for me. In the past, I had always played to the gods but this Hall was so huge that I must have looked like a minute figure from way up there. Nevertheless, I was given the most wonderful reception and the applause was still ringing in my ears as I walked off. When I reached the top of the steps to the exit, I was told to go back on stage and give an encore, as the audience simply would not stop clapping until I obliged. I was so thrilled that there were tears of joy in my eyes as I performed. *The Sunday Times* critic, who reviewed the Festival, reported that:

Jackie Toaduff's solo clog-dance rivalled that of Mr. Antonio's famous 'Zapateado'

Then it was back to the pit again, where I entertained my fellow workmen with countless stories of my trip to London.

In all, I gave sixteen solo appearances at the Royal Albert Hall between 1950 and 1957, while still working down the pit. There was one more solo in 1964, but this time as a professional. On each occasion, I received an ovation and had to give an encore.

After my first Royal Albert Hall appearance, I was invited to dance in almost every dance festival in the country. As they were usually held at weekends, I didn't have to lose any time at work. I couldn't drive, so my journeys to and fro were either by bus or train. Even though it was very tiring, I loved every minute and had the opportunity to meet some extraordinary people.

4

The Princess and the Miner

One particular day in 1954 stands out in my mind. As I was coming home from the pit one day, Bella Brunskill, Ronnie's mother, stopped me in the street just to ask how I was getting on and if I had any exciting engagements in the offing.

"Nothing too special," I answered.

"Well, you're going to be twenty one, next month, aren't you? That's special. Are you having a big party?"

"No," I laughed. "I won't even be having a cake."

"Come on now, Jackie," Ronnie's mother chided, "you've got to have a party. I'll have a word with your mother."

"I wouldn't bother, Bella," I smiled. "There's no way we could afford one."

But Bella wasn't so easily put off. In fact, she went out of her way to make sure that I would celebrate my coming of age in style. She managed to involve the whole street in throwing a party for me. Someone paid for the hiring of the village hall; someone else paid for a band; Bella herself provided boiled ham and pease pudding and my mother made me a birthday cake. Many of the other neighbours baked cakes and prepared sandwiches.

Where the people came from I don't know but it was a certainly a party to be remembered and in the evening, when the dancing got underway, I think that the whole of South Moor must have turned out. I realise now that I must have been very well thought of in those days because everyone chipped in to give me a fantastic day and memories that I shall always treasure. I'd never seen such an array of presents. I must have received about twenty hairbrush-sets, an abundance of socks, enough hankies to last a lifetime and one very special present, a beautiful suitcase. Little did I imagine how useful that suitcase was going to be. I took it to places I could not at that time ever have dreamt I would visit. And to top it all, the following week I was honoured again, as my pal Ronnie was married, having asked me to be his best man.

The next year, in 1955, I received a very special request. Her Royal Highness Princess Margaret was to attend the Annual Ball at Cecil Sharp House, Regents Park, London, the headquarters of the English Folk Dance and Song Society and I was invited not only as a guest but also to dance for the Princess. What an honour that was! I readily accepted and proudly travelled to London, having hastily acquired a dress suit, shirt and bow tie for the occasion. It was arranged that I should stay with an ex-local woman and friend of our family, Doris Lyons, who now lived in Cricklewood.

When I arrived at the Ball, very excited to put it mildly, I was warmly greeted by the Kennedy family and some of the dancers who had been on the Denmark tour with me. Princess Margaret had not yet arrived.

"Are you feeling nervous?" I was asked.

"No, not a bit," I replied, but underneath I was becoming more and more tense and had to keep telling myself, "She's just like everyone else."

Quite suddenly, the band stopped, the ballroom doors opened and in walked Princess Margaret. She stood perfectly still while the band played *God Save the Queen*. She was the most beautiful person I had ever seen in my life. She had such a dazzling smile that it actually took my breath away, and she was so tiny – much more petite than I had imagined from her photographs. Her ball gown was in pink taffeta, apparently the first Royal version of the new A-line fashion, and around her shoulders she wore a white ermine cape.

In no time at all, I was told to get ready for my performance. Princess Margaret, Iris Peake, who was her Lady-in-Waiting, Dr. Ralph Vaughan-Williams and Douglas and Helen Kennedy were sitting on a dais no more than twenty feet away from me when I started my dance. To end my performance, I went into my very fast double-shuffle. Her Royal Highness spontaneously started to applaud and everyone present joined in to give me a standing ovation.

As I took my bows, the Princess beckoned me over to speak to me. "I thoroughly enjoyed your performance," she said, smiling. "You're so fast it's as though you have batteries in your shoes! What are they made of, by the way?"

I was so nervous and breathless that, without more ado, I just lifted my foot up to let her examine my shoe, much to the amusement of the whole audience.

Princess Margaret then gave me the most radiant smile and thanked me. "Do you do any other kind of dancing?" she asked.

"Oh yes, I love all dancing."

"Well, thank you very much," she continued. "Perhaps you will dance with me later."

"I would be honoured to, ma'am," I replied and then I returned to the dressing-room, not believing for one moment that her last remark was to be taken seriously.

While I was changing back into my dress-suit, everyone gathered round me asking, "What did she say to you?" From all accounts, it was a most unexpected thing for her to do – stopping a show in that way. I was still in my dressing-room talking, when an official appeared at the door and announced, "Princess Margaret is now ready to dance with you, Mr. Toaduff."

I couldn't believe it. "Are you kidding?" I asked.

"No, sir, she's waiting for you now."

I walked up to the Princess and proudly led her on to the dance floor. "I'm not sure what we're going to do, ma'am," I said quietly.

"Didn't you watch the demonstration?" she asked.

"No," I admitted, "I'm afraid I was chatting in the dressing-room."

"Well, it's quite simple," Her Royal Highness reassured me. "I think we'll be all right - or perhaps you'd rather sit down."

"Oh no, ma'am, I'd love to dance," I replied – and dance we did.

I was terrified that I might stand on her dainty feet but fortunately I didn't and at the end of the dance, the Princess wanted us to dance again – and this time we did it perfectly. When I led her back to her seat, I was asked if I would like to sit on the dais with the Royal party and I was ushered to a seat directly behind Her Royal Highness.

When we sat down, Iris Peake offered the Princess the ermine cape to place around her bare shoulders. It wasn't needed as she was too warm, so Iris turned round to me and asked if I would mind putting the cape on the empty seat next to mine. I took it and just as I was about to put it on the seat, my eyes caught those of one of the lads who had been on the Danish tour with me. He was on the dance floor, looking at me in amazement, so I smiled, put the cape close to my face and blew on it. At that very moment, Princess Margaret and her Lady-in-Waiting happened to turn round, catching me in the act!

The Princess raised her eyebrows in a questioning way and Iris smiled in amusement and gently shook her head.

All the way back to Cricklewood I was practising what I was going to tell the lads at the pit on Monday as I was sure they would never believe my story in a million years. One thing was quite certain - Doris Lyons didn't believe me when I arrived at her house, very, very late.

"Where the bloody hell have you been all this time, Jackie?" she greeted me. "I've been worried sick!"

"I'm really sorry, Doris, but you see Princess Margaret stayed at the ball later than expected and I've been dancing with her."

"Oh, Jackie Toaduff, don't bloody-well lie to me, you bugger. That's not funny. Now go to bed and I'll sort you out in the morning."

"But, Doris, I did dance with her," I protested.

"No, you bloody-well didn't. Get off to bed with you!"

The next morning, however, it was an apologetic Doris who knocked on my bedroom door and entered with an armful of newspapers. All the national daily papers carried a front-page story of the Princess and the Miner dancing. Most of these reports were accompanied by a beautiful photograph of Her Royal Highness in her stunning dress and some newspapers had published a picture of her dancing and smiling as though she was thoroughly enjoying herself.

Doris was flustered. "Oh, pet, I'm so sorry I didn't believe a word you said last night. I honestly thought you'd made it all up. What a wonderful honour, Jackie! Anyway, what was she like?"

"Oh, Doris, she was smashing, really smashing," I enthused, and this was just what I had been quoted as saying in the newspapers.

The following evening, I was invited out to dinner in the West End. As we were passing the Stoll Theatre, we noticed a crowd gathering on the pavement. Up pulled a limousine with the Royal Crest and out stepped, right next to me, Her Majesty the Queen and the Duke of Edinburgh, who were going to see a performance of *Kismet*. It was perhaps wishful thinking, but it seemed that the Queen was looking straight at me and I felt like saying, "Hello, Your Majesty, I was dancing with your sister last night." I had never seen any member of the Royal Family until that weekend and then I saw three at close quarters, so what a thrill it all was.

The next night I was invited on to the BBC Television's *Guess My Story*, a popular game show, where a celebrity panel had to guess the story of a few people who had been in the news that week. Eunice Grayson soon guessed my tale. The actress Hermione Gingold appeared as a special guest in the same show. She had made up a story that she would like to have seen in the press that week: *The Bank of England gives away free five-pound notes.* It was noticeable to me that everyone in the studio seemed to be making a tremendous fuss of her.

"Would you like to sit down here, Miss Gingold?" asked one girl, indicating a nearby chair.

"Yes, I want to sit down, but not there. I want to sit here," (she pointed to me) "next to this lovely young man."

Surprised, I turned to her. "Good evening, Miss Gingold," I said and then came out with the first thought that entered my head: "Would you like a cigarette?" and offered her, quite inappropriately as it turned out, a Woodbine.

She looked aghast. "A Woodbine? No, I think not," she intoned in that well-known disdainful voice of hers.

When I arrived back home, everyone called round to our house, asking me about the Princess and the TV show I had just taken part in. My parents didn't own a television set so nobody in my family had seen me.

True to form, my mother cut me down to size, remarking, "I hope you're ready to come back down to earth now, our Jackie." She and my father didn't seem to be in the least proud of me and for some unknown reason they didn't really want to know about my fantastic weekend.

My work at the pit seemed to become harder and harder as I was moved from one job to another but I could not complain after all the privileges and time off I was getting.

One of the miners I worked with, George Vincent Lee, was secretary of one of the local working men's clubs and he suggested that I should get a concert party together. He named us the 'Tip Tappers Concert Party'. There were six lads - three singers, a comedian, a pianist and myself. George started us off at the Stanley Central Club and, from there, we went from strength to strength, touring all over the North East working men's clubs. We didn't earn much money at all but we certainly had fun.

At this time, my father's health was failing and he was working less and less. All my brothers had married young and were no longer living at home, so now I was the main breadwinner. I worked hard to earn as much as I could but I never seemed to have any money of my own. Most of my wages were given to my mother and the little cash that I kept for myself I would spend when out with my friends.

Late in 1955, Douglas Kennedy contacted me, informing me that seven European countries had each been invited by the South African Government to send a team of dancers and singers to perform at the Pretoria Centenary celebrations and then to tour the Union of South Africa. This tour was to last six weeks, with all expenses paid, although any loss of earnings couldn't be made good. He wanted to know if I could possibly consider joining the tour. I discussed the situation with my parents and in spite of the fact that my loss of wages would be a severe blow to them, they both felt this was a trip of a lifetime - a privilege and a pleasure that should not be missed.

With my mind at ease, I accepted the invitation and preparations were made for me to join the English team of dancers. Tiny Allison kindly put on a Benefit Concert at the 500-seater Co-operative Hall in Stanley to help fund the extra expenses for my trip. And so, in November 1955, I set off on my journey to South Africa.

5

African Adventure

It was dark and foggy when we found the airport in Stansted, Essex. Our aircraft, a Viking 36-seater, was on the runway and looked alarmingly small for the 6000-mile flight to Johannesburg. When we took our seats, I think that all members of the two teams - twenty-one English and twelve Scots – were slightly apprehensive about our future relations with each other. We flew with Trek Airways, an airline that didn't operate during the night, so our trip to South Africa was going to take four days. We re-fuelled in Nice and then, after brushing the mountains of Corsica, Sardinia and Sicily, we touched down for the night in Malta, where we stayed at the luxurious Phoenicia Hotel in Valletta.

We left the plane with just our light hand-luggage and, after checking in, everyone went down to enjoy dinner. Well, everyone, that is, except me. I was refused admission because I wasn't wearing a tie, and a strict rule of the hotel was that gentlemen had to wear jacket and tie at all times in the dining-room. Unfortunately, by the time a tie had been found for me, all the other entertainers had almost finished their meal and so I was ushered to a table on my own and I really felt the odd man out. In fact, I don't think I would have bothered to stay and dine if I hadn't been so hungry. What cheered me up however was that, sitting at the table next to mine, I saw the very popular radio star Wilfred Pickles and his wife Mabel. In no time at all, we fell into conversation. Wilfred and Mabel were very interested to learn all about me and my trip to South Africa and they bought me a glass of wine to wish me good luck with my tour. So it turned out well for me in the end and it gave me something to add to my very first postcard home: *Met Wilfred Pickles and 'Mabel at the Table' and had a drink with them.*

Next stop, Luxor, where we drove straight into the fascinating world of the Old Testament, with patriarchs on donkeys and strings of camels led by brown toddlers. By the time our bedrooms had been allocated, all overlooking the Nile, it was dark but some of us were determined to see the Temples of Kanak and we drove into the darkness in ancient horse-drawn victorias. By the light of burning papers, we sensed rather than saw the vast temple buildings and rows of sphinxes. Guided by unseen hands, which explored our shrinking bodies, we were then shepherded to our carriages and driven through the native market-place back home to our hotel.

When I arrived at my room, two male Egyptian staff, each dressed in a long white robe and a fez, were sitting as if on guard outside my door. They ushered me inside and turned on the light. Immediately, about five or six fair-sized lizards shot up the white painted wall. I hadn't a clue what they were and I emitted such a loud cry that it's a wonder I didn't wake the mummies in their tombs.

"Oh no, do not worry," the two men reassured me. "The lizards are friends, good friends. They kill mosquitoes or flies that might get into your room."

Nevertheless, I slept somewhat fitfully under the mosquito nets that night, always conscious of the fact that those creatures might come near me.

We left Luxor at dawn, amid what seemed to be all the colours of the spectrum, then dropped down into Khartoum for breakfast and Juba for elevenses. Our next stop for the night was Entebbe at a comfortable hotel by the shores of Lake Victoria. There were three other small planes like ours on their way to Johannesburg, one from Germany carrying German and Danish entertainers, one from

Holland with Belgians and Dutch and one from Sweden. The four planes were to arrive at fifteen-minute intervals at Jan Smuts Airport and everyone had been instructed to emerge from their respective planes in dance costumes. Ours was the last of the four and already late. There had been no time for us to change into our costumes on our previous stop at Salisbury in Rhodesia, so we had no option but to change on the plane, although there was hardly any room to move and absolutely no privacy. Just after we'd changed, we ran into some very turbulent weather and I was about the only passenger who wasn't airsick. Wherever I turned, people were crammed together, holding sick bags to their faces. Thank goodness they were leak-proof!

We finally arrived at Johannesburg and were greeted at the airport by thousands of *Volkspelers*, South African folk dancers, singing songs of welcome. The sight of this vast crowd well and truly sobered us. Arriving last, we had not experienced the crescendo of excitement as each plane before ours had dropped down every quarter of an hour to disgorge its cargo of dancers in their national costumes. Soon we were whisked off to our first *braiivleisch*, a barbecue to which most people could do only scant justice on account of the recent air disturbances.

Then we journeyed on to Pretoria, a thirty-mile trip by bus, singing the songs we had all practised in preparation for the many broadcasts that were to face us later on. At Pretoria Town Hall, we re-assembled under our national flags and met our hosts for the week. Each group had been parcelled out to the appropriate Pretorian colony. We were to be guests of the Sons of England, a Masonic body with strong feelings for the old country, while the Scots, of course, were delivered over to the local Caledonian Society. It would be impossible to exaggerate the warmth of this first 'adoption' of European visitors by the Pretorians. They seemed to have been hungering for years for such a welcome invasion.

Our performances were given at the football stadium on a specially constructed wooden platform, and this pattern was followed in nearly all the cities we subsequently visited. The English dancers were particularly well received and Douglas Kennedy wrote of my performance, in the English Dance magazine:

Jackie Toaduff's clog-dancing brought down the house and the unaffected joy that lit his face when premature applause broke out during his very fast double-shuffle, endeared him to everyone.

There was also a massed display by three to four thousand *Volkspelers* at each of the late evening floodlit performances to audiences ranging from 20,000 to 40,000. During the daytime, we were entertained, taken sightseeing and fêted continuously. We never tired of exploring Pretoria, with its avenues of purple jacaranda trees in full bloom.

After five days there, we boarded our special train, which was to take us 5,000 miles over the Union down to Cape Town and back again. There were 25 couples of *Volkspelers* who were to act as our hosts and, what with the European visiting dancers, the dining-room attendants and the sleeping-car stewards, the train load added up to two hundred people. This may not sound a particularly large crowd but we all had to live on that train for three weeks and for many of us the conditions were confined and difficult. The single men were six to a compartment with just one basin in which to shave and wash. It took quite some effort for all six to be ready on time, as often we had to be prepared to step out in full costume on the platform at six o'clock in each morning. There we would be greeted by the local mayor, after which we would march off in procession through the town, knowing full well that we would not be back on the train before midnight.

I am sure that none of us will ever forget that particular train journey, with its moments of peace and pandemonium. The countryside that we had to traverse was often wild and mountainous but always beautiful. Our personal belongings, including the cigarettes, fruit and souvenirs that were constantly being showered on us, were kept in the guard's van at the rear of the train. After each night's performance, we first had to find our compartment, which could be either near or quite far away, depending on how the train had been turned round. Then we would clamber into it, full of a warm sense of arriving home. The staff provided us with food and drink, no matter how late we were and, while we were refreshing ourselves, the train would quietly move off on to the next leg of its long trek.

We travelled through Natal to Pietermaritzburg and Durban where we performed in the rain in both places. Here the country was green and lush, with Zulu kraals in abundance. Afterwards, it was back to the Transvaal, to the High Veld with altitudes up to 6,000 feet, then through the Orange Free State to breath-taking Bloemfontein, where we gave one of our few daylight shows in scorching sunshine. Off again we journeyed to Cape Province, to the coast to Port Elizabeth, then inland to the dry ostrich-farm country. Back to the coast we travelled, to George, where we danced in a natural amphitheatre with a predominately British audience of 10,000 sitting on a hillside and yelling with pleasure when our particular group performed. Cape Town, where we gave two well-received performances, was outstandingly beautiful and then at Stellenbosch, we danced at the famous rugby ground with a mountainous setting that out-rivalled the famous Empire Stadium in Vancouver, British Columbia.

Our train travelled through the high, flat lands of Karroo, where fortunes were being made from wool of the merino sheep farmed there. There had been no rain in De Aar, our next stop, for eighteen months but the day we arrived, the heavens opened and produced five inches in three hours. This was the only occasion when we were unable to perform outdoors but we managed to present two shows in the town hall to the ticket-holders, most of whom had travelled over one hundred miles just to see us.

In Kimberley, closely observed by a man with a pistol, we were allowed to handle smooth crystals, which were only rough diamonds. Later, in Potchefstroom, we were invited to look round a gold mine. We went three thousand feet down one mine and watched the vein being broken up into fragments of rock in which the gold dust was quite visible. Dressed in white waterproof coats and protective helmets, each with its own electric light supply, we trudged through mud and water and rode in small electric trains - just the same as in my coal mine at home, I reflected - except that we looked rather more up-market here in our white gear.

When we came up to the surface again, we saw the molten gold being taken from the furnace by magnificent Basutos dressed in white and proudly bearing themselves like royalty. They poured the rosy fluid from the crucible into a mould, out of which emerged a small brick, worth at the time £ 7000.

"You can take it with you if you can carry it in one hand," we were told.

Many of us tried – certainly all the Scots did – but it was just too heavy.

Next morning we had breakfast in Johannesburg. The city sweepers and dustmen, all full-blooded Zulus, had been given the morning off to dance for us. They had their own special sports ground, where they danced rather than played football. We were given the honour of sitting in one of the grandstands. The Zulus entered in a procession of two hundred, four abreast, dressed in just feathers and beads, and waving spears and sticks. Their chief organised them into a closely packed set with the drummers sitting out front. Warming up with a chorus song, they rose to their feet and began to dance, marking time as they chanted to the drumbeat. Every now and then, they would swing a leg in a high kick, bringing a foot down on the hard sand - two hundred legs all coming down crrumph in rhythmic union like the breaking of a wave. Physically magnificent and completely uninhibited, they made an unforgettable spectacle in the brilliant setting of Johannesburg's sunshine - impossible to describe adequately.

Later that day, they came along to our stadium to see our show, still wearing their dance costumes. They seemed to like the English dancers best and, at the end of my solo turn, they started chanting and applauding. Some were even raising their spears and waving - I think that meant that they liked me! At the end, as they were leaving the stadium, they smiled at me and nodded their heads as they passed.

As a reward for our arduous dance missions through the Union, our train was next routed to the Eastern Transvaal to Nelspruit, where local farmers had offered to take us on a two-day visit to the Kruger

National Park, a game reserve the length of England on the borders of Mozambique. After sorting us out into fifty cars, we were driven off into the Park as the guests of our farmer drivers who fed and housed us. We dispersed into various lanes that wandered through the reserve. Occasionally, our car would meet another and we always stopped and inquired of each other, "Have you seen anything?" Sometimes we were advised as to which route to take if we wanted to see giraffes, cheetahs, or other creatures. Although we knew of the dangers of stepping out of the car unless we had an armed warden immediately at hand, we did take a risk on one occasion, with a short walk to see hippopotami in Crocodile River. That was long before we had seen lions, however, and there was a warden within sight. I found it all very exciting as I had never in my life before seen a wild animal, apart from the rabbits I'd watched during that holiday in Castle Bolton. I hadn't even been to a zoo and here I was, spotting zebra, impala, lion and wildebeest, to mention but a few. I thought that it was just like being on the set of a *Tarzan* film and half-expected to see Johnny Weismuller come swinging through the trees at any moment.

After those two thrilling days and nights, we gave our final performance at the rugby ground at Nelspruit. I remember how warm and balmy the night was as we walked to the train for our final journey back to Pretoria. Our original hosts were all waiting for us at the railway station, delighted to see us again after an absence of three weeks but genuinely concerned to discover how exhausted we were after all our travels.

The other Europeans flew off the next day but our small British plane was delayed for forty-eight hours, which gave us the chance to catch up on lost sleep. However, we had been looking forward to travelling back across Africa with all the other European teams, as by now they had become our friends, some of them very close. We bade them farewell with tears in our eyes and, two days later, we too were emotionally waved off by the Pretorians.

In all, we had performed at seventeen centres and danced to an aggregate audience of 220,000, roughly one tenth of the European population of the Union. Our return journey was almost a repetition in reverse of the outward flight - Entebbe then Wadi Halfa instead of

Luxor.   Our final night was again spent in Malta, where we had a wonderful farewell party with the Scots. We landed at Southend on bumpy grass, far rougher than any surface I had encountered in South Africa and we were greeted with a chill dampness in the air that left us in no doubt that we were back home in England.

I travelled all alone in the train home to Stanley, thinking that the very next day I had to go back down the pit. Instead of being dressed resplendently in white in the gold and diamond mines, it would be back to the coal mine in my old togs and pit boots; instead of all the fine food and wine I had been enjoying, it would be pie and chips and, of course, my pit 'bait' of jam sandwiches with a bottle of water; and instead of ostriches and zebras and the like, it would be pit ponies. Nevertheless, I had some wonderful memories to treasure and no one would ever be able to take those away from me.

6

Royal Ballet, La Fille Mal Gardee and Clog Dancing

The Billy Pit where I worked was closed down and I was transferred to the Morrison North Pit, which was further for me to travel but at least I was able to catch an early morning bus there. I made new friends and this time, my job entailed working with a pit pony – a much harder job than I'd been used to but a better paid one. I had not had any previous experience of handling a pony; to tell the truth, I did not know anything at all about animals, as we had never kept a dog or a cat or any other pet in our household. However, I thought I would be able to manage as I had seen *My Friend Flicka* and *National Velvet* and, of course, the wonderful films starring Roy Rogers and his horse Trigger. Those horses were almost human and loved their owners, so I fondly imagined that my animal would be just like them.

However, when I was introduced to my pony, Dash, he seemed to take an instant dislike to me. He was a tiny black animal and a stubborn monster, as I was soon to find out. If truth be known, I was scared stiff of him when I saw him shuffling about. On our first meeting, he bared his enormous yellow teeth at me – I wasn't sure if he was annoyed with me, laughing at me or smiling as he said to himself, "I'll give this lad a hard time," - because that he certainly did!

"Hello. Good boy, Dash," I said, tentatively patting him on the nose - and the bloody creature nearly took my hand off. I pulled away quickly.

"Don't be scared of him, Jackie," I was told. "Be firm and show him who's the boss."

"The trouble with Dash," old Jack, the stableman told me, "is that he's a lazy little bugger and he doesn't like being in the pit one little bit."

"That makes two of us," I thought.

When I arrived home and told my brothers about the pony, they advised me to take him an apple or a carrot each day. I was determined that Dash was going to like me, so the next day I did as my brothers had suggested.

"Hello, Dash," I said. "Good boy. Look what I've brought for you," and I put a carrot to his mouth. In a flash, the carrot vanished and my hand nearly went in too!

"Hey, you don't want to feed him like that," old Jack advised me. "Put the food on the flat of your hand or he'll have half your arm as well."

It took a while for me to get used to Dash but I eventually handled him fairly well, although he tried my patience on those occasions when he decided to be moody. My job was to fasten him to a tub, which he had to pull to the coalface. Dash had a knack of pulling the tub off the rails when he didn't want to work and, each time he did this, I had to loosen him off and lift the tub back on to the rails. Often, he would run off and I had to chase after him, half-bent, as there was no headroom; I remember that once he even had me pinned up against the wall. I was almost driven to tears of frustration at times, especially when I was tired and wanted to be anywhere on earth except that pit. One day, when he was trying my patience by running off over and over again, I really surprised myself. I shouted at the top of my voice, "Dash, come here, you little bastard. Come here NOW." And would you know – he did.

He finally got to know me and, as advised, I was always firm with him. On those rare occasions when I had a little break, I used to talk to him, telling him how fed up I was and he seemed to understand. I think that he eventually began to respect me – at least he didn't try to bite me any more. There were quite a few rats about and, if Dash spotted one, he would kick and kick and as I didn't like them either, I used to join him with a clog dance and chase them away. Whenever I was away from work on one of my entertaining jaunts, someone else had to work with my pony and, from all accounts, he gave all the others a very hard time.

"How do you handle a pony like that?" people used to ask me. "He's a wild one."

1956 started well for me with an offer of two nights' performances at the Royal Albert Hall. At this show, I was joined by the other dancers with whom I had toured South Africa and we repeated the show we had performed there. Nan Fleming Williams, the brilliant violinist, played for me. She and I had a great rapport both on and off the stage. It was always a joy to work with her, as she understood my every move, so that her tempos were perfect; in fact, we were almost like a double act and off-stage, I loved to joke with her. She had the most infectious laugh and she loved my accent and Geordie expressions.

I was invited to appear on television quite often - *Come Dancing*, *Arenascope* from Earl's Court, *Everybody Swing* and a few magazine programmes like *Home for the Evening*, and, in April 1956, I felt very honoured to be included in *You're Welcome*, for the BBC, a show produced by Barney Colehan and Ronnie Taylor. This was a television programme about outstanding personalities and artists from the north of England to mark the opening of the newly equipped Northern Television Studios in Manchester. It was introduced by Peter Haigh and featured such artists as Edna Savage, Reginald Dixon (the organist from the Tower Ballroom in Blackpool), Len Hutton (the English and Yorkshire cricket captain),

Flotsam (B.C. Hilliam), Owen Brannigan (Tyneside's eminent bass singer), the veteran Lancashire comedian Rob Wilton, the Littlewood Songsters, Alan Ainsworth and the BBC Northern Variety Orchestra, myself and a tribute to the one and only Gracie Fields. It was a memorable evening and the programme was very well received by the press.

January 1957 started with another three performances at the Royal Albert Hall. I was becoming quite a regular dancer at this magnificent building and felt at home there but one of those shows gave me one of my most embarrassing moments. Dancing to a capacity audience, which included Her Royal Highness Princess Margaret and her friend, prima ballerina Margot Fonteyn, I lost my trousers. Well – almost. At the end of my solo turn, accompanied once again by Nan Fleming Williams, I walked off, but the ovation the audience gave us left us in no doubt that we had to go back and give an encore. I felt so proud to receive this recognition, particularly with the Princess and Margot leading the applause. Smartly dressed in my royal blue knee breeches, white silk shirt and white stockings, I felt so happy that I almost floated back to the centre of that famous arena. With the footlights blazing down on me, I took an extra deep bow towards the Royal Box and that's when it happened. My belt snapped and there was just nothing I could do about it. Nan played my introduction and I went into my dance. Everything was fine at first but then, slowly but surely, my pants started to fall down. "Please God, let them stay up," I was praying but down a little bit more they slipped. I could hear a slight ripple of laughter as the audience began to realise what was happening to me. Then as the tempo increased and I went into my very fast double shuffle, my breeches went right down over my hips. As quick as a flash (if you'll pardon the expression), with one hand in front and one behind, I hitched them up and, amid much laughter and applause, I finished my dance 'sailors-hornpipe' style. I just about brought the house down. Nan was standing on stage with tears of laughter in her eyes, so I gave her a kiss and we rushed off together.

Douglas Kennedy was at the top of the steps waiting for me, I thought perhaps to tell me off but he just patted me on the shoulder and said, "Brilliant. You were brilliant."

At the end of the show, Princess Margaret had to leave immediately but Margot came backstage to speak to me and gave me a message from Her Royal Highness, who had apparently enjoyed my performance and told Margot that she thought my dancing was better than ever.

"I was so embarrassed," I told the famous dancer, "and especially with you both out there."

"We loved it," Margot assured me, "and Princess Margaret laughed until there were tears in her eyes when she thought that you were going to lose your breeches."

Margot asked if I had planned the whole incident to get the attention of the press. "It was pure perfection," she said. "What a showman you are!" She also asked me quite seriously if I'd be interested in giving clog-dancing lessons at the Royal Ballet School. She was amazed when I told her that I was a coal miner and wouldn't have time to do that.

"And besides," I told her, "I wouldn't be a very good teacher."

"Well, if you ever feel you can spare the time, you'd be most welcome."

Incidentally, a few years later, I met Wayne Sleep at a dinner party given by the dancer and choreographer Irving Davies, and Wayne was another dancer who asked me if I could find time to teach him some of my steps. Again, I had so many engagements to fulfil that I had to decline.

However, I did manage to give some lessons at the Royal Ballet School. Peter Kennedy recalls how, when he was teaching folkdance at the Senior and Junior Schools there, he persuaded me to demonstrate at both schools. Strange to say, one outcome of my visits was a French ballet, *La Fille Mal Gardee*, which incorporated some of the elements of the North country-garland and clog-dance steps. He also recalled that, several generations later, the North-East style of clog-dancing, which I had introduced to the Royal Ballet, manifested itself in the recent movie *Billy Elliott.*

More dance festivals followed, including some at Oxford, Cambridge, Alnwick Castle, Tunbridge Castle, Malvern College and the Central Hall in Birmingham. I was kept very busy and my concert party was in great demand too. I also appeared at the Oxford Galleries, a well-known dance hall in Newcastle, at the Press Ball together with Hilda Baker, the tiny Lancashire comedienne.

The Five Smith Brothers, a very popular singing act of the 1950s, had been booked to appear for six weeks at the Empire Theatres in Newcastle and Sunderland. *Mr. and Mrs. Smith's Five Little Boys*, as they were affectionately known, were all Geordies and they wanted as much local flavour as possible in their new show *A Wonderful Time* so I was invited to join them in both towns.

Appearing with me on the same bill in Newcastle was a most talented little singer, thirteen-year old Sheila Armstrong. She accomplished great things in later life and became a star of the Sadler's Wells Opera Company. I was brought into the show in the barn-dance segment, which closed the first half. The show was twice nightly and, as I was in only one spot, I had a lot of waiting around to do. I used to watch most of the acts from the wings and learned quite a lot about stagecraft from them. Although the Geordies loved the Five Smith Brothers, it was the second top of the bill, the Scottish husband and wife team, Chic Murray and Maidi, *The Tall Droll and the Small Doll*, who stole the show every night. I spent valuable time with them in their dressing-room and the three of us became firm friends. Chic taught me the art of taking a curtain call, milking an audience and bowing professionally.

After my act in the second half, I had to dash off home on the bus, all the time thinking how much I loved being on that stage and dreading the thought of going down the pit again at four o'clock the following morning. It was quite an exhausting time but being on the receiving end of all the applause and flattering reviews in the newspapers, mixing with the show business crowd and earning fourteen pounds a week made up for the downside of it. Fourteen pounds was a fortune to me then, as I think I was earning about six pounds a week down the pit. On Saturday nights, I was able to stay to the end of the second house and take part in the finale. Some of my mates from the pit saw the show one Saturday night and came backstage to visit me. When I introduced them to all those glamorous chorus girls and to the stars of the show, they thought they had died and gone to heaven.

That spring, John McGee, one of my best friends at the Morrison North Pit, told me that his local pub was organising a day's outing to Morecambe and he asked if I would like to go too. I had never been to Morecambe and I knew that being with John and his mates would be good fun, so I agreed. We arrived at the seaside resort in torrential rain; in fact, the weather was so bad that no one felt inclined to get off the coach. Fortunately, we were well stocked up with Newcastle Brown Ale and sandwiches, so we sat there, eating and drinking, waiting for the weather to clear. Someone pointed out that just near the coach was a caravan with a notice-board sign which read: *Gypsy Sarah will tell your fortune. Step inside for palm or crystal ball readings.*

"Let's go and have our fortune told," one of the lads suggested. One by one, people stepped off the coach and ran through the rain to have their palms read, then emerged from the caravan to tell the others what the future had in store.

"Come on, Jackie, your turn now."

"Oh, no thank you. I don't want to know."

"Come on," they urged. "It's just a bit of fun," and so I was reluctantly forced into it.

When I met the gypsy, she looked at my palms and remained silent for quite some time. This sent shivers up my spine.

"Have you ever had your fortune told before?" she asked.

"No," I replied.

"Well, I'd like you to make a wish but don't wish for the moon because you won't get it," she went on and then added quietly, as if to herself, "… but almost."

"Amazing," she said. "Very soon you are going to have a change of occupation. The job you have at the moment is totally unsuitable for you. The change will be quite extreme, like black and white or night and day. I can see a big stage with two people on it, you and someone else. Definitely two people. Life for you is going to involve much travel by land, sea and air. I've never seen so much travel," she went on, "and, by the way, you have a third lifeline, which is much better than a long lifeline."

To this very day, I don't know what she meant by that last remark but I can say that everything she predicted has come to pass. The change did happen and in a relatively short time.

When I climbed back on to the coach, my pals asked me what she had said. I related what she had told me almost verbatim and I added that I'd like to think she was right. On the way home, I was lost in thought, trying to work out who this other person could be. Who would be on a big stage with me? The only partner I could think of at the time was Tiny, my dance teacher, with whom I had recently danced at one or two charity shows. She used to laughingly say to me, "We'd be able to make a good living as a professional dancing act, Jackie." But Tiny ran a dancing school in Stanley and had domestic commitments with a husband and young son, so she wouldn't be able to leave home. Then I started to think about where my own life was heading. I would soon be of an age when I could leave the pits without having to do National Service; but deep down, I truly believed that I'd never be able to give up coal-mining or even leave home, where I felt I was needed more than ever before.

Back at work, the main topic of conversation was our next outing, our annual holiday. About eight of us had booked for two weeks at that Mecca of the north and favourite fun-resort of all Geordies – Blackpool. We had all heard of the Golden Mile, the Pleasure Beach with the Big Dipper and the Grand National White Knuckle Roller Coaster ride and we just couldn't wait to try them. We had found out about all the best shows running in Blackpool and we had already chosen those that we wanted to see. We also knew from asking those who had been before where all the best clubs and pubs were!

We were soon off by bus to the holiday that was to change my life. Excitement grew as we approached the town and caught our first glimpse of the famous Blackpool Tower. We had comfortable digs in a boarding house in Adelaide Street and I was over the moon because the room that I was sharing had a balcony with a perfect view of the Tower. Immediately opposite our balcony were huge posters advertising the current shows: Alma Cogan at the Opera House, Bob Monkhouse at the Pavilion, Pearl Carr and Teddy Johnson, Bert Weedon – all the stars were there. What I didn't know as I gazed at those posters was that in no time at all I would be working alongside them and indeed would become great friends with some of them.

After we had paid for our shows and visited the Pleasure Beach a couple of times, our funds were beginning to run low. We heard that Uncle Tom's Cabin and the Philharmonic Working Men's Club were both offering two pints of beer to anyone who would get up and sing. John McGee had quite a pleasant voice and could put across a good song, so he and I and a couple of the other lads spent a few happy hours singing for our beer. Alice Richards from Leeds was the resident singer at the Philharmonic Club. She was a likeable buxom blonde, probably in her late fifties and she sang in the style of Sophie Tucker. Our crowd became quite friendly with her and she always seemed pleased to see us.

One rainy afternoon in the club, we were talking to Alice during one of her breaks. She told me that she liked my voice and personality and, when my mates told her that I was also a tap-dancer and a champion clog-dancer, she suggested that I should enter the 'Peter Webster's £ 30 Talent Contest' on the Central Pier.

"If you can dance as well as you can sing," she said, "you stand a good chance of winning."

"But I haven't got any tap-shoes with me," I told her, "so the dancing will have to be out."

"You don't need bloody tap-shoes," John intervened and everybody agreed.

"Come on, Jackie, be a sport. You know that we're running out of beer money."

Much against my will, they forced me into entering. We all marched down to the Central Pier and asked the manager what the procedure was for entering the contest.

"Do you all want to enter then?" the manager asked.

"Oh no, only Jackie."

"Well, what do you do, Jackie?"

One of the lads answered for me, "He's a song and dance man, the best."

"Well that's certainly a bit different. You'd be the only dancer in the contest." He turned to the others. "But if you lot want to come to see the show, you'll have to pay, you know."

"Let's forget it," I said. "If they can't watch me for free, I won't be interested. We're all short of cash."

The manager thought for a couple of minutes before he answered. "All right," he said, "you can all stay at the back but not too much clapping for him, mind."

In the contest, I sang *Mr. Wonderful*, changing the words to *My Miss Wonderful* and I included a tap routine to it; all the ladies loved it. I won that heat and had to return later in the week for the final. We couldn't wait to get back to the club to tell Alice, who announced my success from the stage. "Come up here and give a repeat performance," she called out, so I did and free drinks were delivered to everyone at our table.

When the final came, I think that everybody in our boarding house came to support me and I'm sure that some of the people from the Philharmonic Club were also there. I don't remember the other contestants very clearly but most of them were extremely talented singers. There was also a comedian who, to this day John believes was Les Dawson, an unknown at that time – but it might have been someone who looked like him.

At the end of the show, Peter Webster walked on to the stage to announce the final result. Standing in the wings with legs and fingers crossed, holding my breath, biting my lip, eyes closed, and saying a little prayer, I waited, only to hear Peter call out someone else's name, not mine. My heart sank.

Immediately, a woman in the audience stood up and shouted, "Oh no you don't. If that song and dance man doesn't win first prize, I'll have this bloody theatre closed. It's all a put-up job."

"Hold on, Flo," Peter laughed. He knew her name because she was a local professional club singer. "I was giving the results in reverse order so if you'll kindly sit down, I'll continue. 'So and so' (he called out a name) has won the second prize and, wait for it, the winner of the contest is the song and dance man, Jackie Toaduff."

How everyone cheered!

With my winnings, we went back to the club to celebrate. News had travelled fast. Those who were in the club had already heard I was the winner and applauded me as I walked in. It certainly turned out to be quite a night. All of us got up to sing and, of course, I had to repeat my winning turn.

Stepping down from the stage, I saw a familiar face approaching me. It was that of Frank Swift, the famous goalkeeper, who played for Manchester City and England. He congratulated me and told me that his brother Fred was chairman of the Blackpool and District Concert Secretaries' Federation and could help me to get into the Command Performance of Clubland, an annual show held at the Winter Gardens in Blackpool. This was a prestigious show, presenting the very best acts from the clubs. To be chosen for this event was an honour and it was also an excellent platform for being noticed. There were no fees, Frank told me, but all expenses would be paid.

"Could you give me your telephone number?" he asked.

"Oh, I'm sorry. We don't have a 'phone."

"In that case, give me your address and I'll tell my brother to contact you. You have to be in that show, Jackie."

From beginning to end, it was a wonderful holiday in Blackpool and one that I remember with affection.

7

I Meet Roy and Colin

Shortly after my arrival home, the letter from Fred Swift arrived and I was signed up to appear in the Ninth Annual Clubland Command Performance on January 24th 1958. Jack Rose was the producer and musical arrangements were by Mr. Tommy Jones. This time I travelled to Blackpool alone and by train through the most atrocious weather. It seemed like a never-ending journey and I was both cold and weary when I arrived at the station. How different it had all looked the previous summer. Now it was snowing very heavily and there was hardly a person in sight. I was carrying a very heavy suitcase and was looking for a taxi to take me to Mrs. Moss's guest-house in Adelaide Street, the same street where I had stayed on our holiday. I found a porter and asked where I would find a taxi.

"You'll be lucky, mate," he said. "Have you seen it out there? The snow's half a foot deep, so I doubt if you'll find one. Have you far to go?"

When I told him, he said, "Oh, far enough, but I really think you'll have to walk. Try and flag a taxi down if you see one or perhaps you could hitch a lift."

Outside the station, however, the streets looked deserted so I started to trudge through a very heavy snowstorm, wondering what on earth had possessed me to come. By the time I reached Mrs. Moss's house, I must have looked like a snowman. I rang the doorbell and a man appeared at the door.

"Hello, my name's Jackie Toaduff and I have a reservation here."

"Come in," he said. "Are you in the Winter Gardens Show tomorrow night?"

"Yes I am."

"Well, take a seat in the lounge with the other artists."

I looked down at my soaking coat. "If it's all right with you," I answered, "I'd rather go to my room first and get out of these wet clothes. Are you Mr. Moss?"

"No," he replied, "I'm Roland Roy's manager."

"Roland Roy? Who on earth's Roland Roy?" I thought.

Just then, Mrs. Moss, a very kindly-looking soul, appeared on the scene and asked, "Are you Mr Toaduff?" I nodded. "Good," she continued, "that's everybody here now. Isn't it horrible outside tonight? You look frozen."

"I am. I had to walk from the station. I only saw about four cars and they were stuck in the snow. To tell you the truth, all I want to do is to get out of these wet clothes and go to bed."

"Why don't you dry yourself off and come downstairs? I'm just about to serve dinner. Have something to eat and then an early night."

I agreed and changed as quickly as possible. When I walked into the dining-room, everybody seemed to stop talking and gaze in my direction. I'd never felt so nervous or so unsure what to do. Mrs. Moss came to my rescue.

"Oh there you are," she said. "You look much better now. Would you mind sitting with these two gentlemen over here?" and she led me to the table where Roland Roy and his manager were sitting. I shook hands with them both and introduced myself.

"We met briefly at the door. I'm Colin Edwardes," the manager said with a broad smile, "and this is Roland Roy but all his friends call him Roy."

Although I didn't know it at the time, these two men were to have the greatest influence on my life. That night Roy looked immaculate. In fact, he was the best-dressed man I had ever seen in my life. He seemed terribly aloof and hardly said a word during the meal. Colin did most of the talking. Roy, I was informed, had been a Sheffield tailor who had won a television talent contest on Bid for Fame and he had a great following in the South Yorkshire clubland. He had just signed to top the bill in a summer show in Jersey for four months.

I could overhear snippets of conversation coming from the other tables, where it seemed that all of them were talking about their summer season contracts, their ideas for the next night's show or their musical arrangements. I couldn't help thinking over and over again, "What the hell am I doing in this show?" I'd sent a few piano copies to Tommy Jones, as the numbers that I was to use in the show needed to be orchestrated. It was the first time I would be singing with a full orchestra and I was petrified.

I didn't feel any easier the next morning at rehearsal. All of the acts were very professional and Roland Roy was outstanding. He had a wonderful stage presence and an astonishingly rich baritone voice. I didn't know until that rehearsal that Colin, besides being his manager, was also his pianist and musical director. All the performers seemed to know each other; no one noticed I was there so once again I felt the odd man out and certainly like a fish out of water.

Jack Rose shouted my name for my band call and introduced me to the musical director, Tommy Jones. I told him that I was feeling very nervous.

"No need to be scared from what I've heard about you," replied Tommy.

At the rehearsal, my opening number was a song and dance to Putting on the Style and I finished my act with a clog-dance. When I stepped down, Tommy reassured me with the words, "You'll knock 'em dead tonight, Jackie. They'll love you."

I shall always remember that the only artists who spoke to me backstage were Roy and Colin. They said that they were very impressed, loved my dancing and Roy even gave me a helpful suggestion about my singing, for which I was grateful. I realised then that he was not aloof as I had first thought, just rather shy.

That night, the atmosphere in the packed Winter Gardens ballroom was electric. The overture was well received and then, to tumultuous applause, on to the stage walked two football legends, Stanley Mortenson and Frank Swift, to compère the show. Sadly, just a few days later, on February 6th, Frank was killed in the Munich air crash when he accompanied the Manchester United Babes, reporting the match for the *News of the World*.

It was a great experience being in that show. The Blackpool Evening Gazette reported that it was the best Command Show to date and said of me that I had one of the biggest receptions. Jerry Dawson, the show critic for the Sunday People, mentioned only two acts in his review - and I quote:

Watch out for Roland Roy. This virile Sheffield singer was acclaimed by thousands of club members who, together with their wives and families, were in the crowded Winter Gardens on Friday night. An old-fashioned clog-dance was the applause-pulling gimmick of song and dance man Jackie Toaduff. Tomorrow he will be back working as a haulage hand at a colliery in Stanley, County Durham.

And so I was.

Roy and Colin found it hard to believe that I was a miner and I explained why it would be another twelve months before I would be free to leave the mines. They suggested that I should go over to Jersey for my summer holiday and they kindly invited me to stay at the house in St. Brelade's Bay that they had rented for the season. Colin promised that he would try to arrange an audition for me with Pat and Tony Fielding, who owned the Tams Nightclub, where Colin and Roy were going to work. He told me that the Fieldings might even employ me the following year if they liked my act. At that point, I asked Colin if he would manage me if all went well and he agreed. So here I was – with a show business manager but still working at the pit!

When I arrived home, I didn't say a word to anyone about all the exciting things that had happened to me in Blackpool because I knew from past experience that any mention of giving up my pit work would not be well received.

In the summer, I travelled to Jersey to stay with Roy and Colin for a week and fell in love with the island. They seemed to know every beautiful lane and beach there and already they had made many friends. My live audition was very well received and the Fieldings liked my act so much that, with Colin's help, I signed a contract there for the following summer - my first professional show, with an excellent fee.

As I travelled home on the plane, clutching my contract and reading it over and over again, I was the happiest person in the world. I would actually be appearing in Jersey for four months and I couldn't wait to tell my family the news, hoping against hope that they would share my happiness. However, once I arrived in the house, I was brought down to earth with a bump. They all thought that I was crazy to even think about sacrificing a secure job in the pit, particularly when my colliery manager was so understanding in allowing me time off whenever I needed it.

"But I'll be earning a lot more money," I protested.

"That's fine," replied my mother, "but what will you do at the end of the season? Isn't it going to be embarrassing, asking for your old job back?"

"No, mother. After eleven years in the mines, once I leave, I never want to see a pit again."

"Well, you just think about it. Dancers are ten a penny, you know."

As a matter of fact, I already had given the matter a lot of thought, and I had only to look at my poor father, a lovely, hard-working man still in his fifties yet hardly able get his breath, to see what the pit had done to him. He couldn't walk more than half a dozen steps without having to stop and rest. My brother Ronnie had fared little better health-wise. I had hoped that my family would have wanted me out of the pit, but no. However, whether they liked the idea or not, my mind was clearly made up. I was not going to work in the mine a day longer than I needed to. I was determined that I was not going to end up like them. I had enough of coal dust – it was stardust I was looking for now.

On 27th October 1958, the English Folk Dance and Song Society were holding a ball in honour of Her Royal Highness Princess Margaret, and I was invited both as a guest and entertainer, which pleased me enormously. I wrote to Roy and Colin, giving them the news; they wrote back telling me that, by strange coincidence, Roy had been booked for two weeks in an old-time music-hall production at the famous Metropolitan Theatre in Edgware Road at the very same time. There was another piece of good news in the letter. Roy had been asked back to Jersey the following summer to top the bill at Tams again, so that meant I wasn't going to be on my own there and I could stay with him and Colin.

At the ball, I danced for Princess Margaret, who was exquisitely dressed in her favourite red polka-dot ball gown and once again I had the honour of dancing with her and also with Iris Peake. Roy and Colin had arranged to pick me up in their car after the ball and drive me back to my cousin's public house in Sunbury-on-Thames, where we were all staying. When they arrived at Cecil Sharp House in Regents Park Road, a reporter, who was carrying a photograph that had just been taken of me dancing with Princess Margaret, asked Colin (of all the people in the crowd he could have chosen!) if he by any chance knew the name of the person with the Princess. Of course, Colin was only too happy to give the reporter my name and to tell him all about me.

The following morning, that photograph and story made front-page news not only in every newspaper in Britain but also in the press worldwide. When it was flashed to the newspaper office in Newcastle-on-Tyne, the editor said to Eric Foster, who was working there, "Just look at this. *Stanley Coal-Miner Dances with Princess Margaret.* We've got our front page story for tomorrow."

"That's great," replied Eric, "I know Jackie well. I went to school with him."

"Do you know where he lives, Eric? I bet his folks know nothing about this."

Eric gave the editor my address.

"Well, I know it's after midnight," the editor said, "but I think his parents should be told first. Drive over and give them the news, Eric."

It so happened that, unbeknown to me, my father had been taken into hospital the previous day and he was in a critical state. My mother and sister Norma were in bed and the house was in darkness when Eric knocked hard on the door.

"Oh, God, Norma," said my mother, imagining the worst. "Who's at the door? What's happening? Something must be wrong. I bet it's your Dad. Or could something have happened to our Jackie in London?"

Eric knocked again, harder and longer this time.

"Just open the bedroom window and shout down," Norma suggested to my mother, who by this time was numb with nerves.

She did so, with pounding heart. "Yes? What do you want?"

"Are you Mrs.Toaduff?"

"Yes, what is it?" she asked urgently.

"Are you Jackie Toaduff's mother?"
"Yes, yes. Whatever's happened to him?" she cried.

"I just wanted you to know that he's been dancing with Princess Margaret tonight."

"Oh, I'll kill that bugger when he comes home," she shouted, angry and relieved at the same time.

Eric related that story to me when we met later. He said that the people back at the newspaper office were so amused when he told them of my mother's reaction that they were tempted to report it but, on learning about my father's condition, they thought better of it.

Meanwhile, back in London, Colin showed the photograph to Ernest Rose, who was producing the show at the Metropolitan Theatre and persuaded him to include me in the show. Ernest agreed that I would be an added attraction. A life-size copy of the photo was put on display in the foyer of the theatre – so instead of going back home, I performed in the show for two weeks. London had been exciting and a wonderful experience for me - dancing with Princess Margaret again and seeing myself on the front page of all the newspapers for the second time in my life.

On the way home, I couldn't help thinking what my family and the lads at the pit would make of my London adventure and I was looking forward to giving them all my news. However, my excitement was dampened when I arrived at the railway station in Newcastle, where I was met and hastily taken to the hospital, learning on the way there that my father was dying. I had not realised that his illness had been quite so serious.

The ward sister was pleased that I had managed to arrive in time.

"He's been asking for you and just hanging on to see you," she whispered. "He could go at any time."

All the family members were sitting at my father's bedside and when I arrived, they moved away to let me sit by him. I was so shocked to see the state he was in. He looked so thin and frail that I found it impossible to hold back my tears.

"Hello, Dad, I'm here," I said quietly and took his hands in mine.

He opened his eyes and managed a faint smile. "I'm glad you're home, son. I saw you with the Princess in the paper."

I was carrying the press photographs in my hand luggage. "I've brought these to show you, Dad."

"He looked at them for some time and then said, "Oh, how lovely. I'm so proud of you, son. Get out of the pits, Jackie, for my sake."

Those were the last words that he spoke. Then, he smiled at me, dozed off again and died within the hour.

My father's death made me doubly determined to leave the pit. Any previous slight doubts I might have harboured were dismissed. In fact, I now started to count the days to the time when I could change my life. With Roy and Colin's help, I was preparing a new act for my first season as a full-time professional in Jersey. I needed to buy stage suits and musical arrangements and for those necessities, I needed extra cash. So I got into the habit of staying in the first shift all the time now, starting work at four o'clock in the morning. Each lunchtime, I would come home, have a bath and something to eat, go to bed for a few hours and then, in the evening, work in a pub or a club with my concert party or sometimes on my own. I even entered several *Go As You Please* talent contests, which I frequently won, but working day and night with very little time between was so tiring that I looked forward to the weekends when at least I could have a rest from the mine.

Then, quite unexpectedly, disaster struck. Just three days before I was due to leave work in the pit for good, an incident almost ended my dreams and ambitions. The lads at the pit had always been warned never to travel to the surface in an empty tub as it was considered a very dangerous practice but it was very tempting to do so, as it saved your legs and your back. In some places, when you were running behind your tub, you had to bend to almost double to avoid hitting your back on the roof. Dash and I had reached a stage in our relationship where we were getting on really well and he no longer pulled the tub off the rail, so when no one was around, I would jump into the empty one and ride to the coal face. It was on one of those trips that Dash suddenly stopped and refused to move. There was less than three inches between the tub and the top of the roof so I couldn't get out or even look out to find what the problem was. I kept urging the pony to move. "Go, Dash, go!" but he wouldn't budge. Then I heard the rumble of falling stones. Dash started to back up. Unfortunately, the tub, with me inside, came off the rail and Dash stumbled. I could still hear the stones and I could see the roof above me cracking. There I was, helpless. I started to shake with fear and prayed that someone would rescue us quickly. Poor Dash was kicking and trying to stand. I'm sure that he was as frightened as I was.

After what seemed to be an eternity, I heard a voice shouting, "Oh, God. Look at this lot."

"Are you all right?" someone else called.

"Yes," I answered. "Can you get me out?"

"Yes, don't panic. We'll manage it somehow. This is what happens when you ride in tubs."

When they rescued us, Dash wasn't badly hurt and neither was I physically, but I was a nervous wreck and I was sent home for the rest of the day. I have a vivid memory of how much I was shaking as I emerged into the daylight and to this day, I have a slight tremor in my hands, a legacy of what happened. My mother would not let me go to work the following day and fortunately, I had not arranged to perform that night either, so I had chance to recover from my ordeal. I was able to pack at leisure and daydream about my forthcoming trip to Jersey and my future in show business.

I could have stayed away from work on that last Friday but I decided to go and say goodbye to my work mates and my pony.

When I arrived at the pit, I was told that I wasn't to have my usual work with Dash – but something lighter. During my break, I went to the stables to see Dash but he was already at work with another miner. Jack, the stableman assured me that my pony was unscathed by the ordeal. I had brought a bag of apples for him and left them as a parting gift in his stable, sad that I could not feed them to him myself. I often thought about him and hoped that he was able to spend some free time in fields before he died.

Colin had promised that he would be at the pit head on the last day. The plan was that he would take me home, drive me to Sheffield where we would pick up Roy and then we would all travel to Weymouth before sailing to Jersey. When I stepped out of that cage for the last time, there was no one happier in the whole world. The day was bright, the sky appeared bluer than it had ever done before, the air seemed fresher and I experienced a wonderful feeling of freedom. I looked in the direction of the pit yard, where I saw Colin standing at the gate, smiling and waving at me. As I ran down the steps to meet him, I joyfully threw my cap and coat up in the air and abandoned them for ever, much to Colin's amusement.

I have always maintained that Roy and Colin saved my life for, without their help and encouragement, I would probably have continued working in the pubs and clubs, remaining at home and working as a miner all my life. I wasn't the strongest of lads on the block, weighing only one hundred and twenty pounds at that time, so with the life I was leading in Stanley, I am convinced that I would have been dead by now. But instead, I left my black and white world and exchanged it for a wonderful one of glorious Technicolor – the world of show business, which exceeded my wildest dreams.

8

Happy Days in Jersey

I started my new life with that summer season in Jersey. We had booked accommodation in a farmhouse owned by a charming couple, Hugh and Yvonne Le Breuilly and their two young sons, Gerard and Peter. It was turning dusk when we found the farmhouse, surrounded by an evening mist and my first thought was that it looked haunted. The family made us feel very welcome and we soon settled in. The show opened to great reviews, the Jersey Evening Post pronouncing it to be the best production ever at Tams and we played to capacity crowds every night. We got on so well with the Le Breuillys that we became like one big happy family and I loved everything about the island.

One day, I thought I heard the sound of a piano coming from an old barn on the farm. None of us had ever ventured there but that sound aroused my curiosity so I persuaded Roy to walk over to investigate with me. Sure enough, there was an old piano there but the lid was closed and there wasn't a soul in sight.

How strange! I knew I had heard it playing, although not exactly a tune. The whole atmosphere seemed spooky to me. Roy lifted the lid and started to play. It had a real honky-tonk sound but most of the notes played in tune. That piano proved to be a bonus as it enabled Roy and Colin to start regular rehearsals there. I loved to listen to them and sometimes I couldn't resist joining in. Colin liked the blend of our voices and suggested that I might like to join Roy in his act and sing with him at the end of the show. This I did and every night the audience shouted for more so we obliged with first two songs then four. I also taught Roy a dance routine so that we could dance together and it proved to be very popular. I loved performing at Tams, which was part of the Golden Sands Hotel in St. Brelade's Bay. We soon had a fan club and every night after our show, residents at the hotel used to ask us to join them in the bar for drinks and refreshments. There we met many great characters, some of whom have remained friends to this day.

One morning at the farm, Roy told us how he had woken up the previous night and witnessed by the light of the moon every item of furniture in his room become covered in a mist, almost like a cloth. He had also noticed that there was a very strange, indefinable smell. When he switched on the light, both the mist and the smell had vanished. My first thought was that he must have been dreaming but he assured us that he hadn't. Another night, I heard the ticking of a clock, moving from place to place within my bedroom. I told the other two about it but we didn't say a word about either of these incidents to the Le Breuillys.

Sometimes it was very late when we arrived back at the farm. There was a gravel path from the gateway to the front door of the house and, if you walked on it, it made a loud crunchy sound so when we were late we would open the gate quietly and walk on the lawn so as not to wake anyone. One night, we left the hotel so late that it was breaking daylight when we returned. We made our usual very quiet entrance and whispered our goodnights before silently going to our rooms. My room overlooked the front garden and that same gravel path. As I was preparing for bed, I heard the path crunching. Looking out of my window, I wondered who could be out there. I just couldn't believe my eyes. The gravel was moving but no one was there. I went to Colin's room to ask him to look; hearing our voices, Roy appeared at his bedroom door and we all gazed down in amazement. Colin grabbed a poker and then the three of us crept downstairs, daring to venture outside to take a closer look. We followed the sound up and down the path; it was just as if someone was walking there wearing heavy boots. After a while, it stopped but the experience was quite unnerving.

The next morning, I couldn't hold my tongue any longer. Yvonne was serving us a late breakfast at the table where her two sons were already eating. "I'm sure this farm is haunted," I blurted out rather tactlessly in front of them.

Colin kicked me under the table but the boys had heard and one of them exclaimed, "Oh, mam, don't say we'll have to have the bishop back to bless the place again."

Yes, the farmhouse was haunted. All kinds of weird happenings had occurred there. Funnily enough, the ghost didn't frighten us in the least and we made light of any unusual sights or sounds in and around the farm.

When we heard that Princess Margaret was making a three-day official visit to Jersey, Colin persuaded me to write to her to invite her to our show. I received a prompt reply from her Lady-in-Waiting, which read:

Dear Mr Toaduff,
I am to thank you for your letter, which I had great pleasure in placing before Princess Margaret. Her Royal Highness was very interested to hear that you are now part of a song and dance act in cabaret in Jersey. I have to inform you how sorry the Princess is that, unfortunately, owing to a very full programme while she is in the island, it will not be possible for her to visit your cabaret. Princess Margaret bids me to send you this message with her very best wishes.
Yours sincerely,
Iris Peake, Lady-in-Waiting to Princess Margaret.

We heard that the Princess would be attending a ball in her honour at the West Park Pavilion on her final night in Jersey so on that night after our show, we wore our tuxedos in the hope that we might be able to gatecrash the party. When we arrived, the police at the gate said that they could not let us in. While we were talking to them, they were informed that the Princess would be leaving at any moment. In the distance, we saw Princess Margaret and Iris Peake climbing into their limousine. Colin, Roy and I stood at one side of the gate while the press photographers positioned themselves at the other. Unfortunately, Her Royal Highness was on the press side but Iris Peake spotted me and, as the car glided slowly by, the light in the back of the car was switched on and both the Princess and Iris looked out of the back window, smiled and waved excitedly at me. It had the same effect on me as if they had blown me a kiss.

Quite a number of celebrities came to see our show during that Jersey season. As I recall, the entertainers Tommy Cooper, Al Read and Ronnie Ronalde among others were in the audience. A famous London agent, George Ganjou, also came to the show at least three times and had a few words with me at the end of the show on each occasion. On his last visit, he told me that he had been very impressed with my performance and asked me to make an appointment to see him at the end of the season, as he would try to help me further my career. Al Read too was enthusiastic about our act and told us that he was appearing in a show at the Opera House in Manchester and would be interested in Roy and myself joining him there as a double act.

"Oh, we're not a double act," Roy insisted. "We're soloists."

"But I saw you doing a double act," Al Read replied.

"That was just for a bit of fun."

Al Read laughed. "So why don't you come and have a little bit of fun in my show?"

But Roy was quite determined that he didn't really want to be part of a double act so that was the end of the matter.

Irving Berlin's song *There's No Business Like Show Business* was certainly true in my case, even though I had only been a professional for a few weeks. I absolutely loved being on stage and receiving applause enthusiastically night after night – and being paid for it too. Most afternoons, we would visit one or other of Jersey's many magnificent beaches and for the first time in my life I became tanned with the sun. Tams was closed on Sundays but every weekend we were invited to different places. Among the many new friends we made there was George Seymour, head of the chain of Seymour Hotels on the island, including the Golden Sands Hotel where we were working. He owned a large yacht and, on two or three Sundays, we sailed with him to St. Malo in France. George made us feel very special as he wined and dined us royally. It was there that I was introduced to lobster, wild strawberries and champagne and I'm afraid I've been addicted to these delicacies ever since. It was all new and exciting and I felt that I was beginning to adapt well to my new life.

At that time, Jersey businessman Ronnie Ronald was married to Joan, although they later divorced and he married the celebrity Yana. Every Sunday morning, Ronnie and Joan threw a cocktail party in their beautiful home, which overlooked St. Aubin's Bay. We were fortunate enough to receive an open invitation to all these parties. It was quite exciting for us because new people turned up each week – Lady Docker, Billy Butlin and I remember on one occasion having a long chat with Freddie Trueman. That season, Frankie Howerd was appearing in a theatre in St. Helier but, from all accounts, his act wasn't going down very well with the audiences. Ronnie introduced me to him as he chatted to a couple of fans.

"Ooooo, you're Jackie Toaduff!" Frankie remarked in an affected voice. "Do you know what I call you? Jackie *Toadstool*!" And with that, he and his two cronies had a good laugh at my expense but I'm afraid I was not in the least amused. His words made me blush and feel inferior, so I quietly turned aside. I wondered whether he might use the scene in his act, as he certainly wasn't making the audiences laugh at the time from all we had been told. How strange it is that some people have the knack of spoiling things for you when you are otherwise on a high.

I saw him there on another Sunday morning and he called out in a loud voice, "Hi, how are you, Mr. *Toadstool?*"

As far as I was concerned, this was no longer a joke.

"I'm fine, thank you," I replied coldly, "and, by the way, there are too many ladies about for me to tell you what I call you!"

Joan, Ronnie and the other guests looked rather uncomfortable and the room went quiet for a few seconds. I met Frankie Howerd on one or two other occasions later in the season but he never referred to me as Toadstool again. I think that he realised he had gone too far. I remember him as looking very untidy and miserable and he always seemed to me to be a very unhappy man behind the comedy mask.

Those four months in Jersey flew by and I was reluctant to leave at the end of the season but it was time to move on. Colin had taken several club dates in South Yorkshire for me but he insisted that I pay a call to George Ganjou in London first, to check if he had anything in mind for my future in show business. I went to George's office, feeling quite confident, as I had gained a little weight, was very tanned and looked in good shape. I was warmly welcomed by George, who now looked so business-like compared to the relaxed man I had met in holiday mood in Jersey. As yet, he had not found anything suitable for me and he truthfully admitted that he had been putting all his time and energy into promoting an up-and-coming star, a handsome, talented young man, who was about to knock Tommy Steele off his pedestal. My first thought was that this newcomer must be really special because Tommy was a firm favourite with the nation. All the time I was with George, his telephone never stopped ringing – and all the calls were concerning this new pop star. George managed to put in two calls on my behalf but without luck.

"Call in again tomorrow," he suggested but the same thing happened the next day and the next and the next. Finally, George asked me to call in the following week, by which time he might have found an audition or two for me. I explained that I couldn't afford to stay in London for all that time, so I left him a contact address and telephone number in case anything came up, but that was the last I heard from him. I can well understand now that all his time would have been taken up with his new discovery - the pop star's name was Cliff Richard!

73

At the time, I wondered whether something might have come up for me if I had stayed longer in London but I am a great believer in fate and I am sure that I made the right decision by fulfilling my engagements with Colin and Roy in that great training ground for entertainers - Sheffield clubland. Night after night, I was booked at the same venue as Roy. He was very well known there and had a great following. At first, when I joined him on stage in his act, my 'intrusion' was resented by some of his friends, particularly as most of the audience had come just to see Roy. However, slowly but surely, the audiences warmed to me and before long, every club we played was packed with fans who wanted to see us together. It was a busy time, rehearsing by day and working every night. There were people who followed us to different clubs almost every night of the week, queuing outside for an hour or so to make sure of getting a good table.

We did our fair share of charity work too. Colin organised shows for polio research and between us we raised over £10,000 – quite a sum in those days. It was at one of these charity shows that we were approached by a man from Galt's Scottish Variety Agency, who offered us an eight-week spring season as a double act in the Jack Milroy Show at the Pavilion Theatre in Glasgow. We would be required to perform for fifteen to twenty minutes twice nightly, with a complete change of programme every week and no repeats. We would also have to take part in the opening and closing numbers at each performance, sing and dance in other musical items and be prepared to take part in other comedy sketches. Roy and I still didn't think of ourselves as a double act but as this job was for eight weeks with an extra week for rehearsals, Colin decided that it would be great experience for us. In addition, it was to be well paid, so we signed.

9

Scottish Sights and Delights

It was a cold February day when we pulled up outside the stage door of the Pavilion Theatre, Glasgow and our first communication with the stage manager was to ask if he knew of any suitable theatrical digs for us.

"Look over there," he said, pointing to a sheet of paper stuck on the wall; the paper contained a list of landladies' names and their telephone numbers.

We contacted the landladies on the list one by one but without success; they were all fully booked. With the last name we were in luck. This lady could accommodate us if we didn't mind sharing a large room with three single beds, and there was a bathroom and toilet, which was shared by all the boarders. It didn't sound ideal but we really had no choice so we accepted. We arrived at this quite respectable-looking house and rang the doorbell. A middle-aged female with brightly bleached hair invited us inside.

"Shall we bring our luggage in?" we asked.

"Well, no," she hesitated, "you won't actually be staying in this house. Your accommodation is across the road. I'm Fiona, by the way."

"Can we go there now?"

"No. You see, I'm not the landlady. She's gone to bingo and she won't be back until about ten o'clock. I don't know which your room is, so just relax and I'll make you a cup of tea. She won't be long."

Our landlady-to-be eventually rolled in at about half past ten. I use the word 'rolled' advisedly because it was plain to see that she had imbibed quite a few drams. She was a fat, dumpy woman, wearing an old fur coat and a woollen hat pulled over a shock of bright red hair. She took off her coat, walked over to Fiona's sideboard, brought out a bottle of whisky, poured herself a large glass and downed it in one gulp.

"You're from England, aren't you?"

"Yes," I answered.

"They're not too keen on English acts at the Pavilion, you know. I should know because I used to be a dancer there in my younger days. I've worked with them all," she reminisced, "Sir Harry Lauder, Will Fyffe, Tommy Morgan and all the best comics. I loved working there," and with that she poured herself another large whisky. "Monday first-house audiences are tough enough but it's Friday nights when you'll have to look out for yourselves. The barrow-boys are in then and it's a killer. If they don't like you, you'll soon know about it, so I hope you're good. And for God's sake, don't let them know that you come from England."

"Can we see our room?" asked Colin. "We're very tired. We've had a long day and we need to sleep."

"All right," she replied. "Fiona, take them across the road," and she gave Fiona our room number. "By the way, it might be cold in your room but you do have a fireplace and I sell coal at 2/6d a bucket, if you're interested."

Colin, Roy and I each carried a heavy suitcase up about seven flights of stone steps to the top floor. When we opened the door (there was no lock), we just couldn't believe our eyes. The room was absolutely filthy. One of the beds was resting on an old box and there was actually dirty straw poking out of one of the mattresses. To top it all, the bedding looked grey. The room itself was colder than the air outside.

"Do you want to buy any fuel?" Fiona asked.

"Definitely," I replied, shivering.

And she proceeded to make up the fire.

It went from bad to worse. The bathroom had to be seen to be believed. The grease-marked bathtub looked as though it had never been cleaned since the day it had been installed and the washbasin was full of black hairs. On the wall was a grubby list, headed 'Bath Nights', which allocated a particular night of the week to each boarder.

One look at this room and Colin had made up his mind.

"Don't bother with the fire," he said. "We're not staying."

"That's a typical bloody English attitude," Fiona shouted after us as we trudged down the steps.

We drove directly to the Station Hotel at about midnight and booked in for the night but we couldn't afford to stay there for the season. I happened to be carrying in my luggage a business card belonging to a holidaymaker we had met in Jersey, who had asked us to look him up if we were ever in Glasgow. His name was Jack Cunningham, a carpet salesman, and he and his wife Hilda were delighted when I rang to tell them that we would be appearing at the Pavilion.

"I wonder if you could help us, Jack," I said. "We can't find anywhere to stay," and I recounted our previous night's experience.

"Call me back in an hour," he suggested, "and I'll ask my sister if she can help. She's a widow, living on her own and she might be able to take you in."

An hour later, we received good news. His sister, Nancy Kirkland, would let us stay there but for one week only. He told me that she was somewhat straight-laced and frowned on anyone who drank, smoked or swore. From all accounts, she had no sense of humour whatsoever, so we would have to be on our best behaviour.

When we met Nancy, our first impression of her was not favourable. She was dressed from head to foot in black and her grey hair was tightly permed. Her stern face told us immediately that she would not stand any nonsense.

"Wipe your feet when you come in," she ordered as we stepped into the immaculately clean house. "In fact, you can take your shoes off at the door. Remember that you're only staying for one week. Keep the place tidy, no late nights and no visitors."

We told her how much we appreciated her helping us and asked if she would like tickets to see the show.

"No, I never go to the theatre," she replied, "or the cinema for that matter. In fact, I don't like going out at all. I visit my brother at the week-end but that's just to make sure he doesn't drink too much."

When rehearsals started, we met the extremely talented Jack Milroy, a young Scottish comedian, singer and versatile dancer. From that first meeting, we knew that we were going to enjoy working with him, but if the rehearsals were anything to go by, we also realised that the following weeks were going to be hard work. On the first day, we were handed at least six songs and several dance movements to learn, together with a couple of comedy sketches to perfect – all in addition to our own act. It was like being in repertory theatre, with a complete change of programme every week

As well as rehearsing, Colin was desperately trying to find us accommodation, as the week with Nancy was coming to an end. On our fifth night, however, she came to our rescue and invited us to stay with her for the rest of the season. It was like music to our ears because she was the perfect landlady. Her home was always warm and comfortable and she even volunteered to wash and iron for us.

The show opened and, as we had been warned, that first Monday night was tough but the critic in the evening newspaper the next night gave the show a very good write-up, praising in particular the three Glasgow's favourites, Jack Milroy, Nicky Kidd and Glen Michael and *a talented song and dance act, Roland Roy and Jackie Toaduff in their very first appearance in Scotland.*

Throughout the first week, the stage hands had been putting the fear of God into me with tales of the Friday crowd, so much so that when Friday night came, I was so nervous coming on to the stage that I tripped over my own feet and fell full length on the floor. Roy, who was just behind me, almost landed on top of me. How the audience loved it! They applauded our entrance, mistakenly thinking that we were a new comedy team. In two seconds flat, I was up on my feet and was able to start singing with Roy right on cue. Thankfully, they liked us and my dance on the table-top brought the house down.

The stage manager congratulated us when we came off. "I knew all along they'd take to you," he grinned.

Even Nancy was concerned to know how we had fared. She surprised us by saying that if we could find her a seat she would come to see us the following night. We obliged and she came on that Saturday night and liked the show so much she came every Saturday until the end of the season.

We had just started our third week's show rehearsal when Roy, Colin and I received a message to go immediately to the Galt's office for an urgent appointment. We were wondering what we had done wrong as we walked the short distance to meet, for the very first time, Nellie Sutherland, the woman in charge of the agency. She was quite tiny and had one peculiarity – loose-fitting false teeth that constantly clicked as she spoke. To be honest, all the time we were in that office, I found it difficult to keep a straight face.

We had been called in just to be informed that everyone was very happy with our performances. Nellie told us that Mr. Galt wanted to know if we would be interested in working with Alec Finlay for the summer season, one week in Aberdeen, followed by twenty weeks at the Palladium Theatre in Edinburgh. At the end of every sentence, her teeth click-clicked.

"Well, we might be interested if the salary was increased," Colin negotiated.

With that, Nellie's teeth rattled like castanets. "Oh, I don't know whether we could manage that. Business has been very bad, you know, but I'll have a word with Mr. Galt. Alec saw you in the show the other night and was most impressed. He really would like you in the show with him. He's a lovely wee man and a great favourite with the Edinburgh audiences, and the Palladium's a wonderful little theatre – I'm sure you'd enjoy it there."

Before we left the office, her persuasive tones had convinced us and we signed for the summer season, at an increased salary, to appear with Alec Finlay, who was billed as *Scotland's Gentleman*. Even though Alec held that title, we didn't feel that he could have been more of a gentleman than Jack Milroy, who was a joy to work with. At the end of every comedy sketch we performed with him, Jack would say without fail, "Thank you, boys," as he left the stage. We felt that it should have been us thanking him – for, all the time we were with him, he was teaching us more about the art of comedy.

As the weeks passed, we had become very good friends with our landlady Nancy, who by this time had established herself as our number one fan. She enjoyed chatting to all the other performers too and was on first name terms with everyone. It was miraculous how everything about her was gradually changing - she seemed to be more open-minded with each successive day. Her old black cardigan, dark skirt and thick stockings had now been abandoned for a new wardrobe of brighter colours, more fashionable styles, and she even sported an up-to-date hairstyle. Everyone told her how much younger she looked and thanked us for our part in her transformation. Her relatives told us that her early life had not been easy, as she had spent most of it nursing first her mother and father and then her husband, who had died young; perhaps we were helping the 'true' Nancy to emerge at last!

During our stay, Nancy's Sunday visits checking up on her brother's excessive drinking also stopped. Instead, she now packed a picnic hamper and off the four of us would drive to explore the breathtaking Scottish countryside. Nancy loved everything about Scotland and was so proud of her Scottish heritage that she was eager to show us the country's delightful scenery. With her help, we began to understand more and more why the country had earned the name 'Bonnie' Scotland.

At Nancy's suggestion, we decided perform a Scottish act and set about choosing a selection of Scottish favourite numbers to use during one week in the show. Being a Geordie, mastering these songs was not too difficult for me but poor Roy, a Yorkshire lad, needed help and Nancy came to his rescue, teaching him the correct pronunciations. In no time at all, he sounded just like a native of the Highlands! We even hired the full Scottish regalia for the week; this was costly but the reception we were given by those audiences left us in no doubt that it had been well worth the effort and expense. They warmed to our duets of *Bonnie Wee Jeannie McColl* and *Two Highland Lads Are We*. They loved Roy's *Road To The Isles*, my clog tap routine to the tune of *The Bluebell Polka* and our rendition of *Walking To The Kirk* and *Granny's Hielan' Hame*. At each performance, the audience shouted for more.

Delighted with this success, we decided that, as we would be performing in Aberdeen and Edinburgh that summer, we would splash out and have kilts made for us by the leading Scottish outfitters, Thomas Gordon and Sons. We chose the Wallace tartan, as we all agreed that the black, red and yellow plaid would be seen to best advantage under the spotlight. Prince of Wales jackets and waistcoats were added, together with sealskin sporrans, silver-buckled shoes and skean dhu. Admittedly those outfits were expensive but they certainly paid for themselves, as in later years we were to wear them in shows all over the world. To this day, they are in our possession and the quality is such that they still look brand new.

Nancy was dreading our departure and as we were packing at the end of our Glasgow season, she was so tearful that we insisted she came home with us. We had about six weeks of club dates in South Yorkshire before our return to Scotland for the summer season in Aberdeen and Edinburgh. She didn't take much persuading and we all set off for Roy's home city, Sheffield.

Nancy became an instant success with Roy's three married sisters and his father, all of whom lived in the same street. As she watched us perform our act every night in the various clubs, she quickly became a favourite with our fans too and there was always someone or other who reserved a seat for her.

Colin, Roy and I were still finding her transformation in such a short time almost unbelievable. The same woman who had frowned on alcohol just a few weeks previously was now saying, "I think I'll try a wee sherry." This soon progressed to, "I think I might try a wee gin and tonic," and on quite a few occasions, "I might try a wee dram." I once caught her puffing on a cigarette but thankfully she did not get into the habit of smoking. Roy's brother-in-law, Frank Greenall, who regularly used snuff, even persuaded her to join him in sniffing it once or twice.

The three of us loved Nancy, so much that she became our unofficial mother and remained with us for the rest of her life; she rarely returned to Scotland and then it was only on flying visits to see her brother and his family or to check her house. The longest she stayed was when we opened for the summer show in Glasgow, where she tended to our every need. When it was time for us to move with the show to Aberdeen, Nancy stayed in Sheffield to look after Roy's ageing father and there she forged very strong links with Roy's sisters.

We were extremely impressed when we first saw the Tivoli Theatre in Aberdeen and we were both delighted and flattered when the star of the show, the dapper Alec Finlay, told us that he had been determined to have us in his show after seeing us on stage in

Glasgow. Alec's wife, Rita, and his valet and secretary, Freddie Nielson, were just as enthusiastic in their welcome and promised us that we would love the Palladium in Edinburgh. How right they were!

This small theatre turned out to be the friendliest place we ever worked, as the patrons seemed to have the same seats on the same nights week after week. We soon began to recognise them in the audience and we knew exactly whom to expect on each night. Many fans turned up regularly at the stage door to proffer small gifts. I particularly remember the delicious home-made cakes and biscuits brought by Mrs. Kay who ran the local post office. Hotelier Jack Scott and his two sisters were other regulars and Jack's brother Craig often took us sailing in his yacht on the Firth of Forth. Chic Murray and Maidi, who lived in Edinburgh, would often come along to our dressing-room to sit and chat. Even the local policeman, Willie Brownhill, used to time his nightly round so that he could pop into the theatre to see our act.

During the third week of our show's run, Edinburgh was over-run with tourists, who had come to see the famous Festival. At this time, our production benefited from the added Scottish attractions of the Police Pipe Band, the Scottish Country Dancers and Curry's Waterfall – all at great expense but certainly worth it in terms of adding Highland flavour, and we three were proud to be able to wear our Scottish outfits for the first time in Edinburgh.

We thoroughly enjoyed working alongside Alec, who liked to include us in his comedy sketches. Roy was also called on to sing duets with an excellent soprano, Eve Robbins, and their excerpts from such shows as The *Student Prince* and *Carmen* were extremely well received. I recall that one week we had been asked by Geoff Morris, the show's producer, to perform songs from *The Merry Widow*, with Eve playing the title-role. Geoff had instructed us to face her as she entered and to freeze, not even moving an eyelid. That night, Eve, looking magnificent in a huge picture hat and long black velvet dress, stood for a moment at the top of five steps and then proceeded to walk elegantly down those steps to centre stage, while the orchestra played the introduction to Velia. It was most unfortunate that, at that very moment, Eve's dress was caught on a nail jutting out from the scenery. Undeterred, she continued to walk, giving her dress a colossal tug in order to free it. With that, the dress ripped all the way down the back, revealing her knickers. Trouper that she was, Eve spontaneously burst out laughing and we on stage joined in the hilarity. The audience genuinely loved it but Geoff Morris was not at all amused and we were all in the dog-house that night.

My mother had never met Roy, so I thought it would now be a good opportunity for her to do so. I invited her and her sisters, Ellen and Frances, up to Edinburgh for a holiday during the Festival and ensured that they were given the best seats in the house to see our show. Roy and I were exceptionally popular with the Palladium audiences and the night my mother came, we were given one of our greatest receptions. In fact, we were cheered wildly by the audience as we appeared on stage in our kilts - even before we had started our act. As we finished, the audience was so appreciative that we had to take more bows than ever before, to prolonged applause and shouts of 'encore'. Alec, the main act, who always performed after us, admitted that he found it difficult to follow us that night.

After the show, when my mother and her sisters came backstage to our dressing-room, I was confident that they would be very impressed with us and full of praise after our ovation.

"Well, what did you think, ma?" I asked excitedly.

"Oh, it's a lovely show," she enthused. "That comedian was easily the funniest I've ever seen. He had the three of us in stitches. And the soprano was wonderful. What a voice!"

"We loved those waterfalls as well," chipped in one of her sisters. "They were ever so effective."

"I really liked the kilt that one of those lads in the Country Dance team was wearing," gushed my mother. "It was a sort of crushed strawberry."

Colin, Roy and I exchanged amazed glances, as she went on to heap even more praise – this time on Arthur Spink, a talented accordion-player.

I couldn't keep quiet any longer. "But, mother, what about Roy and me?" I asked.

"Oh, yes. You two looked lovely and clean. You really did."

"And the audience clapped you for ages," added Aunt Ellen.
"Oh, don't tell them that," broke in my mother. "They'll only get big-headed."

So much for family pride!

Our final show of the season was an unforgettable experience. I don't think we'd ever had a bigger reception. After the finale, everyone on stage received presents, which were handed over the footlights by the fans. Roy and I could not believe our eyes when over seventy gifts, including a haggis, were given to us. Alec said that in all his years in show business he had never seen anything like it. He presented us with record tokens and expressed his greatest wish – that we would come back to work with him the following year, with three weeks in Edinburgh followed by twelve weeks in Aberdeen. Alec was just about to begin a tour of Australia with Kenneth McKellar and promised us that, if we agreed to appear with him in Edinburgh and Aberdeen, he would also try to arrange another tour in Australia the following year and include us. As we had loved working with Alec, we signed the Scottish contract and were delighted at the prospect of going down-under, although we didn't want to build up our hopes too much.

In January 1961, we had the honour of appearing for a second time in the Annual Clubland Command Performance in the Winter Gardens, Blackpool, this time as a double act. Among the performers was Lynne Perrie, who went on to achieve fame as Ivy Tilsley in *Coronation Street.*

Our return to the Palladium in the summer of that year gave us tremendous pleasure, as we were reunited with Alec and were welcomed back enthusiastically by both the other entertainers and the audiences. All the theatre critics were generous in their praise of our act and we were doubly delighted when Alec confided in us that he was in the middle of negotiations with Australia's famous Tivoli circuit. It was being agreed that he should top the bill in Melbourne and Sydney in a lavish spectacular celebrating sixty years of the Tivoli. He had specified that he wanted Roy and me out there with him, as he knew that both our own act and also our comedy scenes with him would be enjoyed by the Australian audiences.

Within three weeks of our being in Scotland, Alec received some welcome news from Australia. All was set for him to share top billing with Leslie Hutchinson, better known as 'Hutch' and Freddie Morgan (Mr.Bonjo from the famous American act, *Spike Jones* and the *City Slickers*). The great news for us was that our act was also to be included. Wee Alec, as we affectionately called him, had been as good as his word. As soon as salaries had been agreed, contracts were sent to us and we signed on the dotted line. Also in the British contingent would be Colin, Alec's wife Rita, who would be an extra in the comedy sketches, their friend, Alister McHarg, a well-known Scottish singer and television star at that time, and Alec's valet, Freddie Nielson.

After everything had been arranged, we all agreed that we would sail rather than fly to Australia, a journey that would take about six weeks. As Roy and I had hardly any time away from the theatre, the thought of relaxing on a luxury liner, with the occasional rehearsal thrown in seemed an excellent idea and Alec agreed whole-heartedly. With preparations well under way, Roy and I decided to take our Scottish outfits with us and also to splash out on a new wardrobe, so we were measured for some expensive new suits, both for our act and for the luxury cruise. Next, Colin, Roy and I arranged to have injections; Colin and I suffered no ill-effects afterwards but poor Roy was badly affected with all manner of symptoms - swellings, soreness, listlessness and lack of appetite, although outwardly he looked in good health.

Geoff Morris, who was producing the show at the Tivoli again, wanted all the company to be involved in an excerpt from a show. One week, *Paint Your Wagon* was the selected show and all the men were required to dress in cowboy outfits and sit or lie round a campfire. During this excerpt, Roy had to sit up and sing *They Call The Wind 'Maria'*. One evening, just before we went on stage, Roy confided that he was feeling ill and that as soon as the show was over he was going to bed.

"Have a drop of brandy or whisky; that'll pick you up," I suggested.

"No, I feel sick at the thought of alcohol," he replied.

We walked on stage to take our positions. The scene opened with a rousing chorus, followed by some lengthy dialogue. Just before Roy's solo was about to begin, I happened to glance across at him and was alarmed to see him lying almost flat with his head on a saddle and his eyes closed. My first worrying thought was that he might have died, so I discreetly moved over to him and nudged him gently. To my relief, he woke from what was obviously a deep sleep. Fine trouper that he was, he performed his song but collapsed as we were leaving the stage. He was immediately rushed to Aberdeen Infirmary, accompanied by Colin, as I had to stay to the end of the show. An apology was made to the audience that, due to unforeseen illness, our act had to be cancelled for that night.

I was so alarmed at what had happened that Alec telephoned the hospital for me immediately after the show, only to be informed that Roy was dangerously ill and should have been admitted to hospital earlier. He was diagnosed with hepatitis, probably from an infected needle when we had received our injections. He would not be able to have visitors for a few days as he needed complete rest and it was highly unlikely that he would recover before the end of the season.

I was wondering what was going to happen to me now that we no longer had an act but Alec, his wife and the rest of the company persuaded me to continue with the show as a solo artist. This meant that I had to work very hard to devise a new act for each week. In the event, I did not feel as though I had let down our act as my solo turns were highly praised in all of the show's weekly reviews.

When Roy was well enough to receive visitors, I used to rehearse every morning and then go straight to the hospital to sit with him, usually in silence, as he slept almost continuously. Many people in Aberdeen showed great concern over Roy's health, sending letters and cards to wish him well and some even visited him weekly.

10

Australia – Here We Come!

There had been some concern about whether we should have to cancel our forthcoming Australian tour and so we were relieved when the doctors decided that Roy was making a good recovery and would be fit enough to sail and later perform, provided that he had adequate rest on the voyage. Thus, we were in good spirits as we boarded our ship, the P & O *Iberia*. Alec and Rita had decided to travel first-class but Alister, Fred and the three of us had booked steerage. We soon realised that the *Iberia* was not the luxury liner we had fondly assumed it to be – in fact, the whole time aboard the 'cruise' ship turned out to be a disappointment. Nearly all the passengers in our class were emigrating to a new life in Australia on £10 tickets and there was chaos everywhere we turned.

On the first night, we entered the dining-room and asked the maître d' if we could join Fred and Alister, as we had earlier arranged. We were abruptly informed that we could not and we were unceremoniously directed to an empty table. We were all quite thirsty and wanted to order a drink before our meal but no one took any notice of our signals. We waited and waited, and still we were ignored.

"Excuse me," Colin called to a passing waiter. "Could we have some service please?"

"You can move from there for a start," snapped the waiter. "I'm not serving you at that table."

We stood up and walked over to the maître d' to ask where we should sit.

"You go back and sit where I told you to," he said. "He'll serve you in good time."

So we did and again we waited and waited, noticing that the same waiter was now serving the main course to everyone around us. When we caught his attention, he shouted, "I've told you before, I'm not serving you at that table."

Colin went back to complain to the maître d', as we were all furious by now. Once again he instructed us to remain at the table. We continued to be ignored. By this time, Colin's blood was boiling! It so happened that there was no carpet in the dining room, just thick linoleum, and very near to us was a service station with a pile of plates on a table.

"We are going to get some attention if it kills me," exploded Colin. "Watch me!"

With that, he walked over to the table, picked up the pile of plates, held them up high and smashed them angrily to the floor, making an unholy clatter. The dining-room was stunned into silence. Up rushed the head-waiter and some other staff, inquiring what was wrong.

"Could we have some service?" asked Colin, red-faced with fury and he proceeded to pick up a large glass dish, ready to drop it.

"Yes, yes," assured the head-waiter, as he deftly moved the dish from Colin's hands.

We never again had to wait for a meal on that ship!

It was about a week before we bumped into Alec and Rita. They said that it was rather dull in first-class and they had heard that our antics in the dining-room had caused fun and games in tourist class. The *Iberia* (or the Siberia, as we had jokingly re-named it) provided little in the way of entertainment and it was almost impossible to find anywhere to sit on deck, as the few chairs were always occupied. The weather was not kind to us either and, to top it all, the three of us were very sea-sick. Luxury cruising it certainly was not!

But, if the conditions on board left much to be desired, the voyage itself proved an unforgettable and enlightening experience because of the places we visited en route. Our first experience of life on the sub-continent of India came when we disembarked for a few hours while the ship re-fuelled at Port Said. Traders had flooded the dockside with their wares of leather goods and silver and gold trinkets, even though the night sky was very dark. I have always been a compulsive shopper and, as I rather foolishly smoked in those days, I couldn't resist buying a leather cigarette case and, for fun, both Roy and I bought a fez, which we were to put into good use in later years on stage.

In amazement, we stood on the dockside and watched while an Egyptian magician who called himself the *Gilly Gilly* Man intriguingly made day-old chickens disappear under three or four cups which he constantly shuffled. We spectators had to guess which cup concealed them and he outwitted us each time without fail, whilst entertaining us throughout with his patter and comical antics.

At the break of dawn we slowly sailed through the Suez Canal, where I was mesmerised by the men swathed from head to foot in strange-looking garments, leading camels through the sand. Some stopped briefly to gaze at our ship, possibly perplexed by the strange sight of a happy-go-lucky Geordie ex-miner, who was waving so excitedly at them.

Our next port of call was Bombay, where we stayed for two days. As soon as we docked, our ship was invaded by Indian traders, who set up shop with their souvenirs and stamps in any available space on board. With this introduction, we could hardly wait to venture ashore to explore the city, where we were to witness the most incredible contrasts of poverty and wealth. Wherever we turned, we were confronted by the most appalling sights. First there were the male beggars, many without arms or legs or blind; then we were surrounded by poorly dressed, greasy-haired women begging for money to feed the tiny unclothed babies lolling in their arms. We were taken aback by the sight of so many disfigured children who had, we were told, been deliberately maimed at birth so that they could become more successful professional beggars. In spite of having been warned not to give any money to them, we were so deeply touched that we felt we had to. It was our own fault, therefore, to find that we were then surrounded by increasing numbers of beggars, pawing at us for help.

As we approached the imposing Gateway of India edifice, we saw even more beggars, together with fortune-tellers, spice-sellers, snake-charmers, performing monkeys and men wanting to examine our feet for corns. They were offering to suck out the corns through a horn-like instrument for a small fee, and others were clamouring to clean out our ears with a similar device. Fortunately, we were not in need of their services but we were reliably informed that the remedies were quite painless and very popular.

From the Gateway of India, we walked to the sumptuous Taj Mahal Hotel, where immaculately-dressed staff were on hand to tend to every whim of the guests and visitors. On sale in the hotel shops were magnificent Indian carpets and fabulous jewellery, whilst exquisite brocade saris were modelled in the hotel's public rooms by the most beautiful Indian girls, all of whom would have been worthy contestants in a Miss World competition. Roy and I both bought silk jackets and that evening we were given the opportunity to wear them, as Colin treated us to dinner in one of the many great restaurants in the hotel. After what turned out to be a perfect meal, we stepped into the street to find countless people sleeping on the pavements - these *untouchables*, as they were universally known, were born on the streets, lived there throughout their lives and died there. Apparently, at least 200,000 people were living rough on the streets of Bombay at that time. We were again soberly reminded of the vastly contrasting lifestyles of India's rich and poor.

The next morning, we were up early to take in more sights. All the streets were teeming with people; there were ox carts weighed down with huge cargoes of goods, men selling everything imaginable and women carrying all manner of wares on their heads. I was unable to resist the lure of the antique stalls, where genuine antiques sat side by side with junk and I bought a brass lamp that to this day reminds me of the magic one associated with Aladdin. At another market place, we were astonished to see two naked three-year old children sleeping on the ground with what looked at first like a puppy. On closer inspection, it turned out to be a monkey, which glared at us as we approached and put its arms protectively around its two wards. I asked one of the traders about the welfare of these two children and was told that, like so many others, they just appeared on the streets for a few days and then moved on. Apparently they existed without any kind of parental care. It made me realise that being born and brought up in a poor mining village in the early 1930s hadn't been any hardship at all, compared with the plight of children such as these.

We enjoyed another meal at the Taj Mahal Hotel, unaware at the time that we would be dining there not as visitors but as guests on several occasions in years to come. Walking back to the ship on that second day, we were again deeply saddened by the plight of the homeless beggars, knowing that we were helpless to change the situation.

Our next stop was a whole day at Sri Lanka, known in those days as Ceylon, where we hired a taxi to explore as much as we could of this tropical paradise. We were driven along rough unmade roads through interesting small villages, where friendly-looking people waved and smiled at us. We passed tea plantations and lush greenery on our way to Kandy to visit the Temple of the Tooth, which houses what is reputed to be Buddha's eye-tooth in seven golden caskets. On approaching this temple, we could see from quite a distance the gleaming gold tiles on the roof. In the grounds, working elephants were pulling huge logs and tree trunks. Riding on their backs or walking alongside them were young, turbaned, half-naked young boys, all very reminiscent of one of my boyhood favourite movie stars, Sabu.

Heading back to the ship in the early evening, our taxi driver stopped the cab to point out similar boys, who were washing their elephants in the river. We took a short break to cine-film the scene and the young boys managed to persuade me to ride on one of the elephants, re-assuring me that it would be quite safe. To be honest, I was more than a little apprehensive as I hadn't even sat on a horse before - but there I was, riding in the river on one of these huge creatures, being filmed by Roy and confident that, if Sir Alexander Korda had seen me before he discovered Sabu, that young star might have been out of a job!

Then we climbed back into the taxi and were just a few miles from the dock when disaster struck. A tremendous storm broke out with thunder, lightning and torrential rain, the like of which we had never encountered before. The roads were running wildly like rivers and at one stage the taxi stopped dead, leaving the three of us no option but to get out and push. Soaked to the skin, we pushed with all our might, hoping against hope that the taxi-driver would be able to make it back to the ship on time. The swirling deluge worsened and still we pushed. By this time, we were convinced that we would not make it back to the ship before it set sail, so we urged the driver to try his hardest. Not really sharing our concern, he just grinned and he assured us that we would arrive on time as long as the plugs managed to avoid the water. By some miracle, we reached the dockside just minutes before the gangplank was due to be raised. Thankfully, we clambered aboard and shortly afterwards, we were sailing out of the harbour and moving onward towards Freemantle, our first port of call in Australia.

11

Success Down-Under

From Freemantle, we travelled to Perth, a city that did not particularly impress us at first as we were constantly surrounded by a plague of flies, most of which seemed to find their way into our mouths! Eventually, we arrived at our destination, Melbourne, a truly beautiful place. Our self-catering accommodation was with a Mr. and Mrs. Howell - Roy's surname, by strange coincidence - who owned a spacious house in the suburb of Armadale, just a few train stops from the city centre.

We were all invited to *Paris By Night*, the current show at the Tivoli Theatre. I was completely overwhelmed as I never seen such a lavish production but I was told that our show was to be even more extravagant, costing thousands of pounds to produce. Angus Winneke, the designer, showed us models of the sets for our show and I could hardly take in the grandeur of it all.

During the time that rehearsals were underway, I was contacted by a long-lost cousin, Brenda Reed, who had become quite famous on Australian television as a Channel 7 Adventure Girl. The Tivoli publicity department thought that it would be good promotion for the show if we could be photographed with her, together with koala bears and kangaroos, and arranged for the session to take place at the local zoo. There we met Brenda, a stunning brunette in her twenties, who was dressed all in white for the occasion. First we were taken to the koala sanctuary where we were photographed holding the animals. I found these tiny creatures quite fascinating and was determined to see more of them at some later date. Then we were whisked off to be photographed with the kangaroos. I was quite apprehensive, as they were larger and stronger than I had imagined and I wondered just how tame they would prove to be when we invaded their territory. Brenda had no such qualms, however, and she walked up to them fearlessly, patted them and told them how beautiful they were. One rather large male kangaroo responded enthusiastically to her kind words and began kissing her. At first, she backed off and giggled, "This really isn't allowed, you know." But the kangaroo became seriously amorous and attempted to molest her. As she fell to the ground, the zoo-keepers rushed to her aid. Once on her feet again, Brenda grinned at the press men and said to them, "Well, you can call yourself a 'fair dinkum Aussie' when you've been embraced by a kangaroo," and turning to the kangaroo, she laughed, "Pick on someone your own size next time."

We were well into rehearsals when I heard Hutch in person for the first time and I thought that his performance had tremendous class. He was the first person I had heard sing Moon River and every time I hear that tune, my thoughts take me back to our stay in Melbourne.

Our show was entitled *The Golden Days – Commemorating 60 Years of Variety at the Tivoli.* No expense had been spared on the sets and costumes and we were immensely proud to be part of the production. Sharing top-billing with Alec and Hutch was Freddie Morgan, an American, who, in addition to being one of the best banjo players in the world, was well-known for his crazy, zany antics as the comedy star with the band *Spike Jones and the City Slickers.* 'Rubber-faced' Freddie, as he was also called, was a friendly man, widely travelled in the American theatre and we always enjoyed chatting to him. His greatest pride was the fact that at that time he was the only American to have been made a Member of the Grand Order of Water Rats in England.

There were other memorable entertainers in the show too. Kenet and Jani, who were originally solo classical ballet dancers, performed a hilarious adagio act in a spectacular circus sequence in the show. Another artist was Jandy, a world-famous musical clown, who had mastered just about every instrument you could imagine and combined his artistic playing with eccentric musical clowning. Then there was Greco, a magnificent Greek, who presented a perfect upside-down balancing act on the smallest of tables. The climax of his performance came when, supported by only two fingers on each hand, he juggled three balls in the centre of three razor-sharp knives that he held in his mouth. I remember this trick as being so dangerous that the spotlights had to be turned off to prevent a double reflection of the overhead lights on the gleaming knife blades. Our act followed Greco's and because I was fascinated with his expertise, I used to watch his every movement from the side of the stage. We were particularly friendly with Anne Lane, who also appeared in the show. She was a vivacious TV and radio star in Australia and well known to all the audiences. The renowned Tivoli Orchestra was led by the remarkable Hal Moschetti who arranged our music to suit his full orchestra. All the above acts, combined with the Golden Singers, the Tivoli Toppers, the Debonair Dandies and the Hawthorn City Pipe Band, provided a variety of entertainment on a colossal scale.

Opening night went very smoothly, considering all the problems there had been at rehearsals with the illuminated staircase which stretched the whole width of the stage and the gigantic illuminated glass thistles which flanked either side the lavish set for The *Lauder Story* scene. The whole company, including the Hawthorn City Pipe Band, was required to climb up the back of the staircase and over the top to come into the view of the audience. Timing was crucial and it took hours to perfect this part of the show. The sound of those bagpipes, combined with the noise of thirty dancers who each played a drum, almost drowned the singing of those on stage and we certainly found the noise unbearable at such close quarters. However, the thunderous applause it drew from the audience at every performance made it all worthwhile.

Roy and I were very well received at the Tivoli and both Alec and Freddie Morgan were firm favourites too. The only person who did not particularly appeal to the audiences was Hutch at the top of the bill. He had flown to Melbourne directly from appearing in both The *Talk of the Town* and the *Colony Night Club* in London's West End, where he had become the idol of the 'Coronet Set', which included the Duke and Duchess of Windsor, the Duchess of Kent and Princess Margaret. His smooth vocal renditions of Cole Porter songs and his nonchalant asides were ideally suited to the worldly London crowd but they were far too sophisticated for the Australian audience.

Press reports were mixed. One of them read:

Variety Bills presented by the Tivoli circuit offer entertainment and standards that are among the finest in the world. The Tivoli celebrates sixty years of Variety (Marie Lloyd was on the very first bill) with a review entitled The Golden Days and this is one of the finest presented for some time. The lavish and colourful costumes and settings of Tivoli shows are always outstandingly praiseworthy and the choreography is usually of a very high standard. In the current show, a peak has been reached which will be difficult to sustain in the future let alone surpass.

Ray Stanley, a respected theatre critic, wrote a review of the show in the glossy Theatre-goer magazine and I quote:

It frequently happens that the smaller billed acts steal the thunder from the stars in a Tivoli show and this certainly happens in The Golden Days. There are two talented Englishmen, Roland Roy and Jackie Toaduff who sing and dance together, whilst in solo numbers, Toaduff does a clog dance and Roy does a hilarious send-up of Johnny Ray singing 'On Such a Night'. Versatility would seem to be their hallmark. Their appearance on the bill is all too brief and one feels the Tivoli could do worse than mount an entire show around the talents and personalities of this duo. After the show-stealers, the billed stars – Hutch, Freddie Morgan and Alec Finlay. In the case of coloured singer-pianist Leslie Hutchinson (or 'Hutch', as he is usually referred to), one can but ask was his journey really necessary? Freddie Morgan is great on his banjo and can tell a reasonably original story but his initial appearance lasts nearly twenty minutes, during which time he becomes repetitive for far too long. The Scottish comedian, Alec Finlay, is no better or worse than a lot of other comics. He possesses the features for pathos; a little bit of this quality in his work would put him a few steps ahead of the other comedians. He is at his best away from comedy, in a nostalgic recap of some of Harry Lauder's famous songs.

He went on to praise the rest of the show and top marks went to producer Knox Godfrey, designer Angus Winneke and Winnie Gill who executed the wardrobe.

Within a very short time of that review appearing, Roy and I were informed that we were to change places with Hutch on the bill. Concerned about Hutch's feelings, we questioned the wisdom of the Tivoli management's decision but they were adamant that the change must be made. Hutch, who had never been the friendliest entertainer in the show and who always addressed everyone with an air of aloofness, was not at all happy with the change. For the rest of the show's run, he refused to speak to us or to anyone else, unless it was absolutely necessary.

In the past, we had heard many stories of jealousy among professional entertainers and now we found that we were at the receiving end. After the change of billing, Alec, his wife Rita, Alister and Fred all distanced themselves, even though the move had nothing at all to do with us – but thankfully, the other performers and the audience loved us more than ever.

We noticed that every week an outstanding-looking couple occupied the same two expensive seats in the front row. It was clear to see how much they enjoyed our act, as they cheered us enthusiastically each time we appeared. The man was noticeable because he had only one eye and wore a black patch, pirate-style and his wife was an extremely good-looking, well-dressed woman, who wore dark glasses at all times. It turned out that they were Eve and Andy Taylor, who had emigrated to Australia from Aberdeen many years ago and settled in Burwood, establishing a thriving bakery and cake-decorating business there.

They had met Alec the previous year and decided to throw a party for him and his group. After our first meeting with the Taylors, Roy, Colin and I forged a friendship that was to last a lifetime. They loved show business and, as we were invited to their home on many occasions, we were able to admire how professionally they entertained their many famous guests.

During our comparatively short time in Melbourne, I had grown very fond of the city, the Tivoli Theatre and our house in Armadale. Each evening, I had to leave the house an hour earlier than Roy because I appeared in a sketch with Alec at the beginning of the show whereas Roy was not needed until the first-half finale. On those occasions, I would stroll down our street to the station, passing gardens which were so colourful that I imagined I'd landed in heaven. There was an abundance of orange, lemon, pomegranate and cherry-plum trees – the green juicy plums were a particular favourite of mine. It was hard for me to believe the change in my life; less than two years ago, I had been living in a mining village and working down the pit and now here I was in the star spot of the most prestigious theatrical production that Melbourne had ever witnessed.

All the dancers in the show were excited at the prospect of moving on to our next venue and they assured us that, if we liked Melbourne, we would absolutely love Sydney – and how right they were! We were fortunate in having a fortnight's break before the show started, so that gave us time to find a suitable place to live. We decided to rent an apartment in Kanimbula Hall at Pots Point in the Kings Cross area of the city; it seemed to us to be the equivalent of London's Soho. It was a bustling, buzzing area, with all-night shops, cafés and hot-dog stands; added to these noises, car-owners hooted loud greetings to each other until three or four o'clock in the morning. Kanimbula Hall certainly had its disadvantages, as the constant noise at night meant that we were forced to wear earplugs before we could manage to sleep. Not only that - our apartment was regularly invaded by huge cockroaches. These insects didn't actually come near us, so I was not particularly bothered by them but Roy hated them and sprayed the floor of his bedroom every night before switching off the light. But to compensate, the place had its advantages too, as it was located very near to the theatre and was a wonderful, vibrant area during the day.

Eve and Andy came to Sydney with us for a fortnight's holiday and Andy's highly-developed sense of humour and mischievous pranks made our time with them most enjoyable and entertaining.

On one of the days, the five of us decided to visit Sydney Zoo, going first to the koala sanctuary because I had been longing to see koalas again ever since my encounter with them in Melbourne. We all thought they looked docile and harmless, sitting on the branches peacefully eating eucalyptus leaves or slowly moving up and down the trees. We noticed two young koalas in a pen by themselves and one of them kept reaching up to me and crying like a baby.

"Oh, just look at it," I called to the others. "It looks as though it wants a cuddle," and, without more ado, I made an attempt to pick it up. Unfortunately, it was an inch or so out of my arm's reach.

"Now don't you start getting ideas," warned Colin. "Haven't you read that notice over there? ANYONE FOUND HANDLING THESE BEARS WILL BE INSTANTLY FINED £50."

"But I'm sure it needs comforting," I said.

"Come on, let's have a coffee," suggested Eve and she, Colin and Andy moved off in the direction of the café, but Roy and I stayed a little longer looking at the small koala.

"Hey, Roy," I said, "do me a favour. Your arms are longer than mine. Pick up the koala and take my photograph with it."

"No, don't be stupid," objected Roy. "We'll be fined."

"Oh, go on, Roy," I cajoled. "Look, there's nobody around. I only want to hold it for a minute."

"It might bite," said Roy doubtfully.

"Don't be bloody daft, they're harmless," I urged. "Go on, pick it up for me."

Roy gave in. "All right, I'll do it, but if we get caught, it's you who'll pay the fine. You must be mad."

I must point out that Roy was looking his usual immaculate self that day, wearing an expensive grey silk jacket and tie. When he bent over to lift it up, the koala immediately flung its arms round him, scratching his face very badly in the process.

"Roy, you're bleeding," was all I could lamely say.

"That's great," he answered, giving me a withering look. "Get the damn thing off me, will you?"

This was more easily said than done. Try as I might, I couldn't prise the animal off him. Koalas have huge claws and in no time at all, the back of his precious jacket was ripped to shreds and his face was bleeding profusely.

By this time, more people had arrived on the scene, with children commenting on the state of Roy's face and jacket. A man tried to help me pull the crying bear away, but to no avail – by now, it was terrified and clung on even more tightly. There was a long struggle before we eventually managed to drop it back in its pen.

"I think you're going to need medical attention," my helper told Roy, "and your jacket's a write-off."

"Colin's going to be really mad at you, Roy," I sympathised.

"Mad at ME?" he exploded. "It's all your stupid fault."

"For God's sake, don't tell him how it really happened," I begged, because I knew from past experience how furious Colin could be. "Just say that you caught your face and jacket on some branches of a tree."

The others, who were quietly enjoying refreshments, stood up in horror when they saw us approaching and wanted to know what was wrong. I was just about to lie, when a woman nearby butted in. "I don't think that koala meant any harm, you know," she said. "It was probably scared of you."

"What koala?" shouted Colin, his face growing purple.

"The one that was crying," I answered quickly. "It climbed up its pen and jumped on to Roy."

But Colin knew us too well and immediately guessed who was to blame. "You lying bugger, Toaduff," he bellowed. "Come on, Roy. Let's get you to First Aid."

"You're lucky it didn't have your eye out, Roy," I sympathised, trying at the same time to shift the blame. "You shouldn't have picked it up for me, you know."

On our way to First Aid, Andy joked, "Look, Roy, there's a beautiful tiger in that cage. If Jackie wants you to pick it up, DON'T!" That remark broke the tension a little and Eve, Andy and I all laughed but, at the time, Roy and Colin did not see the funny side.

During the following weeks, we were kept busy with the show, after a highly successful opening night. We gave regular interviews on radio and television and made several personal appearances. We were invited to appear on *The Beth Nichol 2GB Show*, a very popular talk programme. On two consecutive Sundays, we were interviewed by Ken Evans on *Sunny Side Up*, the Number One top-rated TV show at that time. Ken, who worked for the AWA Network at Key Station 2 Channel, became another friend with whom we still have contact to this day.

He lived in a sumptuous pent-house apartment in Kirribilli overlooking Sydney harbour and he often invited us there on Sunday evenings. He had the largest and best record collection I had ever seen and I was in my element, sitting on his balcony, listening to music and watching all the boats and ferries sailing non-stop round the harbour. I first heard Henry Mancini's version of *Moon River* on that balcony, a perfect setting for the music.

One of my favourite actors, Edward Everett Horton, a master of the double take, came out to Sydney to appear on stage in Nina, a French farce. We met him when we were being interviewed on the same television programme and what wonderful tales he had to relate of his experiences working on such films as *Lost Horizon* and *Top Hat* with Fred Astaire and Ginger Rogers as well as other popular

Technicolor musicals. Because we were working, we were unable to see his evening performances so he invited us to a matinée. He was outstandingly good in the play and when we visited him backstage to congratulate him, we asked him to have Sunday lunch with us. He agreed, on condition that he could supply the champagne. By this time, incidentally, the nocturnal noises and the cockroaches had driven us away from Kings Cross and we were now living in a house in Watsons Bay, further from the theatre but much more pleasant.

Eve and Andy travelled to Sydney to be with us for the weekend when Edward was invited. He thoroughly enjoyed Roy's traditional roast beef and Yorkshire pudding for lunch and later, Eve's ribbon sandwiches - a variation on club sandwiches, only more delicious. Throughout the day, he regaled us with fascinating stories of the American stars. When I asked him about Carmen Miranda, he was very enthusiastic both about her and her house parties. He told us that the first time he had been invited to her house, he happened to admire a beautiful tree in her garden.

"Do you have a garden, Edward?" Carmen asked.

"I certainly do," he replied.

Her generosity was such that, two days later, she not only had her tree dug up and sent to Edward's house but also arranged for it to be planted in his garden.

When Roy asked about Nelson Eddy and Jeanette Macdonald and other famous Hollywood people of the day, Edward reminisced about their many kindnesses to him. Apparently, the only star he did not like was Danny Kaye. When the two of them had worked together on a television show, Edward was required to speak with a Brooklyn accent. Danny was constantly interrupting him at rehearsals, pouring scorn on the way in which Edward spoke.

"You just don't get that accent, do you, Horton?" he sneered.

The producers were growing more and more annoyed at all the breaks in continuity that Danny was causing, so when he began jeering the next time, Edward retorted, "Well, Mr. Kaye, I really think that you should go to Brooklyn and listen to the people there.

As a matter of fact, I happen to know all about that particular accent. You see, I was born there!"

One of his other revealing tales was of when he was appearing in the Fred Astaire – Ginger Rogers films. Ginger was both shocked and angry when she discovered that Edward was earning more money for the film than she was. Edward, who was very fond of Ginger, felt that she was right to demand an increase and fully supported her in her claim.

Towards the end of our show's run, headlines in the Sydney newspapers announced the forthcoming appearance of another Hollywood star, the great Jane Russell, who would be appearing in cabaret for four weeks at Chequers, Australia's premier night-club. That was one show I certainly did not want to miss, as I was a fan of hers. I remembered that, during my school days, we were asked to paint a poster of anything we wanted to do later in life. All the other lads in the class chose footballers to indicate their chosen profession but my picture was a masterpiece! I copied a photograph from a newspaper, probably the *News of the World*, of Jane Russell advertising her banned and much talked about film, The *Outlaw.* I painted her in a very seductive pose, lying in a haystack, with her blouse off one shoulder and carrying a whip. In my boyish enthusiasm, I think I must have exaggerated the boobs somewhat, painting them pink with one exposed nipple dark red. Mr. Holmes, the art teacher, was walking round the room, criticising each poster with such remarks as, "Is that supposed to be a football? It looks more like a tennis ball," but when he came to me, he took one look at my effort and his only comment was, "Oh, my God!" Laughing uncontrollably, he grabbed the picture and ran out of the room to show it to the female teacher in the next class. We could all hear their shrieks of laughter through the glass partition that separated the two rooms. Then all the other teachers came along to see it and we heard more hilarity. It was later put on display for all to view and even our very serious headmaster laughed when he saw it.

One night when we arrived at the Tivoli, Alister McHarg greeted us, grinning from ear to ear. He told us that he had been asked to appear in *The Jane Russell Show* for four weeks, in addition to his act in our show.

"You lucky devil," I enthused. "However did you pull that one off?"

Alister turned to me with sheer disdain as he sarcastically replied, "It was nothing to do with LUCK, Jackie. It's called TALENT."

"Well, we're definitely going to book for that cabaret, so will you introduce us to Jane if you have chance?" I asked.

"To tell you the truth," continued Alister in a rather superior tone, "I don't think you have a cat in hell's chance of getting in. It's already sold out."

"Well, perhaps we could come backstage and watch with you from the wings," I went on.

"I'm already trying to arrange seats for Alec, Rita and Fred," he answered importantly, "so don't build your hopes up, Jackie boy. I might ask her to sign an autograph for you. It'll cost you, mind. Anyway, you seem to have a lot of influential friends in radio; you could try asking them if they can find tickets for you."

I knew I was being more and more humiliated but I wanted to see Jane Russell so much that I still tried my luck. "If you do manage to book seats for us and you introduce us, Alister, I'll buy you a bottle of Scotch."

Alister shook his head in mock pity. "I don't need any more, thank you. I'm already well stocked up with drink."

Shortly afterwards, Jane Russell arrived in Sydney and rehearsals were under way for her grand opening.

"Have you met her yet?" I asked Alister.

"Yes, she's lovely. You know that the show's absolutely sold out, don't you?"

"Yes, you told me - but I've not given up yet," I said. "Do you think I could come to rehearsals with you one day?" I continued, well aware that I was now grovelling again.

Alister knew he held the winning hand. "Sorry, definitely not. No visitors are allowed," he lied.

A few nights later, we were all surprised and delighted to learn that Jane, her mother and Dennis Wong, the Chinese proprietor of Chequers, were in the audience to see our show at the Tivoli. The following day, Roy and I were called into the theatre office for a piece of news that left us absolutely flabbergasted. Alister was now to be taken out of Jane's show and we were to replace him. You can imagine what the atmosphere in our theatre was like; it was as though we had committed murder. Alec and Rita were so annoyed that they hardly spoke to us afterwards, even though once again, the decision had nothing at all to do with us. We were under contract and had to obey orders. And poor demoted Alister McHarg could not look us in the face.

As *The Golden Days* had only two more weeks to run, we were contracted out to appear once each night at the Tivoli and three times at Chequers – two with Jane and one spot on our own.

It was nearing the time for *The Golden Days* to end and for us to leave Australia. I felt sad for two reasons; first, because we might never again see the many new friends we had made in Australia and secondly, because our relationship with Alec, Rita, Alister and Fred remained cool because of our popularity with the audiences. We constantly tried to be friendly as we could never forget our gratitude to Alec who had been responsible for our trip to Australia and we still greatly admired his considerable talent. We were both hurt and baffled by their changed feelings. We were consoled by the fact that the singers and dancers and other acts in the show continued to enjoy our company. I knew that I would particularly miss the many laughs we shared with Anne Lane and Monica Shergold. Before *The Golden Days*, Monica had been a principal in the musical show *Once Upon A Mattress* and had also understudied the famous Australian soprano June Bronhill in *The Merry Widow*. Monica's wicked sense of humour enabled her to amuse us night after night with endless jokes, all of which were very near the knuckle! She used to say that I was her best audience as I would invariably guess the punch line as she was delivering it and chortle with laughter. Colin and Roy were much more staid and often tut-tutted, shaking their heads in disgust, which caused Monica and me to burst into further fits of laughter.

During the last week of the show's run, a Peeping Tom climbed a wall at the back of the theatre and peered through Anne Lane's window. Anne had just finished applying black face make-up for her number *Can't Help Loving Dat Man Of Mine*. If you can picture the scene - Anne, with her face blackened and wearing nothing more than a red and white spotted turban, her bra and long-john bloomers, looking up and spotting the intruder - you can imagine the fright he must have had.

She screamed and shouted, "Oh, you dirty blackguard!" and dashed to our dressing-room, the whites of her eyes almost popping out of her head. Within a very short time, we were all laughing, particularly when Monica remarked. "The poor bastard must have had the shock of his life. I bet he thought it was Hutch in drag!"

After the final performance of the show at the Tivoli, many of the other acts and well-wishers had crowded into our dressing-room. I saw Alister passing our open door.

Still trying to be cordial, I called out, "Goodnight, Alister. When are you travelling home?"

"I haven't the faintest idea," he replied, with no friendliness at all in his voice. There was no goodbye from him and he ignored my proffered handshake.

"Will you be coming to see *The Jane Russell Show*? I could perhaps get you a seat," I said, trying to ease the situation.

"That's one show I definitely wouldn't want to see," he replied aloofly.

I was so hurt and disappointed by his rebuff that I then said something completely out of character. "That's a pity. There's a hell of a lot of TALENT in it!" I was hoping that it would remind him of his earlier sarcastic comment to me but whether it did or not, I'll never know because I never saw him again.

What were to have been our last three weeks in The Jane Russell Show were extended by a further three weeks, so we asked the stage manager at the Tivoli Theatre if we could leave our cabin trunk backstage there until it was time for us to sail home. Following *The Golden Days*, the Royal Ballet were appearing at the theatre for just one week and when I found out that Margot Fonteyn was to be the prima ballerina, I desperately wanted to see the show. I was not really interested in ballet as such but I longed to see Margot perform. However, our three shows at Chequers each night were hectic and exhausting and did not give me any time to spare. I remember Colin noticing my sadness and asking me if I would like to have spoken to her again but I replied, "Oh, no. I'm sure she wouldn't remember me."

Then, quite out of the blue, one of the Tivoli stage hands contacted me. Margot Fonteyn had apparently spotted our black cabin trunk backstage and seeing our names in bold white letters on it, she had inquired, "Is that Jackie Toaduff, the clog-dancer?" When told that it was, she continued, "Is he still around? I'd love to see him again."

"Jackie's appearing in *The Jane Russel*l Show just up the road," she was told.

"Do you think that you could get a message to him?" asked Margot. "Tell him that if he has time to come and see me, I'd love to meet him again."

That settled it. Tired as I was, I pulled a few strings and made arrangements for Roy, Colin and myself to watch her from the back of the stalls the following night. It was well worth the effort, as her performance as *Raymonda* was spellbinding. After the show, I mentioned to the stage manager that I should love to speak to Margot if it could be arranged.

"Jackie," smiled the stage manager, "there's already a line of long-lost relatives, government officials and a host of local dignitaries all wanting to have a word with her. You'll have to wait at the end of a very long queue."

When I saw the number of people waiting, my heart sank. "Well, I'm really disappointed," I said to the manager and told him about the message she had sent to me. "Unfortunately, I won't be able to wait because it will soon be time for our own show to start."

"Leave it with me, Jackie," he said, "and I'll see what I can do." With that, he walked to the front of the long line and into her dressing-room.

Within seconds, Margot popped her head round the door and called out, "Jackie, come on in and bring your friends too."

I must say that we felt quite important as we passed that queue of very distinguished visitors. Inside the dressing-room which she was sharing with Lynn Seymore, Margot, wearing a flowered silk dressing-gown and applying cold cream to remove her make-up, told Lynn all about me. "You should just see this man dancing, Lynn," she enthused. "He is marvellous." She went on to relate the story of how I almost lost my breeches in front of Princess Margaret at the Royal Albert Hall and then she impersonated how I had finished the dance with one hand behind and one in front.

"I'm so pleased that I saw your name on the cabin trunk," she went on. "By the way, Toaduff's a very unusual stage name, isn't it? Who thought of it?"

"It's no stage name – it's my own," I replied, "and to tell you the truth, I'm thinking of changing it because I don't think it's such a good name for show business."

"Oh no, you mustn't do that. I think it sounds Scandinavian or Russian," said Margot, "and it's a great name for a dancer."

And so, because of Margot Fonteyn's words, I have always kept the surname with which I was born.

She went on to ask us if we liked the current dance craze, the Twist, and laughingly told us that some English newspapers had printed photographs of her dancing this non-classical dance, much to the disgust of the Royal Ballet officials.

When it was time for us to leave for our own show, she asked us to meet her for tea at her hotel the following day. "I want to know all about your act and also what Jane Russell's really like," she said, planting a kiss on my cheek.

When we arrived back at Chequers, we had to push our way through the crowds, who had gathered as they always did to catch a glimpse of the world-wide famous Jane. I sometimes used to fantasise that those crowds were clamouring for us, but the nearest we managed was when a mother and daughter, who had seen us in *The Golden Days*, asked us for autographs! The Australians loved Jane and so did we, as she was not only beautiful but also a very down to earth and completely natural person off stage. She had travelled to Australia with her mother, an evangelist, who preached at various venues each night while Jane was performing at the club.

Jane's forty-minute act was faultlessly directed by Peggy Lee and presented so professionally by Jane herself that I was drawn to watch it every night. What fascinated me was that every performance was identical; it looked completely spontaneous but every gesture, every arm and hand movement, every wink, every witty aside – all were methodically worked out and the Aussies, believing it to be impromptu, lapped it up. Throughout the world, Jane was famous as a sex symbol but rather than flaunt this aspect on stage, she sided with the females in the audience instead and good-humouredly sent up the men and made the odd joke at her own expense.

She had brought with her only two stage dresses, which she wore on alternate nights. One was black and the other red with sequins, very similar in style to the dresses she and Marilyn Monroe had worn in *Gentlemen Prefer Blondes* - but without the slit up the side and without the plunging neckline. In fact, both of her dresses were long-sleeved and high-necked. We had adjoining dressing-rooms and she frequently came into ours and asked me to zip her into her dress, a task I remember well! On those nights, I often wondered what that school art teacher of mine would have thought of me now and also what my former miner friends would have given to be in my shoes.

Jane's mother was an amusing character in her own right and frequently commented on the fact that her audiences were bigger than her daughter's at Chequers. She hated the red dress intensely and once or twice enlisted my help in trying to persuade Jane that she looked much better in the black one.

We recounted these tales and many more when we went to tea with Margot that next day. She wanted to know all about Jane – in fact, she seemed almost as star-struck as I was!

"What exactly does she do in her act?" she asked.

I told her that although Jane was famous for her acting talents she also had a fine singing voice. Many people did not realise that Jane herself sang in most of her films. In our Australian show, she opened her act with *I Believe in You* and later sang a wonderful arrangement of *Mack the Knife*; at the end of this song, she threw an imaginary knife at the spotlight, which immediately and most effectively put her in complete darkness. She also parodied *Big Bad John*, which she changed to *Big Bad Jane*, with the words:

When Howard Hughes made the film, "The Outlaw"
He flew off in his big plane
And who stuck around to take the blame?
JANE, big bad Jane!

She spoke to the audience about how fond she was of Clark Gable but added that her favourite of all time was "Old Ski-Nose" himself, Bob Hope, with whom she had starred in The *Paleface*. That story led her into the song from that film – *Buttons and Bows* followed by *I Wish I were an Apple on a Tree*. It was with great affection that she spoke of her friendship with Marilyn Monroe, which cued her for the song *Diamonds are a Girl's Best Friend* and then she closed her act with *Bye Bye, Baby*. At the end of every show, there were tumultuous shouts for more but she never once gave an encore.

Margot listened intently to all we had to say and was upset that her tight schedule would not allow time for her to see the show for herself. When we said our goodbyes, this most elegant and graceful of dancers gave me a large photograph of herself, signed with the words "To Jackie, with my admiration of your dancing and with my very best wishes, Margot Fonteyn Arias". To this day, her photograph is one of my greatest treasures, together with fond memories of one of the greatest ballerinas the world has ever known.

The following night at Chequers, Jane also made a tremendous impression on me as she proved herself to be a lady in every sense of the word. The wall between our dressing-room and hers was so thin that we often spoke to each other through it – and, of course, we could hear everything that was said there. That night, we heard such a commotion outside her room. A drunken woman had somehow managed to find her way backstage and was shouting for Jane.
"Come on now. You shouldn't be here, you know," one of the waiters was saying.

"Get your fucking hands off me," she slurred and followed this with several more abusive sentences with a liberal use of the four-letter word . She wanted to f-well see Jane Russell and nobody was going to f-well stop her.

By this time, several more waiters had appeared and were trying to remove her bodily when Jane opened her door, politely asked the waiters to put the woman down and then invited her into the dressing-room.

 "Now, what's your problem, honey?" she asked soothingly.

"Jane, I just wanted to tell you that I won some fucking money at the races today and I want to buy you a fucking drink because I think you're fucking marvellous. Do you want champagne? You can have as much fucking champagne as you can drink."

"Please listen to me, honey," Jane said. "I really hate to hear people swearing. Ladies shouldn't swear – it's not very polite."

Immediately, the woman sobered. "Oh, I'm so sorry, Jane, so sorry."

"Now, I'm delighted that you were lucky at the races today and thank you for your offer of champagne – but I don't drink. Thank you, all the same."

"Jane," replied the woman, "I think you're fucking beautiful."
"Now, honey, you're not listening to me. I've just told you that I loathe swearing."

"Sorry, Jane, sorry." She spotted some photographs of Jane on the dressing-table. "Please could I have one, Jane?" she asked.

"Of course you can. Look, I'll sign it for you. What's your name, honey? Sheila? That's a good old Aussie name, isn't it? Well, thanks for coming to see the show. Now, goodnight and God bless and promise me, NO MORE SWEARING!"

"I promise you, Jane. I really do. I'll never swear again."

But when Jane closed her door, we heard Sheila call out to the waiters, "Hey, you bastards, that Jane Russell's some fucking lady."

Dennis Wong was very keen to extend Jane's contract even further but the star was missing her husband and wanted to fly back to the USA to be with him as quickly as possible. And so, after six glorious weeks, our run at Chequers came to an end and it was time for us too to go home after spending almost a year in Australia. We had booked our passage back to the UK on a Dutch liner, the *Johan Van Oldenbaravelt* (usually known as the JVO). We would be sailing via the Panama Canal and, as we had gone out via the Suez Canal, this journey would mark the first of many 'round the world' trips for the three of us.

12

Homeward Bound

Our send-off from Australia was unbelievably spectacular. To imagine it, you have to think of those big farewell scenes in Hollywood movies. Almost everyone we had met in Sydney plus Andy and Eve from Melbourne came to see us off. We had decided to book a state-room on board for the journey home and so there was enough room to accommodate all our well-wishers. They came with enough champagne and other drinks to last us the entire trip and brought gifts ranging from boomerangs to stuffed toys. Ken Evans presented me with a white koala bear. I don't think there is such a creature as a white one but this koala still looks wonderful and is brought out for display every Christmas. During our final week in Sydney, we had arranged for Ken to join us in the UK for the following festive season and hoped to be able to show him the snow that he longed to see. In the midst of all the booze-fuelled merriment, we heard the announcement that it was time for all those not sailing on the JVO to proceed ashore as the ship would shortly be leaving. I have never liked goodbyes but I think that this must have been one of the saddest. Those months in Australia had been the most wonderful ones in my life, with the shows, the people and the life-style all giving me immense pleasure. As our friends left, we went up on deck and made our way through the crowds to the ship's rail, where passengers were throwing thousands of streamers to their friends and the ship's musicians were playing *Waltzing Matilda* and *Now is the Hour* over and over again. Eventually, the ship began to move and, as the streamers linking passengers and well-wishers finally snapped, this great chapter in our lives was brought to an end.We loved the *JVO*, a fine old ship that contrasted in every way with the *Iberia* on our outward journey. Accommodation, food, crew and other passengers all helped to make it a most pleasant voyage. Even though we had no work to come home to, we were not unduly worried as, modesty aside, we knew how well-respected we were in the Yorkshire and other Northern clublands and that our diary would soon be filled again. We quickly spotted one or two interesting-looking individuals on board but, as our last couple of months in Sydney had been so hectic both socially and work-wise, we had already decided to keep ourselves to ourselves and enjoy a relaxing journey home. This decision not to become too involved with other people's lives was particularly difficult for me!

Our first port of call was Wellington in New Zealand. Andy and Eve, who had relatives there, had already arranged for them to meet us so that we could see something of the city on our all-too-brief stay. Apart from being wined and dined most royally by these good people, my most vivid memory of Wellington was the sight of anglers pulling out one huge fish after another at the dockside. As we boarded the ship for the next stage of our journey, Tahiti, we nursed the idea that we would love to return to New Zealand one day.

As soon as we reached our cabin, we received a message to report to the Radio Room as there was a telegram waiting for us. We had assumed that it would be another bon voyage communication from our Sydney friends and so we were completely taken by surprise to find that the cable had come from the Galt office in Glasgow, asking if we would be interested in a summer season in Dundee with Johnny Victory – and we could name our own fee. We have never found out to this day how the Galt management knew that we were on the JVO because even our relatives had not yet been informed of our whereabouts. To be honest, we did not particularly relish the idea of going back to Scotland immediately on our return and we had heard that Johnny Victory wasn't the easiest of people to work with, as apparently everyone found his temper tantrums and foul-mouthed swearing hard to tolerate. Bearing in mind these disadvantages, Colin bumped up our fee considerably, feeling confident that we had out-priced ourselves. However, to our astonishment, it was accepted. Knowing that we would now have no free time once we arrived home, we decided to forget our earlier resolution to keep a low profile on board; instead, we would make the most of our voyage! A small group of talented musicians played for dancing in the evenings and, looking around us, it was easy to see that we would not be short of dance partners, as the women greatly outnumbered the men.

One night after dinner, we were enjoying a drink before retiring to bed, when our peace was disturbed by gales of laughter coming from the centre of the room. A distinguished-looking, grey-haired lady in her sixties was holding forth, surrounded by a small group of passengers. We thought at first that the old lady was none other than Margaret Rutherford and we kept glancing over to the group trying to decide. After a few minutes, a couple of the men from her party came over to our table.

"Excuse us for invading your privacy," said one of them, " but we just had to ask. Didn't we see you on television and on *The Jane Russell Show*?"

"You could have done," Roy replied rather warily.

"Are you going to entertain on board?"

"No, we're here to relax," I explained, "so please don't mention to any of the other passengers that we're entertainers, as we truly don't want to sing and dance for the next week or two."

His companion, another Australian, joined in the conversation. "You see our friend over there?" he said, pointing to the older woman. "She also thought that she recognised you and she's asked us to invite you to join our table. We're a noisy crowd, I know, but I'm sure you'll enjoy the company."

"Is she Margaret Rutherford?" I asked.

"No, but she's forever being mistaken for her. Come on over now and we'll introduce you and buy you a drink."

As soon as we sat at their table, the old lady introduced herself. "Good evening, gentlemen. My name is Bertha Hallin, the Countess Helene."

It turned out that Bertha was the wealthy widow of a Swedish count and now lived in Boston, Massachusetts, where she was a well-known socialite. She had been everywhere, done everything and met everyone! She had enjoyed our act in Jane Russell's show - and oh yes, she had met Jane, just after Howard Hughes had discovered her. Howard and Bertha's husband were concluding some business deal at the time.

Bertha, soon to be affectionately christened "Auntie" Bertha by us, was an unforgettable character. That night and every other night on board, she wore an impressive diamond tiara. I'm not sure whether they were real diamonds but, with her vast wardrobe of expensive evening dresses, furs, shoes and jewellery, she certainly looked like royalty.

It so happened that we stayed with that small group until Auntie Bertha and the others disembarked at Florida. Auntie Bertha herself did not dance; I tried to coax her on to the dance floor several times but she always declined. In spite of this, she loved to watch me dance with Mavis, an attractive young woman who had also been asked to join Bertha's select party. Every night, Mavis and I took to the floor, dancing to our hearts' content. She had a great sense of fun and was totally besotted with female film stars, impersonating them in their various films. She would be Bette Davies in *Now Voyager*, Joan Crawford in *Mildred Pierce* or Greta Garbo, talking with eyes half-closed and of course in each of the scenes, I had to improvise as her co-star. Auntie Bertha encouraged our friendship in the beginning and she watched Mavis and myself dancing together as intently as if she were a judge in a dance contest. However, she began to change her attitude when she thought that we were showing too much romantic interest in one another and warned me about the fickle nature of shipboard romances. She asked or, to be more accurate, ordered me to cool the relationship. "Just give some of those other women on board the thrill of dancing with you, Jackie," she advised.

Between Wellington and Tahiti, which was our next stop, we crossed the International Date Line. This happened to be on my birthday, the 17th of May, and as we were travelling east to west, there were two 17ths. As soon as Auntie Bertha realised this, she lost no time in organising two days of birthday celebrations for me, with two cakes, two parties, more champagne than we could drink and a non-stop chorus of "Happy Birthday" from both passengers and crew. Strangely enough, I experienced this phenomenon a few years later when we crossed the International Date Line on the same date at the same location. I've often wondered whether it meant that I should add two years on to my age!

To say that I was disappointed with my first impressions of Tahiti is something of an understatement. I had fondly imagined that our landing would be reminiscent of a scene from a Dorothy Lamour film, where smiling Polynesian beauties with colourful sarongs and exotic flowers in their hair would surround us and ply us with fragrant leis. Alas, this image was rudely shattered from the outset as everything was much too commercialised.

At great expense, Auntie Bertha's party hired a small bus with a driver who had agreed to give us a guided tour of the island. He was an enormous, tough-looking Australian – an adventurous guide who drove us through the bumpiest unmade roads we had ever encountered. At one point of the excursion, he put the fear of God into us as we travelled at tremendous speed up and down the narrow, often crumbling paths of very steep hills. It was not the most pleasant of journeys, for the hot, sticky weather made us feel uncomfortable and we were plagued by almost every insect in Papeete. To be honest, I couldn't wait for the tour to end and even when we finally arrived back at the dockside, our discomfort continued because the ride had made our buttocks so sore that we could hardly put one foot in front of the other. I remember thinking that none of us would be dancing that night.

But bed had to be postponed for a while as the indefatigable Auntie Bertha had other ideas. "Come on, everybody!" she commanded. "We must have a drink in Quinn's Bar right here on the dockside."

For years, this hostelry had been a favourite watering hole of seafarers visiting Tahiti and so, in spite of being weary, we all had to agree that it was an excellent suggestion. Auntie Bertha warned us that the price of drinks always rose dramatically for cruise-ship passengers but we realised that we were so in need of liquid refreshment that being overcharged was of little importance in the circumstances.

That first visit to Tahiti did not impress me in the least but in later years we called there on several occasions and with each subsequent visit I grew more and more fond of the island.

Now it was time for us to move on to Balboa, with a chance to see something of Panama City. We had been warned by the ship's crew that the area would not be safe to roam round on foot as there was very strong anti-American feeling there at that time. It was dark when we arrived at Balboa, so Auntie Bertha, Roy, Colin and I decided to have a look around Panama City in the comparative safety of a hired taxi before dropping in at the Panama Hilton, where we sampled our first Planter's Punch. Then it was back to the ship, which was due to set sail the following morning through the Panama Canal.

We were informed that a pilot would board our ship at 6 o'clock the following morning to manoeuvre the vessel through the canal. Roy and I were determined to see as much of this ten-hour passage as possible and so we arranged to meet Mavis on deck at that early hour. There must have been at least twenty ships waiting to pass through but, because the JVO was a passenger cruise liner, we were given priority over the others, probably at great expense! Very shortly, we noticed the Bridge of the Americas, which was still under construction. Roy, Mavis and I were enthralled with the sights along the canal but the intense heat forced us to go inside from time to time. A commentary informed us that many men had died in the eight-year process of building the canal – some from heat exhaustion alone. Perhaps the most amazing experience was sailing through the locks, each one being one hundred and ten feet wide and a thousand feet long. The loch gates opened so smoothly and effortlessly in spite of the fact that each one was eighty feet in height. For most of the journey, the ship was under power but in the locks it was positioned

Jackie today at the Chantry Hotel standing in front of his 'Wall of Fame' of Hollywood stars that he has known and looking through his scrapbook of over fifty years in entertainment

Young Jackie, an aspiring nine year
old song and dance man

The Princess and the Coal Miner
Jackie Toaduff making worldwide headline news,
dancing with HRH the Princess Margaret

Three champion dancers: Jackie Toaduff,
Tiny Allison and Harry Robinson

With his parents at home in Stanley

Drinking with coal mining pals, John Magee,
Jed Harvey and Jimmy Heaton

At the Royal Albert Hall

Colin Edwardes, Jackie Toaduff, and Roland Roy

Two highland lads

Off to a flying start in Jersey

Touring in South Africa with the Barry Sisters, Bob Monkhouse
Barry Kent and The Dudium Israeli Folk Singing duo

Jackie with
local children in Africa

A company of High Spirits, Tony Bandon, Charlie Mazolla,
Colin Edwardes, Roy Toaduff, Burns and Jan, Derek Agutter,
Judi Jones and Jackie Toaduff

With Jane Russell in Australia

Always described as the immaculate Roy and Jackie Toadu

Performing on the QE2

At Sir Billy Butlin's Birthday Party

The Chantry Hotel, Dronfield, Derbyshire

With Jenny Agutter, daughter of Derek Agutter, Jackie and Roy's company manager

With Sir John and Lady Mills &
Margaret O'Brien

With John Craven and his wife, Maralyn

QE2 popular entertainer Joe Loss
with his wife, Mildred

With Ginger Cheek to Cheek

Ruby Keeler visiting at the Chantry Hotel

With Margaret O'Brien

American singer, Margaret Whiting

Lady Penelope
Sitwell,
Roy,
Dame Moura
Lympany,
Jackie and
Lady Mary Henry

With Vincent Price and Coral Browne

With Lord Bernard and
Lady Delfont at the
Dorchester, London

With Archbishop Makarios at his palace in Nicosia

Jackie and Roy with Pearl Carr and Teddy Johnson

Ava Astaire with husband, Richard McKenzie

Roy and Jackie with Patty Andrews (of the
Andrews Sisters) and husband, Wally Wieschler

On Broadway, New York with Gloria Swanson

The American Film Awards, with Ruby Keeler
and Jane Whithers

On Television with Coronation Street actress, Liz Dawn

Their singing partner, Dr. Christian Bernard

At the Beverly Hills home of Gene and Betty Barry

In the bar at the Chantry Hotel with
Michael Cain and
his daughter, Dominique

Dinner at the London Hilton with Donald Sindon, Virginia
Mayo and Margaret O'Brien

With the great Count Basie

In Russia with Barbara Stanwyck

Ship mates Louis Jordan and Jackie

Jack Gilford and his wife Madeline

With Merle Oberon

With Larry Hagman onboard the QE2

The Great George C. Scott

Lunch with Alice Faye in Palm Springs, California

Party time with Roddy McDowell and
Oscar winning star, Louise Rainer

Night of a Hundred Stars, London with
Jane Powell and Jane Russell

Star spot on the Michael Barrymore show

On the QE2 with Rod Stewart and Britt Eckland.

Dinner with James Cagney and Pat

With Vera Lynn

With singing star, Samantha Jones

With Linda Gloria. French singing
star (Les Folies Bergeres)

The Malaysian King and Queen,
His Royal Highness the Sultan of Selangor and
Her Royal Highness the Tengku Ampuan of Selangor

Jackie with HRH Prince Sulaiman Shah of Selangor, Malaysia

"To Jackie, With my admiration of your dancing and all my best wishes. Margot Fonteyn"

Roy and Jackie at home in the prize winning gardens at the Chantry Hotel

by very powerful locomotives known as mules. Halfway through our passage, we entered Gaton Lake, one of the largest man-made lakes in the world. It was here that Mavis excitedly told us that she had just spotted crocodiles and turtles but Roy and I were rather sceptical as we didn't manage to see any.

Our next port of call was the tropical haven of Fort Lauderdale in Florida, where Auntie Bertha informed us that her Chevrolet would be waiting at the dockside so that she could stay for a few days in Miami before driving to her home town of Lexington in Massachusetts. Would Colin, Roy and I like to join her in Miami for our one-day stopover? She needn't have asked! The ship docked early and, after bidding farewell to the others in our little group, we helped Auntie Bertha to transfer her luggage to her splendid cream car. Then she organised a boat ride on the Everglades, where she pointed out the sumptuous homes of the rich and famous and followed this with a visit to Chriton's, her favourite lunch-time restaurant. This establishment boasted that it made the best apple pie in the world but, to tell the truth, I'd tasted much better at home in Stanley.

Finally, we drove to Miami Beach, a resort that completely overwhelmed me. I had never before seen such magnificent hotels and amazing white sandy beaches. We were then taken to The Fontainbleau, the island's premier hotel at that time. Every President since Eisenhower had stayed at this 'Crown Jewel of Miami' as it was proudly called and all the top names in show business, including Elvis, Sinatra and Sammy Davies Junior, had performed there. Even the swimming pool area was famous as it had featured in the Bond movie, *Goldfinger*. Auntie Bertha insisted on treating us to cocktails in Poodles, her favourite bar in the hotel, where she had rubbed shoulders with Lucille Ball and other stars on previous visits. Later, we all enjoyed dinner in one of the hotel's elegant dining-rooms and then it was time for us to return to our ship.

Auntie Bertha asked us about our immediate plans when we eventually arrived in England. We told her that it would be a mad dash to Sheffield to pick up orchestrations and costumes before rushing off to Dundee to appear for fourteen weeks in *Victory Vanities* at the Palace Theatre there.

"Sounds wonderful," smiled Auntie Bertha, " and a good excuse for me to visit Scotland again, so don't be surprised if you see me out front one night." And she was as good as her word, for she turned up quite unexpectedly in the Dundee theatre, giving us the surprise of our lives.

The final lap of our sea voyage was very quiet, compared with the lively days and nights with Auntie Bertha and her little entourage. Nevertheless, we had enjoyed so many moments on that friendly ship that I shall never forget our time there. Incidentally, just after we disembarked, the JVO was sold to a Greek shipping company, who re-modelled it and renamed it the *Lakonia*. It was used briefly for cruises between Southampton and the Canary Islands until, on December 22nd 1963, it was destroyed by fire at sea, while carrying over a thousand Christmas-cruise passengers. One hundred and twenty eight people lost their lives that day and many more would have done but for the bravery of crew-member George Herbert, who in later years became a friend of ours. What remained of the *Lakonia* sank shortly afterwards 250 miles west of Gibraltar, the country to which it was being towed.

13

The Road and the Miles to Dundee

Within forty-eight hours of leaving the ship at Southampton, we were in Dundee rehearsing for *Victory Vanities*. Johnny was everything we had been told about him apart from the fact that Roy and I did not find him at all difficult to work with, even though those stories about his crudeness, his foul language and his explosive outbursts were quite true. His temper flared if he thought that other acts were not pulling their weight or if the chorus girls were chatting instead of concentrating. His reputation was such that his stage colleagues used to compare working with him to sitting on top of Mount Vesuvius. Funnily enough, however, when he had a tantrum or was venting his fury on the whole cast of this Dundee show, he always added, "Jackie and Roy, this doesn't include you," which was embarrassing as I am sure we were just as much at fault as the others. Johnny himself had an amazing memory and expected everyone else to remember his numerous instructions, which varied daily.

Although we were well-prepared for his fiery personality, no one had ever informed us about his absolute comic genius – a talent which completely bowled us over. His ability to improvise on stage, his spontaneous wit and his changing of scripts, scenes and gags on a daily (and sometimes hourly) basis made him without a doubt the most underrated comic in Scotland at that time and one of the very few who did not need to introduce drag into the act to raise the laughs. His sketches were hilarious, thanks to his own highly original material and that of his comedy feed, Hector Nichol, another very talented man.

In every theatre where he had topped the bill, Johnny had always insisted that all his supporting acts should be artists of the highest calibre and this show at the Palace Theatre was no exception. The company included the soprano Sheila Paton, Jan and Kelly Heart who combined crazy antics with memorable harmony singing, dancers David Ellen and Christine Bell (who, incidentally, taught me some very intricate steps in the Twist), trumpeter Johnny Lister, popular tenor Rico Landi, accordionists Forbes Whitelock and Billy Stuart, the Jackson Girls and Chrys St. Dennis, who was another great comedy feed for Johnny.

At last, the final dress rehearsal was over and excitement was beginning to mount to fever pitch on the day of the show's opening – when disaster struck! Johnny had shouted so much during rehearsals that he had lost his voice completely and could not appear. Every seat had been sold as he was a great favourite and crowd-puller in Dundee so, in the final hours before the show, major changes had to be made. Hector bravely took on Johnny's role as top of the bill and roped in David Ellen and myself for the comedy sketches. All of us must have been extremely well drilled by Johnny because that opening night went without a hitch and received excellent reviews from the critics.

Nevertheless, we were all extremely worried about Johnny as at first the doctors feared it was throat cancer but fortunately this initial diagnosis was wrong. His loss of voice was due entirely to strain and stress, which had thickened his vocal chords. Specialists ordered him to rest for twelve months but Johnny, a determined fighter and true professional, was back on stage within two weeks. Roy and I found it a great privilege to work with him as he was a perfectionist, with hundreds of innovative ideas for sketches. It was hard work and we certainly earned our money because he involved both of us more and more in the show each night, so much so that we always seemed to be rehearsing new material. Indeed, we had so much to do that, after arriving back at our digs in Broughty Ferry, the two of us would often go down to the jetty at midnight, armed with a small tape recorder. In that deserted place, we practised to our hearts' content, knowing that we would not be disturbing anyone. One night, we were so involved in our singing and tapping routine that we almost jumped out of our skins when a torchlight shone right into our faces. It was the local policeman on his nightly round.

On seeing us, his face broke into a broad grin. "Oh, it's only you two," he said. "I wondered what on earth was going on. Carry on the good work, laddies. I'm bringing my missus to see you in the show. Don't stay out too long now."

Because we had been in Australia for the previous twelve months, Colin, Roy and I were completely out of touch with both the English pop music scene and the current TV idols. Consequently, when Johnny asked everyone in the company to impersonate a TV celebrity in a parody of *Sunday Night at the London Palladium*, we were completely at a loss. I was asked to adopt the persona of Adam Faith, a young star I had recently heard on record but never seen on TV, and Roy had to imitate Bruce Forsyth, who had risen to great heights in the past year but who was completely unknown to us. Fortunately, Jan Hunt and Kelly Heart came to our rescue. They showed me Adam's moves on stage and taught Roy the distinctive walk of Bruce, together with his catch phrase, "I'm in charge". To the delight of both Johnny and the audience, Roy's impersonation was particularly good and brought the house down at every performance.

These memories of our time in Dundee would not be complete without mention of our wonderful landlady, May Irving, who owned the Tay View Guest House in Broughty Ferry, a popular holiday resort just outside Dundee. Such was her impact on me that I have complete recall of my first meeting with her. Seeing the *Vacancies* sign in the window of her impeccably clean house, I rang the doorbell and was confronted by one of the largest ladies I have ever seen. Her lovely smile lit up the whole of her face and she instantly brought to my mind a photograph I had seen of my grandmother years ago.

"Hello," I began, "have you … oh, you do remind me of someone."

"It's not Marilyn Monroe, is it?" she laughed and I knew from that moment that we would be happy in her house. "Come in and tell me what I can do for you. Are you looking for a job? If so, here's a tea towel," she joked.

"No," I reassured her, "I'm appearing in Johnny Victory's show for the summer season. My two colleagues are in the car and we're all looking for somewhere to stay for a few weeks."

"Bring your friends in," said May. "I'm sure I can fit the three of you in."

"Er, how much do you charge? Will we be able to afford it?" I asked.

"I'm sure you will," she smiled. "We only look expensive. Chrissy," she called out to one of her girl helpers, "come in here and meet this young man."

When Roy and Colin walked in, May cast her eye over their well-tailored clothes, then shook her head in mock pity and quipped, "My God, you poor, poor things. You all look really hard up. How did you get here – in your Rolls?"

"No, we only have a Jag," I replied, truthfully as it happened, and we all laughed.

For the rest of the season, it was a pleasure to live in May's happy house. Each morning, we were awakened by the sound of laughter coming from the kitchen and when May laughed, every part of her body wobbled. She was the widow of the Broughty Ferry stationmaster and, since his death several years ago, she had not had the courage to step a foot outside her house. And now she was so heavy that she could not walk upstairs or lie down on a bed; instead, she slept in a chair in her lounge.

As the weeks went by, May became so fascinated as we talked about our work that she asked me if I would dance for her, so I stood on her small coffee table and tapped for a couple of minutes. Then, seeing how she loved it, I had a brainwave and stopped quite suddenly.

"Now, May." I said, "if you want to see more, you must come to the Palace Theatre."

After much cajoling and encouraging, we managed to persuade her to venture outdoors and eventually to come to the theatre itself. Once she had plucked up the courage to sit in the audience, all her fears were abandoned and, after that night, she came without fail to every change of programme. On the first occasion that she saw the show, our opening number was *Walking Back to Happiness*, which she loved and from that time onwards she sang it constantly in her kitchen. What a happy, loving woman May was and how she filled her house with merriment. In fact, the only time I saw her downhearted was the day Colin, Roy and I left, for then she wept uncontrollably, so much so that we all cried with her.

At the end of the show's run, Johnny invited us to return the following summer for another season with him and he was very disappointed to learn that we could not oblige. We had already signed a contract to top the bill in our own show *Tamsapoppin'* (so named by me!) at the Golden Sands Hotel in Jersey, but we agreed to appear with Johnny again in two years' time.

After Dundee, we managed to fit in a one-week variety show at the Tivoli in Aberdeen with, of all people, Alec Finlay topping the bill. We were somewhat apprehensive about working with him again after the upset in Australia but he was pleasant, if not over-friendly. Unfortunately, the show did not help to re-cement our relationship as all the newspaper reviews reported that Roy and I saved the day in an otherwise mediocre production. Indeed, one critic damned the show as *"most disappointing, apart from Roland Roy and Jackie Toaduff who were notable successes throughout"*.

The Galt office ideally wanted us to appear throughout the year in one Scottish theatre after another but we agreed to appear in only one more variety show, this time at the Palladium in Edinburgh. After a successful week there, we returned to the Northern clubland circuit, as Colin was keen for us to try out new material for our forthcoming season in Jersey. We also found the time to visit our respective families and friends. Roy was feeling very homesick as he hadn't seen his relatives for well over a year and wanted to spend some time with them. On the other hand, I was so thrilled with our new life that going back to Stanley didn't seem as vitally important, even though I had not visited my home town for over four years. Nevertheless, duty called and I spent a few very happy days with my kith and kin, catching up on all that had happened there and describing to them some of the wonderful sights I had seen and the interesting people I had met. While I was there, I bought my mother's colliery house for her so that she would have some security, as there had always been the possibility that she could have been moved out to make way for another pitman and his family. Incidentally, while I was there, I found that my mother still harboured hopes that I might return to my old job at the pit and live in her house for the rest of my life.

But to be honest, I couldn't wait to return to Sheffield and the clubland scene, as working was a continuous joy to me. There was also the forthcoming visit of Ken Evans to prepare for, although we couldn't order the snow he was so longing to see. Nevertheless, it was certainly very cold when he arrived and I wondered if he would be able to tolerate an English winter or if he would be hopping on the next plane back to warm Australia. As it happened, however, he loved it here so much that he made England his home and only returned to Australia for the occasional holiday. He quickly secured a job and worked for various radio stations before moving to the BBC, where he produced, among other programmes, the *David Jacobs' Show*. Incidentally, he certainly had his fair share of snow! That December saw some of the heaviest snowstorms in years and Ken was travelling with us back from one of our club engagements when we were caught in six-foot snowdrifts. We had to keep getting out of the car to clear the snow, so it was fortunate that we had come well-prepared with snow shovels in the boot. In spite of the hard work involved to keep the car on the move, Ken was as thrilled as a child and insisted on a snowball fight while we were shovelling. I can't say that I was too thrilled with this, as I have always been of the opinion that the best place for snow is either on Christmas cards or film sets!

Early in 1963, we were once again approached by the Galt office, inviting us this time to appear for the spring season at the Pavilion Theatre in Glasgow with another popular comedian of the day, Jack Radcliffe, in his show Jack in a Box. Jack, who had appeared in several British films, was very funny but I think I would describe him as more of a comedy character actor than a comedian. As he had his own team of "feeds" with him, he did not need to use us in any of his comedy sketches, so we did not really get to know him well. What I do remember, however, was that he was the person who introduced us to Drambuie. Every Monday morning during the rehearsal break, he invited us to Lauder's Bar next door to the theatre where, over coffee and this delicious liqueur, we discussed the current show, which was being produced and choreographed by Geoff Morris and his wife, Pearl Shaw. It was at one of these coffee breaks that Jack quite unintentionally delivered one of his funniest lines. He told me that my hair was so fair and thin that under the spotlight I looked bald. He explained that he always wore a hairpiece himself and then asked in all seriousness, "Would you like to buy my old one, Jackie, as I won't be needing it any more?"

Roy and I were pleased to find that Jack respected our talents. In the first show, we were Number Five on the programme but for the rest of the run we were moved to the star spot – the last act before the finale. The only other vivid memory I have of that season was that the show opened on March 11th, which happened to be Colin's birthday. He had received several birthday cards which he had pinned on the dressing-room wall, together with the Good Luck telegrams we had all received. We decided to leave them all up, as they were quite colourful and brightened up our rather drab dressing-room. About two weeks into the run of the show, one of the twelve Moxon Ladies (the show's dancing troupe) came to our room just before curtain-up to borrow a pair of scissors. When she saw all the cards, she asked whose birthday it was.

"Oh, it's mine," I joked, as Roy and Colin were not in the room at the time.

"Jackie!" she remonstrated. "Why on earth didn't you tell us?" And with that, she planted a big kiss on my cheek and wished me many happy returns of the day.

Seconds later, the other eleven Moxon Ladies, all leggy and scantily clad, were at our door, kissing me and singing *Happy Birthday, darling Jackie* in wonderful harmony. I was having such fun that I didn't tell them that I had only been joking. At the end of the First House show, however, things went a little beyond a joke. We were all on stage taking final bows when the Musical Director handed Jack Radcliffe a huge box of chocolates for "Jackie Toaduff from the Moxon Ladies". The girls had organised a whip-round during the First House and sent a stagehand to a nearby shop to buy the present. I was totally embarrassed but didn't have the courage to confess in front of the applauding and cheering audience.

As soon as we came off the stage, Roy lost no time at all in telling me how stupid I had been, so I sheepishly took back the chocolates to the Moxon Girls' room and said, "I don't know how to say this, my darlings, but I was only kidding. It's not my birthday. It was Colin's a few weeks ago and those cards were his." I apologised profusely, telling them that I would of course reimburse them for their gift.

At first, they could not believe that I had been so deceitful and were quite annoyed with me. However, they soon perked up when the head Moxon girl said to the others, "Never mind, we'll pretend it's his birthday, shall we, girls?" and accompanied this remark with a knowing cheeky wink to them.

During the Second House, the girls lost no opportunity to kiss me or pat me on the cheek or whisper birthday greetings while we were all on stage, so much so that I began to get the distinct feeling that they were definitely building up to some joke at my expense. After the finale, during which all the men were required to wear elegant tail suits and co-ordinating regalia, the grinning Moxon Ladies linked arms with me, singing "Happy Birthday" and accompanied me up the stairs backstage. I thought that they were going to leave me at our dressing-room – but no such luck. They dragged me past our door and into theirs. I struggled in vain as I tried to escape but there were too many of them. Once in their room, they began to tear the clothes off me and within seconds I was completely naked. Then those wicked girls 'tarred and feathered' me, rubbing cold cream, talcum powder and chocolate all over my body and writing lipsticked obscenities everywhere – including my private parts!

At that time, we were staying in Nancy's house, for she had come to Glasgow to look after us for the season. When we arrived back there, I rushed to her spotlessly clean bath in an attempt to wash off all the grease and dirt. It seemed to take me hours to scrub myself and I'm afraid that the bath was in a sorry state by the time I had finished. I tried my hardest to leave the bath as I had found it but in the end I had to ask Nancy to help me to clean it. She took one horrified look at the dirty, greasy tide mark before pursing her lips and exclaiming, "Och, Jackie, you can tell those Moxon Ladies that they're no bloody ladies in my book!"

The spring season drew to a close and soon we were on our way to Jersey. We were not able to stay with the Le Breuilly family on this occasion as they had moved from the farm to a smaller house. We were fortunate, however, in that Yvonne Le Breuilly managed to find us excellent digs with a young Jersey florist, Robbie Major and her family. The only drawback as far as I was concerned was their massive guard dog, which totally terrified me as it barked ferociously each time we entered the house.

Our show, *Tamsapoppin*', was a great success and we played to packed houses each night. Roy and I were supported by some very talented acts, including international mime artists Jo, Jack and Joni, ace impressionist Ronnie Collis, a delightful singer called Celia Nicholls, the Six Grosvenor Girls and the Ronnie Caryl Orchestra.

Unknown to us, Arthur Watson, the Head of Combined Services Entertainment was in the audience one night. He was so impressed with our act that he asked Roy and myself if we would headline a show for The War Office, entertaining the armed forces, as soon as we were free to do so. And so, as the season ended in Jersey, off we flew out to Cyprus on Roy's birthday, January 9th 1964.

14

Entertaining the Troops

Mirth and Melody, the name we gave to our new show in Cyprus, started off a very busy 1964 for us. The compère was comedian Wally Dunn and other acts included talented singer Alberta Laine and belly-dancer Karin Karina. We were all accompanied by Andy Reed on drums and Colin on the piano. The Commanding Officer who was given responsibility for the whole set up of entertaining the troops was Derek Agutter.

We were the first group of British entertainers to visit Cyprus since the outbreak of the conflict with the Greeks and the Turks. There had been some very nasty incidents on the island over the Christmas period, so much so that all leave and Christmas festivities for the troops had been cancelled. There was still tension in the air but there was hope that, with this show of strength by the British forces, no more major incidents would take place for the next few weeks at least.

It was our job, we were told, to boost the sagging morale of the soldiers and airmen stationed there, as they were all bitterly disappointed to have been denied their Christmas celebrations. We were accommodated at the Ledra Palace, Nicosia's premier hotel, which was also the headquarters of the leaders of the Gloucester

Regiment. It was their men whom we had to entertain first – in the nearby canteen, which had been re-arranged to resemble a night-club. All the soldiers there had been under tremendous pressure, carrying out patrols and we knew that, if duty called, they would have to leave immediately at any time during the show.

Derek Agutter had arranged for us to put on performances for as many servicemen as possible in Cyprus and left us in the very capable hands of our stage manager for the tour, Charlie Mazzola, a happy, smiling Maltese who, together with two willing drivers, one an RAF lad and the other a soldier, took care of all arrangements and looked after our props. We were accompanied by armed guards at all times so we felt perfectly safe – that is, until the night of our first performance which was, to put it mildly, a nerve-wracking experience. We had been forewarned that the troops might be noisy and over-exuberant as they were now making up for lost time drink-wise. As opening night approached, we noticed that Derek and Charlie were looking increasingly apprehensive.

Colin and Andy opened *Mirth and Melody* with a musical number but the audience was so noisy that they could not be heard. Then Wally Dunn bounced on to tell a few jokes, supposedly to warm up the crowd, but after two minutes of performing to an audience that wouldn't listen, he beat a hasty retreat, deciding that it would be a better idea to bring on the girls. Alberta went on to the stage and was given a very hard time, so much so that she came off and burst into tears, telling us that they were just like animals. Karin, our belly-dancer, could hardly hear her music as she danced to loud shouts of "Take 'em off, baby!" It was Wally's turn next and he warned us to get ready to go on at any time as he might have to cut down his act if they heckled him too much, so Roy and I immediately changed into our brand new whiter-than-white suits.

Derek took one look at our outfits and exclaimed, "Oh, no! You can't be serious about going out there dressed like that, can you?"

"Why not?" asked Roy, quite calmly. (I have to admit that by this time I was so nervous I had already been sick in the toilet twice.)

133

"Why not?" answered Derek. "Don't you realise that they're all men out there and that they've been drinking a hell of a lot?"

But Roy stood his ground. "Derek, Jackie and I have played to all-male audiences in some of the roughest, toughest working men's clubs in the country for years so this audience doesn't worry me one little bit."

By this time, I had already taken off the jacket of my suit. "Let's just go on in trousers and shirts, Roy," I suggested rather lamely.

"Jackie, put that jacket on again," ordered Roy with quiet determination. "We're going on the way we always do. If I were a serviceman out here, I wouldn't want to see sloppily-dressed performers. These lads want to see a first–rate show and that's just what we're going to give them from beginning to end."

And so we walked on to wolf-whistles and catcalls but we carried on singing and smiling in spite of the indescribable noise from the audience. Then, as if by some miracle, the noise slowly died down and by the time we were halfway through our first song we had those lads in the palms of our hands. From then on, they were with us all the way. How they cheered Roy's wonderful comedy strip and they just about brought down the roof when I performed my table-top tap dance. During one of Roy's solos, *From Russia with Love*, a soldier walked up to him and placed a sten gun in his hands to make him resemble James Bond. And finally, when we sang *You'll Never Walk Alone*, there was a hushed silence and many a tear shed. At the end of our act, they just wouldn't let us go, so we gave encore after encore, going through our entire repertoire. They still wanted more and blocked our exit, so we re-sang our two opening numbers and at last they allowed us to leave.

Derek was overwhelmed with the reception we had been given and told us that he had never witnessed anything like it before, as the lads were still clamouring for more, stamping on the floor with their heavy boots and clapping at the same time, long after we had left the building.

The next day, Derek was still enthusing over our performance when he introduced us to his very attractive wife, Kit, who bore a striking resemblance to Elizabeth Taylor. Derek, an ex-captain in the Tank Corps had met Kit in Egypt while she was serving as a member of the Women's Auxiliary Air Force. They had married shortly afterwards and now had two children, Jonathon and Jenny. Twelve-year-old Jenny was with Kit when we were introduced and from our first meeting, I knew that she was a very special child, totally unspoilt and with the most expressive eyes I had ever seen. She was later to become the much acclaimed actress and film star, most famous for her classic roles in The Railway Children and Walkabout. At the age of twelve, however, I do not think that she harboured any thoughts about acting, as her great love then was the ballet and she was a boarder at the Elmhurst Ballet School in Camberley. Jenny enjoyed our act and was particularly taken with my dancing. She longed for me to introduce her to Margot Fonteyn on some occasion in the future but sadly I could not oblige as we were never all in London at the same time.

News travelled fast in Cyprus and our reputation went before us in every camp where we played. All the troops were waiting for us with open arms and we couldn't put a foot wrong. Our stay there was certainly a success. It was hard work performing two or three shows each day but rewarding to know that we were giving so much pleasure to the forces.

One day after a performance in Akrotiri, Derek came to our changing room with a message that there was an airman outside waiting to speak to me. "He says he's your brother-in-law," said Derek.

"That's odd," I replied. "I only have one sister and as far as I know she isn't even courting. This should be a very interesting meeting!"

Then in walked a smartly dressed Senior Aircraftsman who introduced himself as Jimmy Easter Bingham. He informed me that he was going to marry my sister Norma on 6th June. When I expressed my surprise, saying that I didn't know she had a boyfriend, he thought that she had already written to tell me that they were engaged. So much for family communication!

Glowing reports about the show came to the notice of Archbishop Makarios, who was the Cypriot President and he invited our company to have coffee with him in the Presidential Palace on our last day in his country. We all felt very honoured that he had taken time out of his very busy schedule to thank us for our war-efforts. He was a most imposing figure of a man, far more charismatic in person than photographs or newsreels of him had suggested. He spoke to us all individually and when Roy and I told him that this was our first visit to the island, he expressed the wish that we might return in more peaceful times. How proud we were when the Archbishop informed us that he had heard very complimentary comments about our act and wished that he could have seen us. Before we left the Palace, he wished us luck with the rest of our tour which was to take us to El Adem, Benghazi, Tobruk and Malta. The morning was a perfect ending to our stay in Cyprus.

That same afternoon, we flew to El Adem, where we were housed in rather primitive army huts and during our first night, we encountered a raging sandstorm or ghibli as it was known locally. So strong was this wind that I was convinced we would be blown away, for sand was flying into our huts at tremendous speed. The next morning we found everything covered with sand, including our bed sheets and hair.

From El Adem, we flew to Benghazi, where we stayed at the Grand Hotel; this was something of a misnomer but at least it was an improvement on the previous accommodation. During our time there, we were invited to ride in a tank, which proved to be both uncomfortable and extremely noisy – not an experience I would care to repeat.

Our final stop in North Africa was Tripoli, where we were taken on a seventy-six mile excursion to Leptis Magna, the ruins of an ancient port near Homs. Whilst not one of the acknowledged Seven Wonders of the World, Leptis Magna was nevertheless worthy of the title. It was founded by the Phoenicians around 600 BC and later inhabited by the Romans. The well-preserved remains of theatres, temples, baths, walls and arches were most impressive and we were allowed to cine film the various sights – a great privilege, as tourists were not even allowed access there.

Our final stop was in Malta, where we entertained the British troops for a week, staying on this occasion at the Astra Hotel in Sliema. From there, we flew home on 16th February 1964 and the next day we were back in Sheffield, entertaining an all-male Sunday lunchtime audience at the Arundel Ex-Servicemen's Club, with an evening family show at the same venue. The following day, Roy and I received the following letter from Derek Agutter:

Dear Jackie and Roy,
I would like to say how much I appreciated personally all the hard work you put in during your tour of Cyprus and you will be pleased to know that there are many words of praise from all sources on the island. I can honestly say that I thoroughly enjoyed having you here and that you worked the hardest and with the least trouble than all the shows since I joined this fraternity.

(With the letter, Derek enclosed photographs which had been taken of us with Archbishop Makarios.)

During that same week, we received several congratulatory letters from authorities in all three countries where we had performed, including one from Group Captain N. Briggs, who wrote from El Adem:
... of the many CSE shows which have been staged at this station, 'Mirth and Melody' was quite outstanding and certainly the best to visit the Royal Air Force, El Adem. My remarks apply to all the artistes but in particular I commend the brilliant entertainment by Jackie Toaduff and Roland Roy.
and this one from Colonel R.F. Arden Close from the War Office:

Dear Jackie and Roy,

I have now received reports from the Command of your recent tour with 'Mirth and Melody', which I understand was your first with CSE. These reports show how much your performances have been appreciated and enjoyed by so many of Her Majesty's Forces serving in Cyprus, North Africa and Malta and I want to thank you for the part you played in this very successful company.

We were also contacted by Alan Goford at the War Office who, after informing us that he had heard glowing reports of our show, asked us to headline another tour in March, this time in Aden, Kenya and the Persian Gulf.

Before that could happen, however, I had one or two engagements to fulfil in England. I appeared in two Dance Festivals at the Central Hall, Birmingham and these were followed by a return visit to the Royal Albert Hall, now as a full-time professional. Accompanied once again by my good friend Nan Fleming Williams, I performed in two evening shows and a matinée, which was televised; for this work I was paid the princely sum of £21 plus £8 expenses. I was particularly thrilled to be dancing in this concert hall, all the more so because Roy and Colin, together with two special friends we had made in Jersey, Alan and Hetty Friedman, were there to watch me. Unfortunately, their seats were up in the gallery, so that I looked to them like Tom Thumb dancing solo in the middle of that majestic arena. The show was brilliantly produced by another friend, Ronald Smedley, who was now working for the BBC.

Ethel Merman, that great star of Broadway, was in London at this time, appearing at The *Talk of the Town*. Knowing that she was a favourite of mine, Alan and Hetty had booked a table for all of us to see her on the Saturday night. As soon as I had finished my performance at the Albert Hall, I was whisked off to the nightclub, just managing to sit down before the lights went down. Full of the scintillating energy for which she was famed, Ethel sang almost non-stop for over an hour. When the lights went up at the end of the show, I looked around the room eagerly as it was my first visit there. I honestly could not believe my eyes when I saw, sitting just tables away from us, the legendary Marlene Dietrich. I remember quite clearly that she looked stunning in a pale blue outfit, with a hair-band in her blonde hair. Although there were others at her table, I told my friends that I could not resist going over to ask for her autograph. They all begged me not to but I was determined.

"She isn't eating," I pointed out, "and she can only refuse. I'd like to get a closer look at her."

Without more ado, I walked to her table with my Albert Hall programme in my hand. "Excuse me, Miss Dietrich," I said, "but could you please autograph my programme for me?"

"Is it for you?" she asked huskily.

"Oh, yes," I replied.

"Well, that makes a change. It's usually for someone else," she smiled. She looked down at my programme. "I didn't know that they had programmes for this show."

"They haven't," I said. "This is an Albert Hall programme. I was appearing there earlier this evening."

Flicking through the programme, she stopped at a photograph of me on one of the pages. She looked at me carefully, establishing that I was indeed the Jackie Toaduff in the photo and then invited me to join her table, where her daughter Maria Riva and her husband were sitting. She wanted to know everything about me and my dancing and her eyes never left mine until, that is, a portly man in his fifties, obviously the worse for drink, approached her with the words, "Marlene, could I have this dance?"

She took one look at him and, using her voice to best advantage, replied," I'm sowwy but I don't dance."

"Oh, come on, Marlene," the man persisted, "I know you can. I want to boast to my friends that I've danced with those famous Dietrich legs."

Her face immediately darkened. She looked at him with the utmost disdain and thundered, "GO AWAY!"

Taken aback by her tone, he beat a hasty retreat and without more ado, Marlene resumed her conversation with me as if we had not been interrupted.

"Tell me, Jackie," she said, "where are you appearing next?"

"Tomorrow night I'm working in Leeds with my stage partner and then next weekend we are off to Aden, Kenya and the Persian Gulf to entertain the British troops there."

I then related to her our experiences on the War Office tour that we had just completed, mentioning in passing our meeting with Archbishop Makarios, which impressed her greatly. "You must be very special," she said and then went on to tell me that she herself had enjoyed entertaining the troops in Africa and other places during the Second World War.

"By the way," she continued, "where is your partner?"

"Over there," I said, pointing in Roy's direction. "You're his idol and all-time favourite, you know. He would love to have met you but he's rather shy."

"Call him over," Marlene insisted. " I'd like to see him."

Roy was quite overwhelmed when I beckoned him over but, in spite of being somewhat tongue-tied, he did manage to express what an honour it was to meet her.

"We've heard a rumour that you might be appearing at the Edinburgh Festival later this year," I said.

"It's not a rumour – I will be presenting my show there but I'll want more musicians than Merman had here tonight."

"Roy and I will be entertaining in Edinburgh for the whole of the summer so we'll definitely come to watch your show. Would it be all right if we called backstage to see you one night?" I added boldly.

"Most certainly," she replied, "but you must say, 'The Merman Show, London' because I may not remember your names."

Roy and I then took our leave although it must be said that Marlene was quite happy to have us there and would have talked to us for much longer. When we returned to our own table, Colin, Alan and Hetty were all agog to know what had gone on and Colin was delighted that I had managed to acquire her autograph. A little later in the night, Hetty noticed that Marlene was leaving and we were all full of admiration as we watched her elegant departure down the steps.

Shortly afterwards, it was time for our second CSE show – this time entitled *In the Mood*. It followed the same format as the previous one apart from the fact that Andy Reed and Karen Karina were replaced by an excellent musical act, Carl and Collette. It proved to be another hectic tour, with flights on most days but a most rewarding one as we were greeted warmly and with unbelievable generosity in every place we visited. Our accommodation along the various posts along the Persian Gulf was somewhat basic but after each performance we were royally entertained by all ranks. We were thanked and toasted in the Officers' Mess, then in the Men's Mess and finally in the Sergeants' Mess, where the sergeants always put on a grand meal or buffet in rooms resplendent with regimental silver and trophies.

At the end of our tour, we were once again congratulated on an outstanding show in each country and Alan Goford was eager to sign us for more work, starting immediately. Unfortunately, we could not oblige as our engagement book was full for the remainder of the year, including TV appearances for me on *Barn Dance*, one of which was with Val Doonican and three Geordie girls, the Barry Sisters. The one engagement that was causing us most excitement at that time, however, was in the USA as this was to be our first appearance there.

15

Green Cards and Goolies

The trip to the United States was courtesy of Auntie Bertha, who had arranged with her Travel Club in Lexington to bring us over to entertain its members at a special evening in Boston. Never one to do things by half, she then contacted the local press to publicise our debut in the USA. and also persuaded two theatrical agents to view the show.

She met us at the airport in New York and drove us to the World Fair, where we saw entertainment on a scale that really impressed us – particularly the dramatic Dancing Waters and the spectacular fireworks display that accompanied the closing number of *Rhapsody in Blue*.

After that first night in New York, we were driven to Auntie Bertha's home in Lexington in readiness for our show that was to be held in the Terrace Room at the Statler Hilton in Boston. Her energy in publicising our appearance had certainly paid off for the show was a sell-out, not only with her fellow club members but also with the general public. The evening was very successful and we were given a standing ovation. There were compliments all round – even the staff and management of the Hilton were effusive in their praise.

At the end of the show, one of the theatrical agents came backstage, eager to discuss future dates and that is when the blow came. He discovered that we did not have work permits and apologised for having to renege on the arrangements he had just made with us. He told us that he would not be allowed to secure work for us and advised us to say, if approached by any other agent, that we were not being paid as our appearance had just been a working audition. Nevertheless, he went on to assure us that, if we obtained green cards, he would be only too happy to book us. However, we weren't desperate for work because we had several engagements to fulfil in the UK and elsewhere, so we didn't apply for permits.

Incidentally, it is quite amusing now to read the write-up of that show in the Travel Club Magazine – and I quote:

The acts presented by these gentlemen were quite varied and included singing and dancing and all other showmanship that goes with the best of professional entertainment. Of course, being from England, they imitated the Beatles – for a laugh only, as their own talents were on a much higher level.

Auntie Bertha insisted on driving us down the east coast to Florida for a holiday. On the homeward journey back to New York, we called at Cape Ann, Ogunquit, Maine, Connecticut and New York State, where we were taken aback by the beauty of the dogwood trees in full bloom. From there we crossed the Tappenzee Bridge over the Hudson River and then drove through New Jersey, Delaware, Maryland and Baltimore, where we had our first experience of staying in a motel - an establishment called The Burgundy.

As we checked in, I was vividly reminded of the Bates Motel in Alfred Hitchcock's *Psycho*. Colin, Roy and I were sharing a room, while Auntie Bertha was next door. The television in our room was not working, so Roy set about trying to repair it but my priority was to have a shower and change clothes as it had been a long journey. All the time I was showering, the theme music from *Psycho* was running through my mind and thoughts of Janet Leigh being attacked in the shower with her blood swirling down the drain were sending shivers down my spine. Then suddenly, without any warning, the television started up at full blast. With my imagination still living the *Psycho* scene, I let out a startled, blood-curdling yell. Unbeknown to me, Colin was also in the bathroom shaving. My scream frightened the life out of him and he immediately pulled back the plastic shower curtain, exclaiming, "What the bloody hell's wrong with you?"

The sight of Colin with his angry face covered in lather and his razor brandished high in his hand almost gave me a heart attack and I yelled so loudly that Auntie Bertha came rushing in from the next room. We later laughed about the incident but at the time I found it a truly terrifying experience.

From Baltimore, we travelled to Washington D.C., where we found that Auntie Bertha's influence did not quite extend to the White House, so there was no invitation to dine with the President! We then stayed in Virginia and Carolina, usually at the Howard Johnson motels, as they served the most delicious chicken pot pie. I have to say that these establishments were very reasonably priced but even so, I could not resist bargaining to get a discount. It became second nature to me to plead poverty at reception desks, explaining that we were three impoverished Englishmen travelling on a budget with our frail old Aunt. The ploy worked every time, much to Auntie Bertha's amusement.

From childhood, I have always been panicky at the thought of close contact with snakes and, while we were crossing the border into Florida, my heart started pounding as Auntie Bertha launched into a graphic description of deadly Diamond Black Rattlesnakes, many of which were in this area. As she finished speaking, one of these large creatures started slithering menacingly across the road in front of the car. Auntie Bertha drew to a halt so that we could see it at close quarters – albeit through the car windows. Colin, however, was not content with this and, grabbing his cine camera, flung open the car door and stepped on to the road.

Auntie Bertha screeched at the top of her voice, "Get back, you idiot. These snakes are deadly and can strike at twice their length."

Our stay in the United States had been incredible and we also managed to visit Toronto and Niagara Falls before boarding the plane for home, stopping en route at Reykjavik, Iceland. Now we were fighting fit and ready once again to join the very talented Johnny Victory in his *Victory Varieties* show. As expected, Johnny had gathered around him an excellent group, which this time included his pretty wife, Betty. There was Jackie Dennis, the impressionist and pop star - the first rock and roll artist, by the way, to appear on stage in a kilt – who joined the cast hotfoot from appearing in the *Perry Como* show. Other members included singer and pianist Nicky Kidd, Gloria Anderson who was billed as *Aberdeen's Ace Accordionist*, the soprano Sheila Paton, six of the Moxon Ladies and Shari and Dahl, a husband and wife act who were also responsible for choreographing the whole show. Roy and I were delighted to be given second top billing.

We never found out exactly why Hector Nichol, who had always in the past been Johnny's right hand man and comedy feed, was missing from the cast but we suspected that he and Johnny had a disagreement. His absence meant that Roy and I were called on to appear in almost every scene, with me replacing Hector in several sketches. I thoroughly enjoyed myself and the bonus was reading the following review in the Daily Express (June 7th, 1964):

Johnny Victory scored a fantastic hit with his new show at the Palladium last night. Seldom does Edinburgh see such a high quality variety cast. Star of the show was undoubtedly Jackie Toaduff with his tap dance act and, with his partner, Roland Roy, he proved to be an excellent singer as well. Other top artistes were Jackie Dennis who showed that he was no back number and Sheila Paton whose singing was well appreciated.

The critic went on to write a few complimentary words about everyone in the company and concluded that it was an excellent cast.

For all of us, it was a show full of fun. One sketch, which I still remember vividly, entailed me appearing as a bonneted, dummy-sucking baby in a pram, being pushed on stage by Roy in a policeman's uniform. Roy had to say to Johnny, "Is this your baby?" right at the end of the sketch to tag it. One night, I was sitting in the pram in the wings, cursing because Roy was nowhere in sight. I could hear him being tannoyed urgently: "Policeman to the stage IMMEDIATELY!" With that, Roy rushed to the pram and pushed it onstage wearing not a uniform of the constabulary but the hussar's outfit which he had not had time to change from the previous scene – together with the policeman's hat.

Johnny immediately saw the funny side and chortled with laughter, as he marched Roy to the front of the stage, announcing, "Ladies and gentlemen, this is the latest thing in police uniforms – English style, of course!"

The more I worked with Johnny, the more I liked and admired him; he was a master of improvisation. In one sketch, I had to wear a pair of very wide-waisted trousers when playing the part of a backward country yokel. I was required to peer down these trousers and start laughing, look at the audience, glance down the trousers again and laugh even louder. Johnny had to walk over to me with a puzzled expression on his face, as if wondering why I was so amused. Then he would pull open the waist of my trousers and explode with laughter, much to the amusement of the audience. Johnny was a great practical joker with all of us and so one night in this sketch, I decided to play a joke on him. I came on stage without my underpants, convinced that he would be surprised and laugh louder than ever. However, my joke misfired because, as quick as lightning, Johnny pulled out a starter pistol and shot it down my pants. Sparks flew inside the trousers and for few seconds I was jumping around the stage in pain – and how the audience loved it!

Johnny's wife, Betty, was another prankster. In one sketch, she was sitting at a late-night bus stop with Johnny, Sheila Paton, Jackie Dennis and me. Each of us had to relate what had happened to us that evening. With an affected aristocratic accent, I had to tell the tale of a lad who had tried to steal my girl friend and my tale ended with the words: "I was so mad, I felt like kicking him in the WALLIES" – the word *wallies* being a Scots dialect word for false teeth.

One night, Betty took me on one side and said, "Say 'GOOLIES', not 'Wallies' tonight, Jackie."

I can say with hand on heart that I had never heard this word before but I had an uneasy feeling about it and stuck to the script. Betty, however, persisted and at every performance, she whispered to me, "Go on, say 'GOOLIES'." I cannot now believe how incredibly naïve I was but one night, I agreed to change the word. The audience was at first completely taken aback, because in the 1960s this was a very risqué word and then everybody exploded with laughter. All the others who had been on stage ran off and left me sitting there on my own, looking bewildered. I looked in the wings – they were all laughing hysterically, none more so than Johnny, who was lying on his stomach, pounding the floor with his fists.

At the end of the show, the theatre manager sent for me with a grave expression on his face. "Jackie," he said, "I have had several complaints from patrons demanding their money back after what they heard tonight. In fact, many of them told me that, although you appear to be a nice enough young man, they will not visit the Palladium again until they hear that I've fired you."

I must have paled visibly and looked utterly dejected, so much so that the manager took pity on me and burst into laughter. He had been in on the joke and thought that it was hilarious!

Johnny had three great passions in life – Bing Crosby, cars and dogs. At the time of this show, his favourite dog was a huge Alsatian that accompanied him to the theatre each night. This animal would always sit quite calmly waiting for its master but one Saturday afternoon, Johnny locked the dog in the dressing-room before going off to a football match. When Roy and I arrived at the theatre, we could hear Johnny cursing at the top of his voice. As we were by now quite used to his tantrums and temper, we thought no more of it. How surprised we were, therefore, when Johnny made his first appearance of the night at the end of the opening number. His usually smart suit was torn into shreds - in his absence, the resentful Alsatian had vented its wrath by ruining Johnny's entire wardrobe. Johnny, however, was a great trouper and walked on to gales of laughter from the audience as he wore shredded suit after shredded suit in each successive scene.

Another disaster in the show occurred during the time of the Edinburgh Festival. As was usual during Festival weeks, Currie's Waterfalls were brought onstage as an added attraction to the finale. The idea was that the whole of the cast should don kilts and sing Scotland the Brave while gallons of water cascaded over the rocks behind us. Teresa Innes, the Scottish stage manager, was in charge of turning on the water and that first night it just did not emerge.

In an extremely agitated state, Johnny made his way to the side of the stage and shouted into the wings, "Where's the FUCKING WATTER? I want some FUCKING WATTER over the rocks!"

"The watter won't start," shouted back Teresa.

"Well, for God's sake, piss on the damn rocks!" thundered Johnny, loud enough for all on stage and probably the first few rows of the audience to hear.

Then, without warning, torrents came tumbling over the rocks so fast and with such force that water gushed right to the front of the stage and popped all the footlights.

"That's my girl!" shouted a relieved Johnny.

Johnny was untiring in his work for charity, especially for the elderly. On one occasion, he had enlisted the aid of everyone in helping him to raise enough money to buy a house for the most deserving old couple in Edinburgh. The pensioners were duly selected and were invited to the Palladium, where the presentation of keys was made on stage. Johnny himself had been to the house and decided to give them a good start by generously filling the cupboards with food and the coal-house with coal, using his own money.

You can imagine his surprise, therefore, when the couple came to see him a fortnight later with the words, "Johnny, we've come back to tell you that we need some more coal now."

I leave Johnny's reply to your imagination!

Without doubt, the most exciting entertainment at that year's Edinburgh Festival was Marlene Dietrich, whose stage craft and sheer presence was a lesson to all who had the privilege of seeing her. Her orchestra was led by the famous Burt Bacharat and her bass player, believe it or not, was a musician from my home town - Bob Smith, better known as "Hicky". At the end of Marlene's outstanding performance, she took a thirty-five minute curtain call, with the whole audience on its feet shouting for more. Rose petals were showered down on her and bouquets of roses and single roses were thrown on to the stage by young male admirers. Marlene loved every moment of the acclaim, first walking off one side of the stage, then reappearing seconds later from the other side, then from centre stage. At one point, she brought a brush on to the stage and proceeded to sweep up the roses. At last, the orchestra left and Marlene made her final triumphant exit.

As we made our way to the stage door, we wondered of course whether the Legend would remember us and spare a few moments to speak to us but when we arrived, there were literally hundreds of fans crowding round. We were just walking away when Lady Luck intervened in the shape of Hicky, who was leaving with Burt Bacharat. He could hardly believe his eyes when he saw me and when he heard that we had previously met Marlene at the *Merman Show* and that she had expressed a desire to see us again, he and Burt accompanied us back into the theatre. Within seconds, she appeared at her door, still in her figure-hugging, rhinestone stage gown, and beckoned us inside, delighted to see us again. We told her how much we had enjoyed her performance and she smiled when I mentioned that I had never witnessed such an ovation in the whole of my life. She seemed genuinely surprised when informed about the throng of people milling outside, waiting to see her.

After we left, I arranged to meet Bob and Burt in the Festival Club, a late-night bar which was opened just during the time of the Festival and we whiled away the rest of the night with a few drinks and entertaining conversation.

Our time in Edinburgh had been so pleasurable and inspirational that I looked forward to working with Johnny Victory again but, unfortunately, that was not to be. Johnny died of a suspected heart attack at the age of 45. His death was a great loss to show business as, in the opinion of many, he had the ability and genius to have become the greatest Scottish comedian of all time. It was an experience and a privilege to have worked with him.

16

In High Spirits

From Scotland, we plunged straight into another CSE tour, as agreed with the War Office. Once again it was our own show, this time entitled *High Spirits*, which was to take us to many places in the Far East, including Singapore, Malaysia, Sarawak, Brunei and North Borneo (now called Sabah). We had chosen Tom Mennard as our compère, as he was a born comedian both on and off the stage. We also engaged a wonderful song and dance girl, Audrey Mann, who was rather eccentric to put it mildly. Whenever we were ready to move to the next camp, she was always the last and always had the same excuse – her packing. This really baffled me as she did not appear to have many changes of clothes off-stage and her stage outfits consisted of flimsy leotards.

On about the third occasion, I asked her, "Audrey, why does it take you so long to pack?"

"It's my damned pillows," she explained.

"Pillows? What pillows?" I asked, rather puzzled.

"Oh, I couldn't go anywhere without my own pillows, pillow cases and sheets. I just couldn't sleep a wink without them. I'd even bring my own bed if I could pack it," she added, laughing.

The lovely thing about Audrey was that she was always laughing and always making us laugh too. She used to call Roy "Ashley", which mystified me until she explained the change of name one day, confessing to me that she was head over heels in love with Roy. "I think he's just like Ashley Wilkes, Leslie Howard's character in *Gone with the Wind*," she sighed.

She also had another name for Gloria Anderson, the talented accordionist we had brought with us from our show in Edinburgh. Gloria was a blonde-haired teenager, quite tiny and very appealing to our audiences and she reminded Audrey of Freda, a character in the St. Trinian's films.

"Little Freda's a real brick," Audrey would say every time that Gloria helped someone.

Also appearing with us was Scott Mackay, a popular musical entertainer, who played the trumpet, sang well, told a good joke and played on the drums with Colin at the piano.

From the outset, our 20,000-mile tour was a great success. Our first port of call, Gan Island in the Indian Ocean, afforded us some insight into what Paradise could be like. Coral reefs, multi-coloured fish, gleaming white sands and clear blue-green waters where no sharks ventured, made it an ideal place for swimming and snorkelling. When we weren't performing or rehearsing, we all made full use of these facilities.

We had the distinction of being the first group of entertainers ever to play on this tiny Maldivian island, where five hundred airmen (and one female from the WRVS!) were stationed. For two nights we performed at the tiny Astra Cinema and were very well received by enthusiastic audiences.

During one of our daytime rehearsals when Roy and I were singing and dancing onstage, we noticed that some teenage boys, who were wearing sarongs, were moving closer to us in mesmerised silence but we thought nothing of this at the time. The next day, we had arranged to spend our day off sailing to another small island so that we could be interviewed on the RAF's radio station there. Just before the boat left the shore, we were amazed to see two of these boys jump on deck, stand in front of us and, without more ado, launch into the most wonderful dancing and singing. Although they shouldn't have been on the boat, they were allowed to sail with us after explaining that they desperately wanted to dance and sing for Roy and me.   In truth, we were all spellbound by their ability to interpret their folklore so professionally and movingly. Flight Lieutenants Eric Paisley and Cliff Farrel who were sailing with us were amazed as they had never heard any of the natives either sing or dance before and told us that we must have inspired their performance. Perhaps this was true because just before we left the island, the boys, accompanied by Wing Commander Geoff Moss, presented both of us with beautifully-crafted model balsa wood sailing boats, similar to those that were used to sail round the islands.

From Gan, we flew by RAF Comet to Changi in Singapore, where we were met by Captain Rene Maby who escorted us by military bus to the Adelphi Hotel. We didn't know it at the time but our journey happened to coincide with the final night of the Chinese New Year celebrations, with the traditional firecrackers exploding in the sky and raining down non-stop from the multi-storeyed modern blocks of flats. Convinced that the noises were from machine-guns firing down on us, I threw myself on the floor of the bus, screaming, "Get down, Roy," much to the amusement of the armed guards. They thought I was joking but I was deadly serious!

We loved being in Singapore and were captivated by the sights, the people and the shopping.   One day, Roy and I were all but dragged into a tailor's shop a few doors from our hotel. The owner offered to make us each a suit within twenty-four hours. We were slightly sceptical but agreed to have two suits each, as the cost was most reasonable and the materials were superb. We were measured there and then and before we left, the tailors had already started on the cutting. There was another fitting later that day and, early next morning, the suits were delivered in smart suit-bags to our hotel. The other men in the show were so impressed with the cut of the suits and the quality of the materials that they also decided to place orders at the same shop.

Our tour then moved on to Kluang in Johore State, where we stayed at the Paramount Hotel, a rather seedy-looking establishment in a decidedly unsavoury area. This surely must have been a brothel, as young girls were constantly moving in and out of the hotel and I myself was propositioned by them on several occasions during the twenty four hours of our stay.

From there, we moved to perform at the old trading port of Malacca. Roy and I were extremely hot when we arrived and decided to take a shower. I must explain that the building where we were to perform was a long wooden hut which did not boast a stage. Word had already reached the camp that a stage would be needed because of the dancing in the show – and some of the troops had been roped in to construct it. We were not to know of the resentment that our request had caused but while we were showering, we could hear raised voices from the other cubicles.

"Who in hell are these guys anyway?" grumbled one voice. "Asking for a stage indeed!"

"I've no idea," came the reply, "but they've made enough demands."

I immediately turned the shower to a drizzle so that I could hear everything being said.

"All this fucking extra work just because one of the bastards does a bit of dancing. He'd better be fucking good or we'll give the bugger a hard time."

Having heard all this, my heart was pounding and it was the toilet I needed, not the shower, but Roy and I were too scared to venture out of our cubicles until the men had left.

Still shivering with terror, I told Tom Mennard what we had overheard and I suddenly brightened up, realising that I wasn't the only dancer in the show. "Oh, Audrey tap-dances as well," I said with relief, "so she'll need the stage too."

Tom shook his head, "No, she'll be all right. It's you they'll be gunning for. Oh and, by the way, Jackie," he continued, with a twinkle in his eye, "when you make announcements on the stage, try to disguise your accent. I've been told that they hate Geordies in this camp."

"Don't have me on, Tom, please," I gulped. "They loathe me already and they haven't even set eyes on me yet."

In a way, we were all dreading this show, none more so than yours truly but as it turned out, our fears were completely unfounded. The only worry we had was that not just the stage but the whole building might collapse, as the troops not only clapped and shouted for more but also stamped with all their might, hammering their heavy boots into the wooden floor. Soon, everyone realised that the building was actually moving and the Officer-in-Charge announced that he was going to write in his report that Roland Roy and Jackie Toaduff almost brought the roof down - literally!

We were taken by taxi to our next venue in the Cameron Highlands, where we were to perform for servicemen, their wives and civilians. We had to endure an ascent of thirty-seven miles of hairpin bends (1,700 in all) before we reached the township. Until that ride, we had never understood the true significance of car-sickness. And we were even more sick when we arrived and discovered that there was no piano for us.

"Is a piano really necessary?" we were asked.

"Well, we can't sing and dance without music," was our dismayed reply.

"How about performing to records? We have a wonderful selection of different kinds of music - Eartha Kitt, Bing Crosby, Gigli…you can take your pick."

We just couldn't believe that this ridiculous suggestion was meant to be taken seriously. It reminded me of the first time this had happened to us, when we were entertaining in the Persian Gulf. On that occasion, the piano was so full of sand that it was unplayable – but the situation was quickly remedied when a replacement piano was flown in at great expense from another post on the Gulf.

There was no such luck this time, however, because there was just NO piano. Fortunately, Gloria Anderson's accordion came to the rescue. Gloria played for Audrey, whilst Colin, who could also play this instrument, accompanied Roy and me, with Gloria turning the pages for him. It occurred to me then that, if we ever fell on hard times, we could always make ends meet by busking in front of cinema queues.

In spite of everything, the show was a great success with the audience but it taught us a salutary lesson. From that time on, we always checked in advance that a piano was available in any place where we would be performing.

We returned to Singapore via Kuala Lumpur and then flew to Sarawak. For some unknown reason, on this trip I suddenly developed an inexplicable fear of flying. This did not augur well for me because I knew that in the near future we would often be flying twice a day.

After the show in Sarawak, we were told that we had a very early flight the next day. Everyone else in our company went to bed early but this fear of flying was preying on my mind so I decided to have a drink in the Officers' bar before retiring for the night. A very inebriated airman who was propping up the bar insisted on buying me the drink and we fell into conversation. I say, "conversation," but he was so drunk that I found it difficult to understand him. I downed my drink and stood up to leave.

"No, don't go," he said, pulling at my jacket. "Get him another one, barman."

"No thanks, mate, not for me," I protested. "I have a very early flight tomorrow and I'm not looking forward to it. To tell you the truth, I'm scared stiff."

"Scared? There's nothing to be scared of," my new friend slurred. "Look, what's your name?"

"Jackie," I told him.

"Jackie, now don't you worry. I'm on your flight tomorrow. I'll look after you. Trust me. I'm your pilot."

This last remark almost finished me off and I hoped against hope that he was lying. But no, he really was in charge of our plane and fortunately seemed to have sobered up the next morning. He flew us safely to our next stop, from where we drove deep into the jungle to Balairingin, accompanied by armed guards front and rear. This was dangerous territory almost on the Indonesian border where only two months previously a band of terrorists had ambushed and killed seven British servicemen; these native Indonesians were themselves then rounded up and killed.

We were given a rousing reception by our audience, the Argyll and Sutherland Highlanders, especially when we sang one or two of their favourite Scottish songs. It was during this performance that I had yet another shock. I had just come off stage, where Roy was now delighting the audience with The *Scottish Soldier*. I was feeling hot after my hectic tapping routine so I decided to open a window in the dressing-room. As I did so, an oriental-looking soldier wielding a gun suddenly sprang up at the other side of the window and stared menacingly straight into my eyes. Terrified, I emitted an ear-splitting yell, which immediately brought another gun-carrying soldier to the scene. It turned out that the first soldier was in fact an ally. He was guarding the outside of the building while we were performing but he certainly gave me the fright of my life.

After that incident, I felt uneasy for the rest of the night in Balairingin. I think that perhaps I'd seen too many jungle war films in my youth. The humidity of the place made me feel ill and the constant loud chirping of crickets, tree-frogs and cicadas kept me awake all night. It was a relief to fly to Brunei early next morning.

Here we enjoyed some free time, which we spent visiting the famous mosque in Brunei's capital and Kampong Ayer, the largest water village in south-east Asia, where the inhabitants live in wooden huts on stilts submerged in water. Although there was dire poverty in this area, the people were very hospitable and invited our company into their homes. The other entertainers politely declined the offer but I felt that one of us at least should accept the kind invitation and so I stepped inside one of the houses. I remember that there were some children sitting on blankets and there seemed to be buckets everywhere, some filled with water, others with food or cooking utensils. Apart from a mirror and a couple of photographs on one wall, there were no ornaments or furniture. The stench inside was quite overpowering and so, after a short while, I thanked the lady who had invited me and made my excuses to leave.

We also enjoyed a fascinating sail on a long, narrow motorised boat, almost identical to one I had recently seen in a James Bond film. Along the river, we passed jungle longhouses where several families lived together. One or two of the inhabitants were apparently head-hunters - needless to say, I didn't want to be invited into any of those dwellings! Nor did I relish the idea of falling into the river as it seemed to be alive with evil-looking snakes.

This tour had been quite hectic and we were all tired when we all returned to Britain in a Bristol Britannia via Bombay and Istanbul. All, that is, except Audrey Mann, who had been offered a season at The Cockpit, a famous night-club in Singapore. Some weeks later, we received a letter from her in which she seemed to be thoroughly enjoying her stay. Since then, however, we have heard nothing. I like to think that she might have found another Ashley out there.

17

First Shaking, Then Sheikhing!

We were met at the airport in London by Alan Goford who told us that our tour had been an outstanding success with the troops and that our return was eagerly awaited. No sooner had we arrived home from London than the telephone rang. It was Derek Agutter with an invitation to begin another CSE stint in Cyprus.

Thus began two new tours early in 1966 –*Running Wild* and *Rise Above It* with the support of a first-class company. First there was Judi Jones, a fine singer with an appealing personality, who had already performed in Cyprus for the War Office when she supported Stan Stennett, a popular radio and television star in the 1960s. She had also sung with several big bands including Cyril Stapleton's, and just before joining us, she had been resident singer at the London Hilton Hotel. Another act on the tour was Berns and Jan, an instrumental and vocal turn. Berns, who excelled as a drummer, had also worked with Cyril Stapleton, in addition to touring with Chipperfield's Circus. Jan, his pretty, red-haired partner, who had sung in summer shows with almost every leading television personality, added her talents as accordionist to our show. Our compère was Tony Brandon, a gifted entertainer, comedian and impressionist. He was a decided asset as he had appeared on the radio several times and also in two long-running BBC television series. He had previously compèred shows for the Rolling Stones, Acker Bilk and Gerry and the Pacemakers. In addition to all this, he had enjoyed success as a freelance DJ with Radio City, the pirate radio station based on a fort on the Thames Estuary and he later joined the BBC's Radio One and Radio Two as a DJ.

Derek Agutter and Charlie Mazzola greeted us warmly at the airport in Cyprus and then we were driven to the Ledra Palace Hotel in Nicosia, again with a strong army escort. This hotel, which had now become the Headquarters of the United Nations, was to be our home for most of our time in Cyprus. I felt quite important being able to rub shoulders with such distinguished men as General U Thant, the United Nations' Secretary-General. I later boasted to people that the great man spoke to me once and then jokingly added that he told me to get out of his way!

My room in the hotel was immediately above the main entrance, where General U Thant's limousine seemed to be permanently parked. One evening, before we were leaving the hotel to give a performance, we were all informed that we would not be offered any food at that particular venue. This took us aback as we were usually expected to socialise after the show and to be guests at a superb meal or buffet. We knew that we would arrive back at the Ledra Palace long after the dining-room had closed but the management promised that a tray of food and a flask of tea or coffee would be left in each of our rooms. Tony asked for his tray to be left with mine as he didn't want to eat alone. When we arrived back that night, Tony was most impressed with my superb room, particularly when I opened the huge French windows to let in the night air.

"Now for the food," said Tony eagerly. "I'm starving." With that, he walked over to the tray. "Bloody hell!" he exploded and, without more ado, he threw the tray right out of the window. There was an almighty crash.

True to form, I started to tremble. "Tony, what on earth did you do that for? I'm sure that I saw General U Thant's car outside, just under my window."

"I don't give a bugger," retorted Tony. "That tray was covered with ants and I hate bloody ants! We couldn't have eaten that food."

"Tony," I said, my hands shaking and my heart pounding, "somebody will definitely be up here in a minute. We'll probably be arrested."

"Well, I don't care. I've completely lost my appetite now. I'm going back to my room. Goodnight."

I was terrified. I rushed to Roy's room to relate to him what had happened. This didn't help matters in the least, as Roy merely shook his head sadly and prophesied, "Well, Jackie, I don't think this will do much for your reputation, will it?"

But strangely enough, I did not hear another word about the incident and often wonder whether Tony had gone down that night to apologise.

We were a happy band of performers on that tour but most of the company seemed to keep themselves to themselves. The one person who spent most time with the three of us was Judi. She loved to go shopping with me as I was an old hand at bargaining with shopkeepers. In fact, she and I spent so much time in each other's rooms that everyone connected with our company assumed that we were in the middle of a big romance. Just for a laugh, we kept up the pretence but the truth was that Judi had a boyfriend back in London and ours was a purely platonic relationship. Nevertheless, to this day our friendship remains very special.

After a few days in Nicosia, we moved to the Limassol area, where we were given a full free day between two of the shows. Roy had previously bought a tourist information book on the area and, reading from it, he informed us that no one should miss the opportunity to visit the Kykko Monastery high up in the Troodos Mountains, where the monks loved to welcome visitors. We agreed that it would be an interesting excursion and so Colin hired a Mini for five of us – Roy, Colin, Judi, an airman dentist called Peter May and me. The early morning was so gloriously hot that all the men wore shorts and Judi donned a flimsy dress. Little did we know then that we were setting out on a journey that we would never forget!

Colin drove the Mini and Roy sat at the front with him to navigate. We drove along happily, singing, chatting and admiring the various sights as we climbed higher and higher into the mountains. After several miles of twisting and turning into various roads, we came to a crossroads but unfortunately there were no signposts there.

"Now which road do I take?" asked a perplexed Colin.

We got out of the car and investigated. It was agreed that one of the roads looked reasonably well-used so we made our choice. However, after driving along it for several miles, we found that it suddenly petered out in front of a dense forest.

Always a master at stating the obvious, I piped up, "I guess you've taken the wrong road, Colin."

Colin gave me a withering look and remarked wryly, "Oh, yes, Jackie, and which road should I have taken?"

"Well, let's go back and I'll show you," I volunteered brightly.

At this, Roy spluttered with indignation. "Listen to Jackie and we'll be even further in trouble. He has no sense of direction. He could get lost in his own house!"

Back at the crossroads, we took another route and once again came to a dead end. By this time, we had been driving for hours and darkness was beginning to fall. We had long ago abandoned the idea of visiting the monastery – all we wanted was to find our way back to Limassol but this was proving impossible. We saw some lights in the distance and headed in their direction, passing a small, abandoned village. There was no sign of life anywhere but we kept on driving.

"We've had it now," decided Colin. "We've almost run out of petrol. I think we'd better try to sleep in the car until day breaks tomorrow."

We were all shivering in the parked car as the night air was decidedly chilly but we huddled together to try to sleep. I kept thinking that the other members of our company back at the hotel would be wondering what had happened to us. We hadn't mentioned our plans to visit the monastery to anyone but I felt sure that the army would have already organised a search party.

At daybreak, we stumbled out of the car - cold, stiff, hungry and thirsty. The air was silent – no bird sang, no branch stirred. My imagination went into overdrive. By now, I was sure that we were going to perish in those mountains. I could imagine helicopters flying overhead, searching for us in vain. I could picture the headlines in the newspapers back home:-

CSE ENTERTAINERS MISSING, PRESUMED DEAD, IN CYPRUS

Judi was the only one among us who remained totally unconcerned. "Don't worry," she frequently consoled me. "We'll be found. We're in a clearing and anyone flying overhead will be sure to see us."

We each decided to walk in a different direction for five minutes to see if we could find any houses or signs of life but this proved to be futile. Then, while we were puzzling out what to do next, lo and behold, we heard the engine of a vehicle approaching us. When we saw a Land Rover driving towards us, our first thought was one of extreme relief. This was quickly replaced by one of sheer terror, however, when four huge, menacing-looking men, two of them holding guns, jumped out and confronted us grimly. Even the courageous Judi grasped my trembling arm in terror and we all thought that the end had come.

The unsmiling men spoke no English but made it quite clear that we had to explain ourselves. By exaggerated miming, we showed them that we had no petrol and that we were innocent tourists.

Eventually, this satisfied them, thank God. We discovered that they were forestry workers who had spotted our car tracks and decided to investigate. They siphoned some of their petrol into our tank and then led us out of the forest, down paths that were only the width of the car and with sheer drops over the side.

When we reached civilisation, we called at the nearest garage for petrol. It was only then that the full realisation of how lucky we had been was brought home to us. The garage owner told us that the area into which we had strayed was out of bounds, as it was used as a hideout for terrorists. He couldn't believe how we had escaped being shot.

We limped into the Corinthia Palace Hotel, stiff, hungry and exhausted – and, to cap it all, not one person had realised that we had been missing!

As I hobbled to reception to collect my room key, the Commanding Officer marched briskly towards me. "I say, Mr.ToadRuff, I have a request for your show this evening. "Does anyone in your troupe sing *Climb Every Mountain?*"

"Climb Every Mountain?" I spluttered. "We've just bloody well done that and, by the way, the name is ToadUFF not ToadRUFF – although I must admit that I am feeling pretty 'ruff' at the moment."

That evening, after hot baths, food and sleep, all of our performances were completely relaxed and it seemed to me that Roy's rendition of *Climb Every Mountain* was the finest he'd ever given.

After the mountain incident, our admiration for Judi just grew and grew. We realised that nothing was ever too much trouble for her and we never heard her grumble about anything. Her singing was superb and her act was very popular with everyone. When we flew over to Malta on the next leg of our tour, Frank Manzie, her boyfriend at the time, came out to see her and they often invited me to join them on excursions. In Malta, we gave one of our very few performances for the Royal Navy and they were so appreciative that they invited our company on board a battleship, where we were plied with food and drink. Frank, Judi and I stayed longer on board than the others because we were having such an enjoyable time. Before we came ashore, we were presented with three sailor hats as mementoes of the visit. As Frank and I were already wearing white shirts and trousers, we quickly donned those hats and were suddenly transformed into Frank Sinatra and Gene Kelly. What fun we had on the way back to the hotel, dancing and singing *We're Going on the Town* and *New York's a Wonderful Town*, jumping on walls, and swinging round lamp posts, with a laughing Judi trying to keep up with us.

A few weeks later, back in Cyprus in a new show *Rise Above It*, Judi and I happened to stroll down to the local park in Limassol one warm Sunday evening. The surrounding streets were packed with young Cypriot men walking up and down. Inside the park, there was a little café where drinks and snacks were sold and where a jukebox took pride of place in one corner. Just in front of the café was an open paved space, probably used for dancing on festive occasions. I chose *Zorba's Dance*, one of my favourite records of the day and Judi and I couldn't resist moving to the music on the paved area, improvising with our own version of the Greek dance. In no time at all, we were joined by two or three of the young Cypriots, who linked arms with us and danced. At the end of the record, someone put in another coin to play it again. As if from nowhere, more and more boys swarmed into the park until the dance area was filled with hundreds of male dancers plus Judi, the only girl in sight!

When Judi and I left the park, the dance music stopped and the Cypriots all followed us back to our hotel, begging us to go back but we were very tired by this time. They remained outside the hotel and when we appeared on the balcony, we felt like royalty as they were all cheering and urging us to join them. That was a very special night.

Another memorable occasion on that tour was in Bahrain when Roy, Colin, Judi and I decided to go to the beach for a swim. I suggested that we should then walk along the beach to have a closer look at the Sheikh's Palace, which we could see in the near distance. Roy volunteered to remain behind on the sand to watch over our belongings while the three of us took a stroll. We were in the process of admiring the Palace when three men, dressed in spotless white robes approached us. My first thought was that they were going to arrest us because Judi and I were wearing the skimpiest of swimsuits and Colin was just in shorts. In fact, quite the reverse happened; the Sheikh had seen us on his security cameras and was curious about who we were and what we were doing in Bahrain. He had requested that we should go to the Palace to take tea with him.

"Now? But we're not suitably dressed," we protested but we were assured that our clothes were of no importance as the Sheikh had personally requested our presence. We followed the men into the magnificent Palace, which reminded the three of us of something out of *Kismet* or the *Arabian Nights.* We were then introduced to the Ruler of Bahrain, His Highness Sheikh Isa BinSulman Al-Khalifa, a small, portly man, dressed from head to foot in black and gold flowing robes. He smiled broadly, shook each of us by the hand and indicated that we should sit. The opulent gold and cream furnishings seemed to be too grand for us to sit on in our beachwear but the Sheikh insisted. I just wished that I had been carrying a camera that day and I wondered what my old pals down the pit would have made of it all.

He was a most gracious host, delighted to learn that we were professional performers from England in his country to entertain the British forces. He was also most impressed that Judi was the resident singer at the London Hilton, taking a short break to appear in our show. We were served tea, cake and biscuits, all flown in from Harrods and served on solid gold trays with the most exquisite china we had ever seen. We then excused ourselves, telling the Sheikh that we had to go back to our friend who was guarding our clothes on the beach. As we were leaving, His Royal Highness ordered one of his servants to cut some carnations from the Palace gardens to give to Judi.

Poor Roy had been sitting alone on the beach for nearly two hours and, as it was almost dark, he was worrying about what had happened. He was so relieved to see us that he didn't even show his annoyance!

When we arrived back at the hotel and related our adventure to everyone, we were told how privileged and lucky we had been to be asked into the Palace – but not quite lucky enough, as the Sheikh usually presented his guests with Rolex watches.

"Perhaps he will, next time," I said quite confidently.

"Has he invited you back then?" asked our amazed friends.

"No, not yet," I rejoined, "but with our kind of luck, you just never know!"

18

Sour Grapes in South Africa

We had been home only a couple of days after the tour, when Derek Agutter telephoned to give us some exciting news about his daughter, Jenny. She had been spotted by a Disney talent scout at her school and had been selected to appear in the film *Ballerina.* We were all delighted to learn of her success and even happier when soon after that, Derek rang again to tell us that Anthony Quayle and Sylvia Syms had been so impressed with the first rushes of Jenny that they had insisted on her joining them in the film *East of Sudan.* Miss Agutter certainly had star quality, even as a child!

Another performer with star quality was Lex MacLean. Within a week of our returning home, we had the privilege of appearing with Lex for twenty-seven weeks at the Glasgow Pavilion. He was another comic we had been previously warned about. "Be on your guard. If he takes a dislike to you, you're out," we had been told on more than one occasion. We personally knew of two well-known and well-loved acts that Lex had fired and we actually witnessed him dismiss a young impressionist who had nipped out of the theatre for a drink during the show. Just before he was due to appear on stage, this young man could not be found anywhere in the theatre so Roy and I were summoned to the wings to take his place. The impressionist arrived split seconds before his entrance and was ready to rush on stage, only to be stopped and fired on the spot by Lex.

At that time, Lex was Scotland's favourite comedian and probably Britain's highest paid comic although he was almost totally unknown outside his native land. His shows were always a sell-out, with a capacity audience at each performance, and the material needed to be changed only once every three weeks – always a sign of a first-class entertainer. The costumes and sets used in his productions were decidedly more up-market than those of his contemporaries, whilst his supporting acts and his feeds had to be of the highest calibre.

For this particular show, Lex had employed three double singing acts, including Roy and myself, all appearing in the second half of the programme. The other two acts were brothers Bob and Jack Young, who were very talented vocalists and instrumentalists, and married couple George Cormack and Irene Sharp, a popular Scottish duo. Lex told us all that he wanted the act that preceded his final nightly solo spot to be so fantastic that the audience would be yelling for more. Consequently, the three singing acts were always anxious to be given that prize-slot billing and it became almost like a friendly singing contest. Happily, out of the nine changes of programme during the run, Roy and I managed to win the coveted spot five times.

Some of the artists on the show were very popular with the Glasgow audiences as they had worked alongside Lex for several years. These included instrumentalist Ronnie Dale, glamorous personality-girl Margo Bentley, singer Helen Randell, whose voice out-rivalled Shirley Bassey's and two feeds, Carr and Vonnie. Incidentally, one of the stagehands for this show was a pleasant young lad called Ian, who used to chat with me most nights while I was waiting in the wings for my cue.

"I'd love to be on the stage," he said on one occasion.

"Well, you're in the business now," I replied.

"Yes, but I mean I'd love to go out there and perform."

"Can you sing, Ian?"

"Not really."

"Can you dance?"

"I'm afraid not."

"Can you act or tell jokes?"

"No, but I'd still love to give it a go."

He was always so enthusiastic that I used to think to myself, "Well he might not think he has any talent but he's certainly got all the ingredients." And would you believe it – just a few months later, I switched on the television and there he was! He had teamed up with a young dancer called Janette and was now one of the famous duo, the Krankies, an act popular with all ages throughout Britain for many years.

Contrary to what we had been told, we found that working with Lex was extremely enjoyable, although we often had difficulty in understanding his broad Scottish accent, particularly when he spoke at full speed. Roy had been roped in to join Lex in some of his sketches and often had no idea what the comic was saying. Lex told me one day that he had specifically chosen Roy because of this, as he could say whatever he liked and Roy, not understanding, would keep a straight face – which added to the comedy. He often had a joke at my expense too, especially during the Friday night second-house finale when he would hand me our pay packet on stage, saying, "I don't know whether you're worth all this money I'm paying you, Jackie. Try and polish your act up for next week, and you and Roy must try to smarten yourselves up." This last remark always caused a laugh with the audience, as by now Roy and I were renowned in the Scottish theatres for our sartorial elegance.

While we were appearing with Lex, a South African impresario called Ronnie Quibel visited us backstage. He wanted us to sign up for a six-week tour of South Africa at the end of December in a show starring Howard Keel. We agreed. Before we left the Glasgow Pavilion, Lex expressed a strong wish for us to perform again with him in the near future but, as it turned out, whenever he asked us, we had always been booked for other engagements. In fact, we never played in Scotland again and Nancy Kirkland, now firmly established as our friend and housekeeper, finally cut off all her ties with Scotland when she arranged to sell her house in Glasgow.

We were now looking forward to the South African tour and I was particularly excited as I was keen to renew friendships with the many people I had met there on my previous visit. Unfortunately, Howard Keel had been forced to withdraw from the show as he still had film commitments. He was to be replaced by two American females, the Barry Sisters (not to be confused with the Geordie Barry Sisters), completely unknown to English audiences but very popular in the USA, where they were frequent guests on the chart-topping *Ed Sullivan Show.* On the tour, they were to share top billing with Bob Monkhouse. Also with us were Barry Kent, who had recently starred as Lancelot in Camelot at Drury Lane, and The Dudium, an Israeli male folk-singing duo. The line up of three singing double acts, a ballad singer and a comedian who also sang, seemed a most unlikely casting for a variety show, but when we opened at the Civic Theatre in Johannesburg on Christmas Eve, none of us had any qualms about this.

On opening night, our act was in the first half of the show, preceded by The Dudium and Barry Kent and followed by Bob Monkhouse. It was an excellent first half, as we all received enthusiastic ovations and Bob Monkhouse had the theatre rocking with laughter. The whole of the second half was devoted to the glamorous Barry Sisters, apart from a brief appearance by Bob who had written a brilliant finale to re-introduce all the acts. It was unfortunate that the Barry Sisters did not really gel with the audience, even though they were beautifully attired and gave extremely polished performances, with songs in different languages. This rather negative response to the duo happened again in the second house and we noticed that their manager, Manny Pine, who was married to one of the sisters, was looking decidedly unhappy.

After the show, Bob's first wife, Liz, came backstage to congratulate everyone. "I loved it all," she enthused and, pointing to Roy and me, she said, "and these two stole the show. Did you hear the audience when they walked down in the finale? They were great."

Her remarks did not go down too well with Manny, who had a face like thunder and even Bob's usual grin faded a little.

Success does not always pay, however, as we found to our cost the next day. The company was informed that there were some changes to be made in the running order and there were to be several cuts in the programme. Barry Kent was now to sing only two songs and our act was to be drastically cut to twelve minutes. Roy and I were devastated and went to the office to air our grievances.

"Why on earth have you shortened our act?" we asked. "You must have heard the applause we received."

"The trouble is," we were told, "you were too good. Also, the Barry Sisters were not very happy with your performance as they felt there were too many similarities between your act and theirs. You made a suit change during your act and they also had a change of outfit in theirs."

Roy and I stood there open-mouthed in astonishment. Some further explanation was surely needed. We stood our ground and waited.

"Well, gentlemen," said the manager at last, "the truth is we are paying such a lot of money to the Barry Sisters to top the bill that we can't afford to have anything that detracts from their performance or upsets them in any way. I fully understand why you are unhappy with the change of programme but we are willing to pay your full salary for the entire run if you want to leave the show now. We'll send you back to England on first-class tickets. Or, if you prefer, you could open the show with the twelve-minute act and then be free to leave each night as soon as you've finished it. There will be no finale in future, as they've forced us to cut that as well. Take it from me, the Barry Sisters will not be invited back here again, but you two would be welcome at any time in the future – you could even top the bill for us."

We put our grievances behind us and decided to stay with the show for the next few weeks. I have to admit that it was money for old rope because we left early each night, made full use of the facilities in all the first-class hotels where we stayed and enjoyed party after party.

After this alteration in the programme, Manny went out of his way to be friendly towards us. On New Year's Eve, he told us that the Barry Sisters wanted to invite the whole company to a champagne party. The two sisters were ordering the refreshments and drinks for everyone and had also made arrangements for the music. We were all quite happy to accept their hospitality. The next day, however, Manny asked Colin for a share of the cost.

"But I understood that it was an invitation," said Colin, quite bluntly.

"Well, it was meant to be but it cost more than we expected so we're asking everybody to chip in."

And, after all that, the fare at the party was very mediocre and the music was from a record-player!

In fact, Manny's somewhat miserly ways became a joke as the tour progressed. Colin, Roy, Barry Kent and I fell into the daily habit of dropping into nearby cafés and, more often than not, who should show up just after we'd started eating but Manny.

"How's the food?" he would invariably ask.

"Delicious," we would chorus. "We can thoroughly recommend it. Are you going to eat with us?"

"No, I'm not very hungry," he'd reply. "I'll just have a taste of yours if you don't mind." Then he would proceed to help himself to something from each of our plates.

Bob Monkhouse, on the other hand, made a favourable impression on all of us. The more we saw of him, the more we admired his considerable talents as a performer and 'sketcher' – in both senses of the word, as he not only wrote very amusing sketches but also was extremely gifted in drawing. I used to notice that when we were all talking, he would often whip a small notebook out of his pocket and start writing at full speed. I asked him about this one day and found that when any amusing thought or observation occurred to him, he always jotted it down. Incidentally, it was Bob who suggested that we rename our act, as he felt that 'Roland Roy and Jackie Toaduff' was quite a mouthful and so, thereafter, we became known as 'Roy and Jackie Toaduff'.

Before the end of the run, there was a dispute between the Barry Sisters and the management. The sisters had worked it out that they were expected to give two more shows than had originally been agreed on and they refused to oblige. On those two nights, Roy and I were asked to replace them as top of the bill and everyone was delighted with our performances.

A few days before the show closed, Bob received some wonderful news – he was to take over as compère in the popular show *Sunday Night at the London Palladium.* We were all happy for him and wished him every success. Roy and I also were given some exciting information. Apparently, the Grade office in London had received excellent reviews of our act in the show and asked us to call in to see their agent on our return.

19

What an Impact!

Colin had arranged for us to fly back home via Rhodesia, so that we could visit the spectacular Victoria Falls, a sight definitely well worth the stopover. Once in London, we called into the Grade office as their agent had requested and we were optimistic that we would secure a summer season, possibly in Blackpool. However, when we arrived, the agent told us that the headliners for the season had now been selected and as they were all singers, no supporting singing acts would be required. He apologised and went on to tell us that he could definitely arrange some club dates for us instead. He suggested that we might like to appear at a "fantastic club" in Doncaster, The Scala. He emphasised that the salary would be excellent but when he mentioned the sum, Colin immediately opened his briefcase and brought out a contract that he had previously signed with The Scala - for twice that amount!

"We happen to be favourites at that club," said Colin, handing over the contract to the manager. "In fact, Roy and Jackie topped the bill on its opening night."

When the agent saw the figure written down, his eyes almost popped out of his head. "Well, there's no way I could find that sort of money for you. I've hired Cilla Black to appear with Frankie

Howerd at the Prince of Wales Theatre and that's more than she's getting."

We were quite downhearted as we left the office; if we had known that Grade's promise of a summer season was not going to materialise, we could quite easily have booked ourselves into a summer show but now it was too late. We were consoled with the thought that we would certainly be welcomed with open arms on the club circuit, as we always packed in the crowds. I often think that fate was on our side at that time because, while performing in the clubs that summer, one of our engagements was at the Golden Butterfly in Ingoldmells, about two miles out of Skegness. It was there that we met Stuart Hammond, a young man who was to become a very important person in our lives.

At a period when most of the holiday summer shows were complaining of poor attendances due to the ever-increasing attraction of television, Roy and I were playing to packed crowds every night at the Golden Butterfly. It was the first time we had appeared in Skegness and we were relatively unknown there but word of mouth recommendations quickly spread among both holiday-makers and locals, and we received standing ovations at every performance. In fact, we made far more money for the club than any other previous acts had done since it opened. The local press reviewed us as *The Golden Boys* at the *Golden Butterfly* and fans came time after time to see us, with hoteliers arranging for large parties to visit our show. The popular DJ, Pete Murray, was making a holiday programme in Skegness at the time with Peter Jay of Anglia Television and a host of other television personalities and they all came to see us on the recommendation of Bob Monkhouse. Johnny Hurt, a local fairground owner, also became a fan and insisted on opening up the dodgem car rides for us at three o'clock one morning, after we'd recovered from our midnight show. We were joined on that funfair by Julian Jorg, Phil Kelly, Sandy Lane and Jimmy Ryder, all well-known professional entertainers and we certainly let our hair down.

The management at the Golden Butterfly bent over backwards to please us, and Stuart Hammond, the catering manager, fed us like royalty with all our favourite dishes cooked to perfection and served with style. Business was becoming so brisk towards the end of our run that a partition had to be opened for the first time in the club's history, so that a further two hundred punters could be accommodated.

The general manager of the Derbyshire Miners' Welfare Club, J.S. Chisnell, wanted us to appear in Skegness for the full season, a request that was reiterated by members of the Board of Trustees a few days later. As it happened, however, we had already signed another contract with Tams in Jersey.

In a matter of weeks after our departure from Skegness, Barbara Castle brought the breathalyser law into operation. Drivers were now being stopped and tested so frequently that they were becoming reluctant to venture out to late night, out-of-town venues. This certainly had an adverse effect on the Golden Butterfly, even though it wasn't too far from Skegness. Business dropped so dramatically that the club was forced to close and all the employees there were made redundant.

Stuart rang us to give us the news and asked us to look out for jobs for him in the Derbyshire area, as he could not find any suitable work in Skegness. That week, we happened to be performing in and around South Yorkshire so we invited him to stay with us so that he could look around for himself. Stuart gratefully took us up on the offer, touring the job centres by day and accompanying us on our club dates each night. He immediately made himself useful, taking care of our extensive wardrobes, carrying and setting up our sound equipment and, in fact, becoming so indispensable that we offered him a job as our road manager until he could find something more suitable.

Our entourage was growing. We already had our housekeeper Nancy, our own manager and pianist Colin and now Stuart. As well as taking on the duties as road manager, he was also chief cook and bottle-washer. He soon became such an integral part of our lives that we realised that we could not do without him and so we asked him to join us permanently. He agreed and so great has been the friendship that he is still with us today. At the time, however, I am sure that he didn't realise what a task he had taken on, as we had just embarked on an extensive tour of one-night stands – often two clubs in a night – intermingled with weekly engagements.

It was a tiring time for Roy and me too in 1968 and, without the help of Colin and Stuart, we couldn't have managed. There was no such thing as a night off and during the day, we had to rehearse new routines and new songs to keep up with the ever-changing hit parade; added to this, we were preparing for our forthcoming Jersey summer engagement.

When we arrived in Jersey, our first task was to find accommodation. Once again, we were fortunate in our choice. For the whole of the season, we lived in the parish of St. Clements, in a stone cottage attached to a farmhouse belonging to a lovely young couple, Charles and Maureen Hamil and their three children, Barry, Glen and Lynn. This family could not have been kinder to us if we had been relatives and, even to this day, they treat us like family members whenever we visit. It was quite usual for us to find on our doorstep a basket of freshly-dug Jersey potatoes, fresh vegetables and Jersey tomatoes. Next door to the farm lived Jack and Mary Hanson, owners of the Eden House Hotel. Most Sundays, Jack and Mary invited us all over for lunch and a refreshing dip in their swimming pool. It was here that Stuart taught the Hamil boys to swim.

I have to admit that before our show at Tams opened, Roy and I were worried because, initially, rehearsals were anything but smooth. Billy Forrest, a Birmingham agent, had signed a group of musicians to provide the musical backing for the whole show. When this group arrived and rehearsals began, we felt that there was something not quite right.   Roy and I watched the other acts and they were obviously struggling so much that we started to worry about the standard of their professionalism. When our turn came, however, we quickly realised that it was not the entertainers who were at fault - but the backing musicians. These lads were eventually forced to admit to us that they couldn't read music!

"Just give us two or three days," they pleaded, "and we'll be able to do it."

But this, of course, was not acceptable and a frantic search started for replacement musicians. This was proving an impossible task and we were just about to postpone the opening night when luck intervened at the eleventh hour in the shape of the Anna Dell Four, an extremely talented musical quartet.

The show itself was a highly acclaimed success and we played to capacity audiences each night. *The Jersey Evening Post* was full of praise for our act, dedicating a full broadsheet page to us. Under the eye-catching headline **WHAT AN IMPACT**, the report also reminded readers that we were back in the place where I had started my professional career. We had a strong supporting cast, including Mike Burton, who later became a popular television personality. An all-female group, The Gaytones, added their talents as trombone players and singers; Maurice French and Joy brought gasps and applause from the audience with some breath-taking manoeuvres during their balancing act; and true glamour was provided in the shape of the Jean Belmont Grosvenor Girls. One night, there was also a special midnight performance for charity where we shared top billing with the renowned pianist Semprini.

Our stay in Jersey was enhanced by the number of pleasant duties we had to perform in addition to our work at Tams. People called on us to open various garden-party events, to judge beauty contests and to topple piles of pennies that had been collected for charity. However, one task that I should never wish to repeat was to act as a judge in a baby show and I would urge anyone who has been asked to undertake a similar duty to steer clear! Before the actual competition, every mother without exception smiled at us and flattered us with complimentary remarks about our act, our appearance and anything else they could think of. To us, all the babies looked beautiful but only three could be selected. After the winners had been announced, those lovely maternal smiles turned to frowns and grimaces. Within our hearing, there were sarcastic mutterings all round. "What the hell do they know about babies, anyway?" was the general drift of their remarks. Roy and I were only too anxious to beat a hasty retreat on that day.

During this season in Jersey, we made many new friends, one of them being the inimitable Tommy Cooper, who came to see our act four or five times. We spent quite a few pleasant hours chatting and drinking with him and watching close-ups of some of his card tricks. Each time we met, Tommy told us that he was very keen for us to work with him in the near future.

Two other people who became friends were Sir Billy Butlin and his wife, who owned a house on the island and frequently brought friends and relatives to see our show. We were often invited to their home and one occasion that I particularly remember was a garden party in the grounds, where the food and champagne were of the highest order. Many of Sir Billy's celebrity friends had flown in from the mainland for the party but, strangely enough, he spent much of the day with Roy and me, constantly ensuring that we were being looked after and posing with us for press photographs.

One of my idols as a youth was the orchestra leader Geraldo, as our family had always enjoyed listening to his music programmes on the radio. At Sir Billy's suggestion, Geraldo, or Gerry as he was affectionately known among friends, caught our act at Tams and the next day we were invited to lunch with him at the Little Grove Hotel, where he and his wife were staying on holiday. During the meal, Geraldo offered us various engagements, including work on cruise ships. This invitation was later to lead to twenty years of glorious cruise-ship life, with all the travel and glamour that it had to offer.

That season, we topped the popularity poll in the *Jersey Evening Post,* and we were proud to be voted Best Cabaret Act in Jersey 1968 by readers. The next year, Pat and Tony Fielding brought us back to Tams, where once again we topped the poll for best cabaret act.

Jersey itself will always hold a special place in my heart and not just because it gave me my first break into professional show business. I have always loved everything about the island - the climate, the beautiful scenery and beaches, the success of our performances at Tams and, most of all, the wonderful people we have met there on each visit.

20

Knights and Nights to Remember

It was early in 1969 when our first cruise-ship work began. Geraldo had arranged a short season for us on the *Empress of England*, a ship owned by Canadian Pacific. We would be sailing from Liverpool Docks to Montreal, Canada. It was a quite a voyage!

Roy and I had been allocated an inside bunk-bed cabin, as far forward on the ship as we could possibly be. My first impression was that we had done well as it was en-suite, with considerable wardrobe space. After looking at the Bon Voyage cards and basket of fruit that had been sent to us, we unpacked and then went to meet the Cruise Director and other artists, all of whom had been entertaining on board for some time. They welcomed us, assuring us that it was a very happy, friendly ship and that the food was superb.

After these formalities, Roy, Colin and I went on deck to watch as we sailed from the docks, but we didn't stay long as it was bitterly cold, with a strong wind blowing. Later, after cocktails in the bar and an excellent evening meal, we decided to have an early night. The weather was worsening and, as we walked along the uncarpeted floors of this rather old but nevertheless elegant ship, we could not stop laughing as we were buffeted from side to side with every step.

In no time at all, we had climbed into our bunks and I was soon asleep, rocked no doubt by the creaking and rolling of the ship.

Suddenly, I was disturbed by Roy who had jumped out of the top bunk, switched on the light and was attempting to reach the bathroom as he was feeling sea-sick. It was then that I noticed our cards and fruit – they were scattered all over the floor. At that point, the force of the rolling was so great that I was propelled out of my bunk and could hardly stand. Adding to the confusion, the wardrobe doors swung open with a clatter and began moving back and forth. I could hear Roy's retching in the bathroom and, as I was trying to steady myself, I heard a tremendous crashing outside our cabin. To my horror, I saw water rushing in under the door.

As was usual with me, panic stations set in and I cried out, "Roy, Roy, we're sinking. Come on! Put this life-jacket on and let's get out of here."

There was no answer from Roy so by now I was terrified. "Roy, come on. The water's flooding in and we're definitely sinking."

"I can't go anywhere," gasped Roy. "I'm dying! You go, Jackie."

There was another series of crashes and I stumbled to open the cabin door. What a sight met my eyes! Those crashes had been caused by nothing more than the flower vases that had been left outside all the cabins as was customary each night. They had all rolled down to our room. And what about that tempestuous sea, hell-bent on flooding our cabin? It was merely the water from the vases!

The next morning when I related what had happened, all the other entertainers were highly amused, particularly when they told us that the storm had been a very mild one. I found out that their cabins were situated midship, where there was very little movement and so we immediately arranged for ours to be changed. Needless to say, before every subsequent voyage we made, we always requested midship accommodation.

We made several more trips on the *Empress of England* and also on the *Empress of Canada* and found that it was quite usual to be entertaining famous people on board. Sir Harry Britain was one such passenger and a lively one at that – aged over 90 and swimming every day in the ship's pool. One day, he asked us if we could sing *The Road to Mandalay* for him. As it happened, Roy knew the song well and included it in our act that same night. How surprised he was to have Sir Harry join him on the stage and sing it with him, much to the delight of the audience.

Sir Boyd Rochford and his wife were two other friendly titled passengers. They didn't miss a single one of our shows while they were on board and joined us for tea almost every afternoon.

But perhaps the character I remember most of all was a man, who was accompanied by a woman I mistakenly assumed to be his wife. After he had seen our show, he invited us for a drink and introduced himself as Roy and his companion as Mrs. Newman.

Once at the table, we started chatting. I asked him, "And where do you come from, Roy?"

"I live in Southern Rhodesia," he answered.

This piece of news started me off enthusing over the country. "Oh, I've been there," I said eagerly. "In fact, I was there last year and visited the Wankie Game Reserve and Victoria Falls. If you haven't been there, I can thoroughly recommend both of these places. You'll love them."

After that first meeting, I would always greet him with a cheery, "Hi, Roy, how are you doing?"

"I'm fine, Jackie," he would reply.

Then, some time later, we received a party invitation, which read:

Sir Roy Walensky and Mrs. K.G. Newman request the pleasure of the company of Roy and Jackie Toaduff for cocktails on Sunday, 8th February at 12.15pm in the Hampton Court Lounge.

Sir Roy? I gulped. I had been addressing him like an old friend for days and now I found out that he was not only titled but also the former Prime Minister of Southern Rhodesia and Nyasaland! When I saw him, I immediately apologised for having addressed him so informally but he put my mind at rest by saying that there was nothing to apologise for.

He came to see all our shows on board and was particularly impressed by our Scottish act, especially Roy's rendition of *My Love is Like a Red, Red Rose.* He asked if Roy had recorded it, as he would like a copy for his collection. Unfortunately, Roy hadn't but we bought a recording of Kenneth McKellar singing it and sent it to him after he had disembarked. In his letter of thanks, he emphasised that, if we were ever to plan another trip to Rhodesia, we had to be sure to inform him in good time so that he could offer us hospitality. He was indeed a great character and obviously a hit with the female sex for, in December1972, I read in the newspaper that 65 year-old Sir Roy had just married - not Mrs. Newman, but 32-year old Valerie Scott, a former organiser for the British Tory Party.

By this time, Roy and I had been stage partners for almost eleven years, headlining shows around the world and appearing on the Australian TV network, but we had never appeared together on television in our own country. Perhaps this had something to do with the fact that we had never entertained as a duo at a London venue. Wherever we performed, people always asked us the same question - "Why haven't we ever seen you on TV?" Sometimes, we received a backhanded compliment such as, "You should have your own TV show – we've seen much worse than you on the box, you know."

Our nearest engagement to the capital was at The Barn at Braintree in Essex, about which Peter Hepple of The Stage newspaper wrote in his Nightbeat column:

April 2nd 1970. Out at The Barn in Braintree last week-end, where apparently the whole of metropolitan Essex congregate to judge by the volume of business, occurred a raiding foray into the Home Counties by that remarkable Northern act, Roy and Jackie Toaduff. Why remarkable? One reason is that they are better known in Australia and South Africa than they are in London. Another is that they have the enviable ability to create an instant party atmosphere, based not so much on what they do but how they do it. The act has immense heart, vitality, gaiety and magnetic professionalism. It's one of the best acts I've ever seen and London doesn't know what it's missing. It will have to miss it for the rest of the spring and summer for the boys have been signed for the Palace Lido, Douglas in the Isle of Man, where doubtless 2000 people a night will be agreeing with every word I have written about them.

Indeed, we had been topping the bill for years at nightclubs up and down the country, where other headliners in other weeks in these same clubs were invariably TV favourites or well-known recording stars. Some of our supporting acts were also television stars and yet we had never had the opportunity to prove what we could do to entertain a wider audience. In the clubs, we constantly felt that we had to go out and prove that we could hold our own against these more famous people – and we always did.

"One of these days, we will be on television," I used to say to Roy and, sure enough, that day came with an invitation to appear on the popular game show *The Golden Shot*, hosted by Bob Monkhouse. This was our chance – or so I thought. We knew that we would not get very much time to perform but, nevertheless, we were still disappointed to be told that our performance could last only two minutes and we wondered how best we could show our talent in that short period. Colin came up with the idea that we should sing a selection from *The Sound of Music* and devised a bright medley, timed to perfection. Having practised this, we were further dismayed when the show's producer, Dickie Leeman, insisted that we should include some clog-dancing. What were we going to do? To begin with, we didn't know how to fit it in with the chosen music and secondly, Roy could not clog dance! We really should have refused to appear there and then. However, we knew that there would be a large audience nation-wide and so we approached a song-writing friend of ours, Barrington Brown. He composed a number just for us, entitled *The Boy with Clogs On*, an extremely fast number with tongue-twisting lyrics, leaving me a few seconds at the end to include a few simple clogging steps. Sadly, it was all so different from how we usually performed. I think that it must have been Bob Monkhouse who put our names forward to be included in the show because it was quite obvious that the producer had never seen either the content or the unique presentation of our work. Even the TV Times billed us incorrectly as *Rae and Jackie Toaduff – Comedy Dancers*. No one spoke to us in the studio and I don't think that there was a rehearsal. I don't remember much about the show other than that it went out live. We had to leave as soon as our spot ended because we were appearing for a week at a club in Birmingham.

Whilst in that city, I managed to fit in a solo appearance for two nights at the Central Hall during the EFDS Festival of Dance. Ron Smedley, who reviewed this Festival, wrote:

Jackie Toaduff is a little heavier than he used to be but his dancing is still light and adept; it is a funny thing to say about a clog-dancer, but he really is a delicate performer. There's nobody quite like him. He's got real quality.

Needless to say, television producers didn't shower us with offers of other shows after our two-minute debut on *The Golden Shot*, but we were still in demand on the club circuit and so we forgot about TV and London, concentrating all our efforts on wowing audiences, especially in the north of England, where the money was astonishingly good.

Another popular and lucrative area was in South Wales, where we were always given an enthusiastic reception in the clubs. After each performance, the audiences used to sing the Welsh National Anthem and *We'll Keep a Welcome in the Hillside* especially to show us just how much they had appreciated our act; this display of gratitude invariably moved me to tears.

If you recall, Auntie Bertha, the Countess Helene from America, had promised that she would come over to see us on a regular basis and she was as good as her word. We saw her every year and on this occasion she descended on us while we were in South Wales. As usual, she soon made herself known to the locals and I have vivid memories of her holding court in a small pub in Bedlingnog. She was dressed in all her finery, surrounded by all the local men of the village, who had come just to see her. Never before had they been so close to the rich and famous – and they showed her as much deference as if she were a member of the Royal family!

I had always worshipped from afar that star of stars, Ginger Rogers. She had just arrived in London from the USA in a blaze of publicity, to appear in the Jerry Harman musical *Mame* at Drury Lane, with our old friend Barry Kent as her co-star. Of course, I longed to meet my idol but Barry confided in me that, although Ginger was a very pleasant and friendly person, he didn't feel that he knew her well enough to knock on her dressing-room door and introduce me. Nevertheless, I couldn't wait to see the show and, at the first opportunity, I made the trip to London. Ginger had received mixed reviews for her performance but I thought that she was wonderful and just as glamorous as in her films. She worked hard too, as she was never off the stage for more than three minutes at a time in the whole show, with twenty-nine costume changes to boot! After the show, I went backstage to congratulate Barry and we chatted for so long that at last he said, "I think we'd better get out of here now, Jackie, or we'll be locked in. I'll give you a lift to your hotel."

When we reached the stage door, it was pouring with rain, so Barry asked me to wait until he brought his car round, as it was parked some distance away. No sooner had he gone than the old Toaduff luck put in an appearance, for who should emerge from the theatre but Ginger!

"Hello," she smiled and we fell quite naturally into conversation, as though we had known each other for years. I told her that I loved her performance and that I was a friend of Barry. When she asked what I did for a living, I explained that I was in show business as a song and dance man. She was well and truly interested in everything I had to say. Barry's car and her taxi arrived at the same time.

"I have loved talking to you," she said, giving me a peck on the cheek. "Please come and see me again and make sure that you come backstage to talk to me. Good night and God bless."

"My God," said Barry, once we were in his car, "She certainly seems to have taken a liking to you. I've been working with her for weeks and that's more than she's ever said to me!"

It was a few months before I was able to see the show again and this time I went with a girl friend of mine and managed to get two seats on the front row. As Ginger took the final curtain, she curtsied and blew a kiss directly at me. I wasn't sure whether she had recognised me or not but I couldn't go backstage on this occasion, as my friend had to rush to catch the train home. Ginger and I met again a year or so later – but more of that in good time.

Roy and I loved working in the Isle of Man and quickly became addicted to the Manx kippers supplied to us each week by Douglas's favourite fishmonger, Mr. Curtis. Roy knew how to cook them to perfection and we often held kipper parties after our shows, for friends who visited us during the season.

When our work there finished, we appeared before H.R.H. Princess Margaret at a charity ball for Dr. Barnardo's at the Winter Gardens in Blackpool. It was compèred by Stuart Hall of BBC television fame and our supporting act was Cy Grant, the calypso singer, another TV favourite.

After our performance, Lady Pilkington, who had arranged the evening, came backstage to inform all the performers that Princess Margaret would like to meet them. "I do believe she knows one of you gentlemen," she said.

"Yes, it's Jackie she knows," answered Roy. "He's even danced with her on a couple of different occasions in the past."

Lady Pilkington turned to me. "Well, she seems to be very fond of you. I must say that Her Royal Highness wasn't in one of her better moods until you appeared."

Roy was very nervous about meeting the princess and asked how he should address her.

"Just remember to call her 'ma'am'," reassured Lady Pilkington.

Princess Margaret spoke very briefly to Cy, a little longer to Stuart and then, when she saw me, she beamed, extending her hand. "Hello, Jackie. It's so nice to see you again. I didn't realise that you were such a good singer and I didn't know that you had such a talented brother. Is he really your brother?" she asked, searching Roy's face for any similarity of features.

"No, he's my father!" I answered cheekily and she began to laugh.

"What a good friend!" she said to him. She went on to tell us how much she had enjoyed our performance, particularly Roy's selection of Ivor Novello songs. "You're very talented. Ivor would have loved you."

Before she left, she asked me if I would be taking part in the EFDS Annual Festival at the Royal Albert Hall.

"I haven't been asked yet," I smiled.

"Oh, I expect you will be," she replied.

With that, she departed, leaving Roy and myself with memories of a wonderful evening, where we had both been made to feel very special by a beautiful princess.

21

The Chantry

Roy and I had often toyed with the idea of owning our own nightclub and in 1970 the chance to do so came one night after we had been performing at the Park Hall Country Club in Derbyshire. We were enjoying a post-show drink with the owner and his wife when we mentioned how much we liked the club and how fortunate they were to own such a lovely house in such beautiful surroundings.

"Why don't you buy it from us then?" asked the owner. "We've had enough and we'd like to move."

We thought at first that he was joking but the couple left us in no doubt about the seriousness of their decision to sell.

For the next week or two, we could hardly think of anything other than becoming owners of Park Hall, a magnificent house set in ten acres of land. It had been restored by Sir Francis Pole in 1715 and, in the past, such well-known celebrities as Lord Byron and Dame Edith Sitwell had not only stayed there on frequent occasions but also agreed to have bedrooms named after them.

However, although the building itself was impressive, it was clear that the interior needed renovating and redecorating and we began to wonder whether we could afford to purchase it. We discussed the pros and cons with various friends, particularly Albert and Betty Kemp, whom we had met when they were on holiday in Jersey in 1969. They encouraged us to take the plunge and further suggested that they could sell their own lucrative fruit and fish business in Harrow and come into partnership with us. They had already seen Park Hall, as they had travelled there to see us performing earlier in the year and they too had fallen in love with the club. In no time at all, their enthusiasm had them organising how it might be run. Stuart could be in charge of catering and Nancy of housekeeping, while Albert could be the manager, with Betty as the hostess. This would leave Roy, Colin and me free to continue with our show-business commitments and at the same time perform at our own club whenever we were available; we were also to assume responsibility for booking other acts to appear there. We all agreed that this was an ideal plan of action.

We knew that this partnership would be a happy one, as both Albert and Betty were so friendly. Albert, with his ability to make people welcome, his infectious sense of humour and his expertise as a dancer would make a wonderful manager and Betty would be the perfect hostess. The Kemps had four sons, all living at home; two of the boys, Tony and Edward, were in show business and had already appeared on television and stage and in films. Tony had played Alec Guinness's son in the West-end production of *Voyage Around My Father* and the juvenile lead in *Equus* with Ronald Lewis. He had been given the starring role in *Cry Wolf,* a film for the Children's Film Foundation, the lead in a Hungarian film, *The Boys of Paul Street*, and had played Richard Harris's son in *Elizabeth R.* Edward, an accomplished dancer, had also appeared as Alec Guinness's son - in the film *Cromwell.* He was given the part of Glenda Jackson's son in *A Touch of Class* and later performed in *Starlight Express* for eight years, playing every male part, including the lead.

After we had made final arrangements to go into partnership with the Kemps, Albert and Betty sold their house and business and moved to Derbyshire. Deposits were paid for the purchase of Park Hall and the contracts on our side were fully signed. We were now the proud owners of our own club – or so we thought. The news quickly spread and our wide circle of friends all wanted to become members. The future looked very promising indeed.

Just after signing, Roy, Colin and I set sail on the *Empress of England* for another working trip to Canada but not before we had chosen the new furniture, drapes and other furnishings for the club. Our happiness knew no bounds and our excitement grew by the minute as we kept reminding each other that, after this trip, we would be moving into a mansion! Then on that first day at sea, all our hopes were dashed. We received a radio telephone call from a very distressed Albert, who informed us that the deal was off.

"That can't be true. We've signed the contract," said a bewildered Colin.

"Yes," explained Albert, "but the owner didn't sign and now he is selling it to someone else who has put in a higher offer."

"You could put in another bid as well," Colin suggested.

"I've already tried that, I'm afraid," said Albert, "but I was too late. We had no idea that this was going to happen. He's already sold it."

When the news had sunk in, we were so unhappy that we would have jumped ship had it been possible. We found it difficult to disguise our misery in public, and in private it was even worse because we couldn't believe how we had all been let down. One day, Roy and I were sitting in one of the ship's lounges, still bewildered by what had happened, when Geraldo's sister, Betty Friedentag, accompanied by a rather distinguished-looking lady, joined us. Betty had travelled with us before and, sensing that all was not well, asked us to tell them what was troubling us.

We related the whole sorry tale and, as we finished, Betty's friend asked, "Whereabouts in Derbyshire is this club?"

"Park Hall in Spinkhill," I replied.

With that, she gave a slight smile, shook her head gently and reached out to touch us. "Well, boys, all I can say is that you don't know how lucky you've been not to get it. You see, the place is cursed. I know this for a fact because I used to own it. It broke my heart when I was forced to leave it and on the day of my departure, I kissed the step and personally cursed the damned place. Nobody who has lived there since has ever prospered and, mark my words, nobody ever will. Not only that," she went on, "it would have cost a fortune to put the place right. I know for a fact that the roof needs replacing and that in itself will cost thousands of pounds. There are also several major faults with the building. And to cap it all, Park Hall is haunted."

Slightly appeased, we passed on all this news to Albert and Betty but I have to admit that we were still sad about having been let down so badly.

When we arrived home after our work on the ship, a clairvoyant friend of ours telephoned me to say that she had heard about Park Hall and realised how downhearted it must have made us. "Be glad the sale didn't go through, Jackie. The building's been cursed, you know. I'm ringing to tell you that there is another place in Derbyshire just waiting for you. It's called the Chantry Hotel in Dronfield. You must go to see it now. It has your name all over it!"

"Are you an estate-agent as well as a clairvoyant?" I quipped.

"No, I am most certainly not. Listen to me. The Chantry is the hotel for YOU."

When I related this conversation to my colleagues, they were not at all impressed; in fact, Stuart was the only one to show a glimmer of interest. I, however, had a very strong feeling that we ought to at least visit the Chantry and so I tentatively broached the subject with Stuart.

"Do you happen to know where Dronfield is?" I asked him.

"Sorry," he replied, "I've never heard of the place."

"From what I've gathered, it's half-way between Sheffield and Chesterfield," I said. "Come on. Let's go and have at look at this hotel which is supposedly waiting just for us."

Although the night was cold and wet, Stuart somewhat reluctantly agreed. When we reached Dronfield, we drove up and down the streets trying to find the hotel but to no avail. In those days, it was more like a village than a town but even so, the people we stopped to inquire about the hotel's whereabouts had never heard of it.

"I think we must have been conned," I concluded.

"Well," said Stuart, "I don't know about you, but I'm ready for a drink. Let's call into this pub."

And so we walked into the Green Dragon, which was empty, probably because of the foul weather. When the landlady, Ethel, served our drinks, we fell into conversation with her.

"Do you happen to know of a hotel called the Chantry in Dronfield?" I asked her.

"Why, yes," she said. "It's just next door. Are you thinking of buying it? It's a place that is crying out for love and attention. You must come back in the daytime and look at it. As soon as you see it, you'll probably realise how it's waiting for someone like you."

As we stepped out of the Green Dragon, the night sky was pitch black but Stuart and I wandered up to the front of the Chantry to have a look at the outside. I walked up to the front door and the most amazing thing happened. I turned the knob and to our surprise, the door groaned open. We ventured in and then, in the glow of Stuart's cigarette lighter, I saw a light switch. We could not believe our luck when the lights came on!

I have never been the bravest of individuals but curiosity filled me with courage and I persuaded Stuart to explore this eerie, three-storey building with me. From what Ethel had told us, we now knew that it had not been lived in for almost a year and we could see from the outset that it was in a dilapidated condition. Rain had been collecting in the entrance hall for months and there were large cobwebs everywhere we looked. It reminded me of the jilted Miss Haversham's room in Great Expectations, which had remained untouched for years.

Ethel had also told us that the last owners had left in a hurry on Christmas Day of the previous year and when we ventured into the kitchen, we were given proof of this. A turkey had been left in the oven and it was now dried up and covered with dead maggots and flies. Not only that, every shelf of the cold-room was also blackened with insects – crawling this time. The kitchen table was strewn with bottles in which foul-smelling milk had puffed up to twice the size it should have been. The ceiling was covered with grease and the whole room was indescribably filthy.

From the kitchen, we made our way up the creaking staircase - an experience in itself as it was as frightening as a scene from an Alfred Hitchcock movie.

"I think we should leave now," faltered Stuart.

Although it was decidedly spooky and I was by now quite terrified underneath, something forced me to want to investigate further. "We'll just have a quick look at the bedrooms," I said.

In spite of the cheap fixtures and furnishings, these rooms at least looked more promising and my mind was made up. Although this hotel needed time and money spending on it, I knew instinctively that this was the place where I wanted to live.

We returned home and, bubbling with enthusiasm, I related to the others what we had seen. Unfortunately, my eagerness to impress them was not as infectious as I had hoped because they still showed no interest. It took all my powers of persuasion to coax them into viewing the Chantry the next day.

We arranged to meet the estate agent there and, before he arrived, we took the opportunity to look at the hotel and its grounds. We could see that the gardens were completely overgrown and in front of the main entrance was a tacky wishing-well, inexpertly constructed out of wine bottles. Strangely, the front door was now locked and so we peered through the dirty windows to look at the bar and dining-room. When the estate agent arrived, he opened up and found it hard to believe that Stuart and I had been inside the previous night.

"But that's impossible," he protested. "I'm the only one with keys and they have never been out of my possession."

How strange that was!

Once inside, it did not take long for the others to agree that the Chantry definitely had potential. The main building was Georgian with large Victorian-style bay windows. The estate-agent informed us that parts of the house dated back to 1250AD and that in the past, the Chantry priests had stayed there when visiting the nearby parish church; this accounted for the hotel's name.

Albert and Betty also liked the building and once again asked if they could become part-owners with us. We agreed of course and so, on December 17th 1970, we signed the contract.

Our first task was to either sell or dispose of all the furniture and furnishings, and, from then on, the place became a hive of activity, with carpenters, plumbers, electricians and decorators buzzing around to ensure that the whole house was completely refurbished. Colin, Roy and I missed all this activity, as three days after signing, we set sail from Southampton to New York on our first Cunard ship, the *Carmania*, and from there on to the Caribbean. In all we were away for five months. We loved entertaining on this ship and were pleased to miss the worst of the English winter but we were also keen to return to Dronfield, as we were anxious to see what progress was being made at the Chantry.

When we finally arrived home, we were delighted with what we saw. No expense had been spared – this was certainly going to be an exclusive hotel of the highest order and we had managed to secure the services of an excellent chef. Within a month of our returning home, our hotel was opened to the public and it was quickly established as the 'in' place to wine and dine. It attracted many celebrities and sports personalities, with Michael Caine and George

Best among our first guests and an impressive number of television stars who came to stay or visit soon after we opened.

Business started to boom and we were seriously considering the idea of giving up show business altogether. This was not to be, however, as offers of great engagements started to flood in. One which I particularly remember was an invitation to appear at the Victoria Palace in a Sunday night star-studded charity show for the Variety Artists Ladies' and Children's Guild. Heartthrob singer Malcolm Roberts was to top the bill in the first half of the show and the New Seekers in the second. However, during rehearsals, Malcolm and the orchestra leader, Ivan J. Dozin, had a disagreement, which ended with Mr. Dozin refusing to play for Malcolm and the singer walking out. Mr. Dozin then suggested that Malcolm's place should be taken by Roy and me. The write-up in The Stage was full of praise for our top of the bill performance, stating that our streamlined act thoroughly deserved 'the tumultuous ovation' it received.

On the occasions when we were back at the Chantry, however, it was becoming increasingly obvious to all of us that management was somewhat overcrowding the building. Albert and Betty had bought a house in Dronfield but they and their family spent most of their time at the hotel. As Colin, Roy, Stuart, Nancy and I were living on the premises, you can imagine how the eleven of us were often under each other's feet. We also realised that, with so many mouths to feed among the proprietors, the Chantry could not hope to make a profit in the dining-room. We all sat down and discussed the situation very amicably and it was decided that we should buy out Albert and Betty and their family. They were in full agreement and so they sold their house in Dronfield and moved back to the south of England, where they purchased another business. Our friendship with them was not adversely affected in any way and they regularly came up to stay with us. Unfortunately, Albert has since died but to this day Betty remains one of our closest friends.

22

From Sea to Shining Sea

We had just arrived at the Chantry to enjoy a couple of days between engagements when the telephone rang. It was Charles Munyard, speaking from Geraldo's office.

"I don't know what you fellows did on the *Carmania,*" he said, "but the feedback has been absolutely fantastic. Gary Brown, who is the booking agent for acts on the *QE2*, says that Cunard are so impressed by what they've heard about you that they want to engage you for two weeks on the great liner itself."

We explained to him that we were fully committed with other work until the end of August and then we intended to retire from show business in order to concentrate on our hotel.

"RETIRE?" Charles almost exploded. "Don't be so ridiculous. You've no idea how much demand you are in at the present time. And who in their right minds would turn down a chance to perform on the greatest ship in the world? Most entertainers would give their right arm for the opportunity. Whatever you do, don't think of passing up this chance of a lifetime."

We told Charles that we would have to think about it but his telephone calls were so persistent that we eventually agreed to work for the two weeks.

And so it was that in August 1971 we sailed from Southampton and embarked on a journey that I shall remember for as long as I live. Stepping on to the *QE2*, we were over-awed; we had worked on some fine ships in the past but nothing stood comparison with this beautiful liner. We were met by cruise-director John Butt, who took us on a tour of the public rooms. He showed us the cabaret rooms where we would be appearing. We were to open in the Queen's Room in the First Class lounge and, when John saw how its sheer opulence had rendered us speechless, he said, "Yes, this room is fantastic, isn't it? Nevertheless, I have to tell you that for most entertainers it's a nightmare. Just look at the chairs. They are so big and comfortable that the people almost sink into the floor and they find it physically impossible to applaud. So don't worry about it if the audience doesn't seem to be responding, as it's quite normal – it won't mean that they dislike your act."

However, at the end of our first appearance in the Queen's Room, we were rewarded with the greatest of accolades – a standing ovation! The talented Jimmy Bence, whose band had accompanied us that evening, was overjoyed. "You do realise that you are the first entertainers ever to have been given a 'stander' in this room, don't you?"

Word of our success reached Cunard in New York and immediately a message came back from them insisting that the *QE2* was not to let us go after the two weeks. When the cruise-director informed us that Cunard wanted our contract extended, we were well and truly in a dilemma. We had really wanted to concentrate on our hotel, but we were told our appearance in the Queen's Room had been so unbelievably successful that we owed it to ourselves to stay. So, instead of the two weeks, we ended up working on the ocean wave for almost twenty years!

As it happened, this was the best decision we could have made, because it opened up a new and exciting chapter in our lives – and one that brought with it a legion of new fans and friends. Within a very short time, we began receiving fan mail from all parts of the USA and indeed from all over the world. Many of the people who wrote were world travellers and they actually requested our future itineraries so that they could book their world cruises to coincide with our appearances.

In the 1970s, cruising on one of the Cunard liners was probably even more glamorous for entertainers than it is today. Quite apart from the plaudits on stage, the rewards were many and varied. There was always plenty of room to perform, with first-class lighting and amplification. Stage-management was of the highest order and we had the privilege of working with such excellent bandleaders as Joe Loss, Jimmy and Harry Bence, Jackie Sprage, Rob Charles, Ronnie Caryl, Mick Urry, Don Lang, Trevor Knowles and Jack Hawkins, to name but a few.

Success breeds success and soon there was great demand for our services not only from other leading cruise companies, but also from the charterers for maiden voyages and other prestigious cruises. In fact, in 1975, we entertained on no fewer than three world cruises - on the *QE2* for Cunard, the *Rotterdam* for Holland America and the maiden voyage of the *Royal Viking Sea* for the Viking Line. I think that this was established as some kind of record and it certainly involved a tremendous amount of organising. Other maiden voyages where we entertained included the *Royal Viking Sky*, the *Cunard Adventurer*, the *Cunard Princess* and the *Cunard Countess*. This last liner was launched by Janet Armstrong, wife of Neil Armstrong of moon-landing fame. We had the honour of being introduced to him but we were all briefed not to ask him any questions about the moon. I remember him as being a quiet, unassuming man, almost to the point of shyness. When he shook my hand, I was slightly taken aback by the roughness of his skin, as it was unexpectedly rough, the texture being almost like crocodile leather.

Working the great liners gave us an entrance into socialising not only with the rich and famous – royalty, heads of state, leaders of industry, film stars, best-selling authors - but also with some great characters at all social levels. We travelled throughout the world, not always by ship as we sometimes had to fly as far as Australia, New Zealand or India and wait for our ship to dock. On these occasions, we were always accommodated in 5-star hotels. The ships were usually reliable in the dates they were to reach us but sometimes there were delays and on those occasions, the shipping companies we worked for made arrangements for us to fly first-class to the port of call. The three flights I remember most vividly were those on Concorde from Rio, Barbados and New York. Even though I still hadn't fully overcome my anxiety about flying, I have to admit that I felt perfectly safe on those planes. On board ship, we were always given Officer status, which enabled us to enjoy all passenger privileges – all that is except gambling, although I must confess that I occasionally slipped into the casino to play the slot machines. We also dined first-class and wealthy passengers would sometimes send expensive wines or champagne to our table.

It was as though we were living the lives of millionaires and being paid for it too! We visited so many wonderful places that had previously been just magical names in geography books – the Taj Mahal, the Pyramids, the Game Reserves of Africa, the Great Barrier Reef and the People's Republic of China, and we shopped in New York, Hong Kong, Singapore, Sydney and Rio.

For me, one of the best things about working on the *QE2* was the fact that we were constantly sailing in and out of New York and I never failed to wave to the Statue of Liberty on each occasion. New York itself captivated me; I loved the vibrancy of this city. The Manhattan skyline was one of my favourite sights, especially at night with its millions of lights. I had sung about Broadway for years and now we actually had the chance to jostle with the crowds in this famous area.

We never missed an opportunity to take in a Broadway show when we were in the Big Apple. One evening we went to see Jane Russell in *Company* and, after watching her performance, we went backstage to congratulate her. We wondered whether she would remember us, for it had been ten years since we had worked with her in Australia, but she recognised us immediately and we reminisced about our time at Chequers. She told us that she was enjoying her success in *Company* but confessed that she found Elaine Stritch, from whom she had taken over, a hard act to follow.

Not long after that evening, I was on the gangplank ready to board a Royal Viking ship, when I came face to face with Elaine herself, just as she was disembarking. We spoke at the same time – I asked her if she was Elaine Stritch while she wondered whether she had met me before. We both laughed.

She looked me up and down and said, "That's a very smart suit you're wearing. Are you in show business too?"

I gave her a brief history of what I had been doing and explained that I was going on board to entertain. Then I mentioned that I had just seen *Company* and reported what Jane had said about her.

"How nice of her," said Elaine, "and what a pity you and I are just passing. I should like to have chatted with you longer. When you are in London, please get in touch. I'm living at the Savoy."

I saw Elaine recently in her one-woman show *At Liberty* at the Old Vic and was quite tempted to go backstage to have a chat, wondering whether she would have remembered me after all that time. However, I thought better of it when I saw Elton John sitting just behind me, as I felt sure that he would be going to visit her.

The one Broadway show that I wanted to see above all was the revival of the 1925 musical *No, No, Nanette,* starring Ruby Keeler and Jack Gilford. At the time, it was the 'must see' show and tickets were like gold. Everyone who had seen it was talking about Ruby, who had been a Zeigfeld Broadway star in the late 1920s and early 1930s. She had also appeared in a string of Busby Berkeley musical films, including the original starring role of Peggy Sawyer in 42nd Street. In real life, Ruby had been the wife of Al Jolson from 1928 to1939 but their marriage was turbulent. After their divorce, she met and married the great love of her life, real-estate broker and builder John Lowe and then she retired from show business, devoting herself to raising a family of three daughters and a son. She also had custody of Sonny, the boy she and Al Jolson had adopted. During this period, she was often quoted as saying, "There's more to life than show business."

However, after John Lowe's death in 1969, Ruby was gradually persuaded back into the spotlight and so it was that in 1971, at the age of 60, she starred in No, No, Nanette. Her performance was acclaimed as a triumphant return after an absence of over thirty years. The praise from the critics was not just generous – it was euphoric. Her old fans were thrilled and she succeeded in capturing the hearts of a host of new young admirers. The only word I could use to describe Ruby's performance on the three occasions I saw the show was SENSATIONAL. Her rapport with Jack Gilford was so moving that I, like the rest of the audience, applauded until my hands were sore.

One afternoon, I decided to have lunch at the famous New York restaurant, Sardis and who should be sitting at the table next to mine but Ruby and her son, John junior. I could see that they had finished their meal and wondered if I might be bold enough to ask if I could take a photograph of her. Taking my courage in both hands, I told her how much I had enjoyed her films and how I had been bowled over by her performance in No, No, Nanette. She was delighted and readily agreed to let me take her photo.

"I have a better idea," she suggested. "Why don't you join me in the photo? John will take it with your camera."

Little did I know at the time that this snap would be the first of hundreds of us taken together because, in a very short time, Ruby and her co-star, Jack Gilford, were to become two of my closest friends. In fact, Ruby always maintained that Roy, Colin and I were instrumental in giving her a new lease of life – but more of that in the next chapter.

23

Our Friendship with Ruby Keeler

No, No Nanette continued to enjoy success and so, some two years later, it was decided that the show, still with Ruby as the lead, should go on tour. During this tour, Ruby took a short break in order to visit her daughter Chrissie and family in Montana. While she was there, she became ill so she was taken to the nearby hospital; she had an aneurysm and remained in a coma for almost two months. She underwent complicated brain surgery and it was doubtful that she would survive the ordeal. However, Ruby's unshakeable faith in God together with her strong will to live pulled her through. She endured hours of painful physiotherapy both in the hospital and at home. Her determination was such that, some months later, she was able to take a cruise on the *SS Rotterdam*. It was here that I met her again.

Whilst on board, I caught sight of a physically handicapped lady, walking very slowly with the aid of a stick and accompanied by an attractive young woman. Although she was now vastly changed from the slim Ruby I had met in the restaurant, for she had gained quite a lot of weight and was paralysed down one side, there was no mistaking that beautiful face and those sparkling blue eyes. Later that day, when the young woman happened to be on her own, I asked her if her companion was in fact Ruby.

"Yes," she replied, "she's my mother. I'm Kathleen, by the way."

I explained to her that we were entertainers on the ship and that we were appearing that night. "We'll include a selection from *No, No, Nanette* if you can persuade your mother to come and watch," I concluded.

Kathleen agreed enthusiastically.

"Do you think your mother would mind if we announced that you were both in the audience?" I asked. "No one seems to be aware that she is on board."

"I'm sure that Mom would love it," said Kathleen.

That night, we told the audience that we were dedicating our next selection of songs to a very special person. "This lady is not just a star," I said. "She's a superstar and, in fact, she is with us tonight in the front row. The selection we are going to sing is from the show that this great lady made her own – No, No, Nanette. She is, of course, Ruby Keeler."

At this, the room erupted, with the whole of the audience rising to its feet. Ruby stood up and was rapturously applauded for at least five minutes. Ruby cried, the audience cried, the orchestra cried and it goes without saying that Roy and I were in tears too. There was so much love coming from everyone that it was almost like an opening night on Broadway.

After the show, Kathleen thanked us, saying, "You'll never know what a wonderful lift this has given Mom. You have made her so happy."

The next morning, there was a thank-you note from Ruby too and, for the rest of their journey on board, the two of them spent quality time with us every day. When they were ready to disembark, Ruby insisted that we exchanged addresses and telephone numbers and made us promise that we would keep in touch. She extended an open invitation for us to stay in her magnificent Palm Springs home.

Over the following months, our friendship grew even stronger, so much so that I approached Cunard with a suggestion that they might engage Ruby as a celebrity guest to be interviewed on the *QE2*. Cunard contacted her and she agreed, thus beginning a new career. It was usually the Cruise Director's job to conduct such interviews but because John Butt realised that we knew far more about her than he did, he asked if I would like to do the honours. Even though the job of interviewing was new to me, I was enthusiastic and asked Ruby if she would rehearse with me.

"I'm glad you asked," said Ruby. "I'd feel much more confident if we could run through the questions you're going to ask me. I'll talk about everything except – and I really mean this – I don't want any questions about Jolson."

"Oh, Ruby, that's not very fair," I protested. "You know that the audience would expect me to ask you about him. After all, you were married to him for eleven years."

"But, Jackie," replied Ruby, "I never ever mention his name. Do you know, my children didn't know that I had been married before until they were almost in their teens." She went on to relate that they only found out then because one of her daughters had come in from school, quite distressed because someone had told her that her mother had been married to 'a black man'. "It was then," she said, "that I had to explain to them about my previous marriage to Al. I told them that he was a white man who blacked his face on stage."

"I understand what you mean, Ruby," I said, "but you do realise that if I leave him out, you'll have the audience shouting out questions about him."

Ruby looked apprehensive. "Well, what sort of things would you be asking?"

"Nothing too personal," I assured her, so we tried out a few questions.

"It has been quoted many times that Al Jolson was the greatest entertainer in the world. Did you think he was?"

"Why, yes, of course I did. He told me so. EVERY DAY!"

"Did Al sing a lot at home?"

"Yes, he did. If he opened the refrigerator door and the light went on, he would burst into song."

"Did he sing in the bath?"

"Jackie, I really don't know. I never took a bath with him!"

And that was how we became almost a double act – with me feeding the questions and Ruby showing her natural wit and her ability to play for laughs with perfectly timed delivery. She also knew how to turn on the pathos to full effect. The audience loved her.

I asked her about Dick Powell, her co-star in many films. "You and Dick were such a loving couple on the screen. Did you fancy him in real life?"

"Oh, what a question! Yes, I loved him but just in the same way as I love you, Jackie. Jolson of course was intensely jealous of him but then, he was jealous of every man I worked with."

The audience soon found out that her life with John Lowe had been much happier and that she treasured her children and fourteen grandchildren.

Each time that Ruby appeared, she was given a standing ovation and so it was that her new career on the high seas became a permanent feature of the Cunard cruises, enabling us to travel the world together. She was allowed to bring a companion at all times and over the years we met the whole family, staying at their various homes in California. Ruby's neighbours in Palm Springs included Bob and Dolores Hope, Ginger Rogers, Frank Sinatra, Lucille Ball, Mary Martin, Kaye Ballard and Alice Faye.

The first time we saw Alice was when Ruby had arranged for Roy and me to have lunch with the two of them at the exclusive Springs

Country Club. We would all be meeting at the club and Ruby had said to us, "If you arrive first, keep a look-out for Alice, as she hates to be on her own."

Minutes after our arrival, Alice appeared at the entrance so I jumped up to greet her. She looked every inch the glamorous star she had been in her Technicolor films. She smiled at me and said, "Now let me guess – you must be Jackie. Am I right? I've heard such a lot about you; I feel I know you already. Ruby never stops talking about you. Now where is the lovely Roy?" When she saw Roy, she greeted him like a long-lost friend. She was just as down to earth as Ruby and we soon began to feel that we had known her for ages.

By this time, Ruby had been over to England and had stayed at the Chantry, which she loved. Alice was full of enthusiasm for our hotel too even though she had not seen it herself. "I'm coming to stay with you because Ruby raves on about it all the time," she said.

Alice had a delightfully dry sense of humour. When I asked her if she'd worked with Al Jolson, she replied. "I certainly did – at 20th Penitentiary Fox! Jolson was the greatest guy in the world to spoil anybody's day! I don't know how Ruby lasted eleven years with him because I couldn't have stood eleven days."

Sadly, Alice did not visit the Chantry. On the only occasion when she came over to England, we were all in Spain. Ruby, however, stayed at our hotel six times in all. Once she brought another fun-loving lady, the popular comedy actress Penny Singleton, star of the series of Blondie films. At the time of her visit, Penny was seventy going on twenty and displayed her fitness by performing cartwheels on our lawn. "Come on, Ruby. It's your turn now," she shouted.

"No thanks, Penny, I think I'll sit this one out," laughed Ruby.

Perhaps the most memorable time we spent with Ruby was when she brought her favourite niece, Patty Keeler, to stay with us. Their visit happened to coincide with the opening of 42nd Street in London's Drury Lane Theatre. While at the Chantry, Ruby received a call from Helen Montague, the executive producer of the forthcoming show. She and David Merrick, the producer, extended an invitation to Ruby, Patty, Roy, Colin and me to attend both the opening night and the after-show party at the Savoy.

We were given the Royal Box for this spectacular musical and, at the end, the cast took several curtain calls. Then quite suddenly and unexpectedly, the spotlight turned on Ruby; at this point, the whole cast and the orchestra leader turned to her and bowed. When the audience realised that Ruby was there, they gave her a great ovation. To say that she was surprised was an understatement – in fact, she looked in shock.

I nudged her. "Ruby," I whispered, "stand up. The spotlight and applause are for you."

Still dazed, she rose to her feet, with tears streaming down her face. It was a moment to be treasured.

That night, outside the theatre and then at the Savoy, Ruby was constantly surrounded by cast members, photographers, press and fans. I noticed producer David Merrick sitting in a corner, looking rather downcast as no one was chatting to him. It was indeed Ruby's night. As she danced with me at the party, she told me that the Savoy brought back other memories because the last time she had danced there was with Al on their honeymoon in 1928.

Three years later, we met Ruby at the Savoy again. She was in London for one day only, having just completed a movie-cruise with June Allyson, Virginia Mayo, George Murphy and David Gest (who, at the time of writing this, has just separated from Liza Minnelli). Ruby had arranged a dinner party in the Riverside Room with June Allyson, June's husband and George Murphy and his wife. Roy and I were asked if we would like to join them – an invitation which we readily accepted.

As a lad, I had always made a point of seeing films which featured June Allyson, because she was one of my favourite stars. I even went so far as to write to her to request a photograph. And now, here I was, dancing with her. She was just as friendly and as bubbly as in her films.

George Murphy proved to be a most modest man. When I told him that he was a great tap-dancer, he laughed and replied, "Do you want to know something? I was a great – in fact, THE GREATEST faker in the business." But this remark, I am sure, was all part of his modesty.

Believe it or not, Ruby had never seen The Jolson Story, which starred Larry Parkes as Al and Evelyn Keyes as Ruby. I really thought that she ought to see it and so on one occasion when I knew that both she and I would be on the *QE2* together, I made a request for the film to be shown on board.

When Ruby found out, she was adamant that she still did not want to see it.

"But, Ruby," I pleaded, "it's a wonderful movie and you would love the music. I'd really like you to see how beautifully Evelyn portrays you on screen."

Ruby started to weaken. "Would it truly mean so much to you for me to see it?" she asked. When I nodded, she went on, "All right but I'll only go into the cinema after the lights have gone down and I definitely want to leave before the end."

That night, Roy, Colin and I escorted her into the darkened cinema, and even before the titles had finished rolling, there were tears in her eyes. In fact, she cried all the way through, soaking not only her own handkerchief but ours as well.

After the film, she had to admit that it was well worth seeing. "But there wasn't a lot of truth in it," she said. "Nevertheless, I thought that Scotty Beckett who played Al as a boy was superb and I couldn't get over how much like Sonny, our adopted son, he looked."

There are so many tales I could relate about Ruby that I am sure I could fill a book with them. I was once chatting to Michael Stewart, who regularly travelled on the *QE2*. He was the man who wrote the musicals *Bye Bye Birdie*, *Hello Dolly* and *Mack and Mabel*. I suggested that he should write a musical about Ruby. "There are so many successful shows like *Mame, Dolly* and *Irene* that I'm sure that Ruby would be an excellent vehicle for you," I concluded.

Then Michael said something that saddened me. "Jackie, you and Roy should write it. I'm very ill and I'll never write another show. But you two could do it. You have arranged your own act to perfection and, in many ways, a musical is the same sort of thing. You just have to concentrate on choosing the songs – there doesn't need to be much in the way of script. Try it."

But we were always too busy.

Ruby, who called us 'her boys', used to ring us two or three times every week and she always stayed on the line for at least an hour at a time.

"Think of your telephone bill, Ruby," I used to say.

"Why? Does it bother you?" she'd always reply. "Don't give it another thought. It's my bill and I'm certainly not complaining."

Then one day there came a call that we had secretly been dreading. Ruby opened the conversation with the words, "When are you all coming to see me? I miss you so much."

"Rest assured, we'll be with you in summer, Ruby," I replied.

There was silence for a few moments and then Ruby spoke. "Jackie, I'm afraid that summer will be too late. I have been diagnosed with cancer of the liver and I'm dying."

There was no hesitation on our part. We booked flights immediately and were soon at her bedside in Palm Springs. She had grown so painfully thin that she was almost unrecognisable. Yet even though she was so ill, she remained the perfect hostess. She wanted to make sure that we were comfortable and her friends Alice Faye, Ginger Rogers, Kaye Ballard and other famous names all rallied round, entertaining us so that Ruby would be pleased. Sadly, we watched Ruby become weaker by the hour. We stayed on because we wanted to be with her to the end. One day, I accompanied her son John to the Holy Sepulchre Cemetery at Costa Messa in order to choose her final resting place and then we sat with Ruby and her family for the final mass. We postponed our flights for yet a further week but she clung on to life and so we had to bid farewell to our special darling Ruby. I believe that my final few minutes with her were some of the saddest in my life. Just after we left, she died - on February 28th 1993, at the age of 83.

Shortly after the funeral, I received a moving letter from her niece Patty. In it, she wrote of the great love Ruby had for Roy, Colin and me and of the great affection she had held for Derbyshire in general and for our hotel in particular. In the letter, Patty also described how she herself had placed in the casket the small photograph of the hotel, which Ruby always kept at her bedside. And so it was that part of Dronfield - a picture of the Chantry in a blaze of red tulips and yellow daffodils – was taken to the grave of a great Hollywood Legend, Ruby Keeler.

24

Islands in the Sun

As far as I was concerned, working on luxury liners was the most enjoyable job in the world. Every ship that we worked on had a special, individual character and special characters too! Most of the passengers were very wealthy and several of them were somewhat eccentric. Whichever ship we were booked to work on, we knew that we should meet up with old friends, fellow artists and shipmates. All the shipping companies treated us with great respect because we never let them down and our act always went down well with audiences. It was inevitable that sometimes we had to put up with resentment or jealousy from a few of the other entertainers – usually those with acts that did not have much substance or were badly put together. Some of them classed us as 'corny' but this didn't cause us any concern, as we were well aware that some of the greatest acts in the business were similarly categorised.

Occasionally, we were criticised for being too popular. Once, I remember coming off the stage, having received three standing ovations in one hour. Back in the dressing room, we found the female singer, who had opened the show with a twenty-minute spot, sitting there sobbing. "Whatever's wrong?" we asked.

"I'll tell you what's wrong," she cried. "Anyone who stays on stage for an hour like you do is bound to get a standing ovation. It's just not fair."

And this was from a girl who had no more than a dozen songs in her entire repertoire!

Our accommodation on board also drew resentment from one old 'friend' of mine, Frankie Howerd. It so happened that we had been given a splendid suite, complete with bar on the boat deck of the *QE2*. We put this to good use, regularly entertaining friends and special passengers. One evening, Frankie managed to invite himself. On seeing our suite, he said, "Oh, very nice, I must say. It's much better than the cabin I've been given." This was understandable as he was on board for only a few days and scheduled for just two performances, which had not been very successful. His rudeness knew no bounds. "How much do you earn in a week?" he asked.

I couldn't believe his cheek and quickly replied, "Not as much as you, I'm sure."

"Well," he complained, "you seem to be working all the time – I'm not!"

The next day, the cruise director told me that Frankie had stormed into his office, complaining that our accommodation was far superior to his."

The cruise director had defended us. "Roy and Jackie are on board for much longer periods than you," he said. "They are firm favourites and always give the audiences what they want. And everybody likes them offstage too, so they are great PR people for the company."

As Frankie was rather unsociable offstage and his stage appearances on board did not appeal in any way to American audiences, I think that he quietly admitted defeat on this occasion.

The few unfriendly entertainers, however, were greatly outweighed by the many artists who delighted in our company. One of our favourites was Samantha Jones, a fantastic singer with a great personality to match. She had been a member of the *Three Vernon Girls* group in the 1960s and then branched out on her own, recording several albums. I think it was her wicked sense of humour that first attracted me to her. We are still the best of friends and chat to each other on the telephone almost daily.

Although life at sea fully satisfied me, Roy often grew bored with performing on board and insisted that we did one or two summer seasons at our favourite night-clubs on dry land. One of these summer seasons was in Jersey - this time for Frank Thomasson, who owned the West Park Pavilion in St. Helier. The room where we were to perform was huge and totally unsuitable for the intimate ambience of cabaret. We were reluctant to sign the contract but Frank made us an offer that we found hard to refuse. Before signing, however, we contacted Billy Forrest, the agent who used to book us at Tams. We wondered whether Tony Fielding would be able to match the fee so that we could enjoy a season at Tams instead. Billy asked us how much Frank had offered.

"How much?" he spluttered. "Accept Frank's offer immediately. There's no way in which Tony Fielding could match that figure."

And so we signed. About a week after we had made our commitment, Pat and Tony Fielding turned up at the Chantry to try to book us for Tams, unaware of the fact that Frank had already engaged us.

Unfortunately, our choice of venue that season was a mistake on our part and we endured rather than enjoyed our time there. In fact, it was a show that we hated more with each passing week and among ourselves we quietly agreed that its title *Grin and Tonic* should have been more aptly renamed *Grim and Bear It!* From the outset, things started to go wrong; on opening night, the sound-system failed. The following day, the newspaper critic headlined his review thus:

The Toaduffs Pull Show Through First Night Amplification Problems

He went on to write:

With such accomplished and professional entertainers as Roy and Jackie Toaduff on the Bill, it doesn't really matter if there is trouble with the amplification – and there was plenty of that last night at West Park Pavilion! Roy and Jackie are undoubtedly the stars. They are professional to the extreme and they don't need a supporting act.

As the show went into its first week, we realised that we had done ourselves no favours by agreeing to appear. The whole set-up was chaotic, with Frank Thomasson failing to put in a single appearance.

To begin with, we had no say in who would be appearing in the show with us. We knew from past experience that a family show should always include a line of glamorous female dancers but this show boasted only one girl, who had apparently featured once on Opportunity Knocks. She sang reasonably well but opened the show with only four numbers. There was a comedian whose scanty material did not warrant the time he spent on stage and an impressionist who was fired for constantly using bad language – a habit that offended most of the audience. In the company, there was a country and western entertainer, who sang about four songs (very badly I might add). This man also acted as an assistant to a dreadful clairvoyant who was appearing in the show. The assistant used to walk among the audience asking for personal items, such as driving licences, passports or identity cards.

"No rings or other jewellery," the clairvoyant would say. He used to put on a blindfold (through which he could actually see!) and give almost the same predictions at every performance. As the assistant lifted up an object, the clairvoyant spoke mysteriously. "The name (so and so) is coming through to me. Do you know who I mean?"

"Yes, that could be me," a trembling voice from the audience would reply.

Then came the melodrama. "Be warned. You are going to be involved in an accident," he would say in saddened tones, "yes, a serious accident." Then he'd pause so that everyone could feel the full impact of his words. "However," he continued, "this accident will not be fatal – but you will be an out-patient for a long period. Next object please." Then he would pass on to someone else, giving further dire warnings. One of his regular predictions was, "I feel a pain in the lower regions. Have you seen your GP recently?" The whole act was a sham – and closed the first half of the show, which ran for two hours! There was a fifteen-minute interval and then it was our turn to perform. Indeed we felt it was our duty to try everything in our power to make the audience feel happy, as almost every night, the clairvoyant shocked them with his gloomy and often frightening forecasts. So pessimistic was he that we would often see people leaving the show in tears during the interval! Eventually he had to be told to lighten his patter, as it was very difficult to lift the mood of the audience for the second half.

Half way through the season, we were not at all surprised to learn that the Pavilion had been sold – and we did not meet the new owners. In fact, the only redeeming feature of our stay in Jersey that year was that we found another wonderful place to stay. Eileen and Lesley Stock, who owned Le Taillis Farm, rented half of their beautiful granite-built house to us. They were a delightful couple, with two lovely daughters, Miranda and Sheena. Eileen and Lesley were both exceptionally good cooks and the very thought of their delicious meals still makes my mouth water. They also let us use their boat and if we managed to catch any fish, they always cooked them for us.

These days, we often reminisce about our last working season in Jersey. The show might have been a disappointment but the company of the Stocks was great fun and we met up with our previous landladies and their families on a regular basis.

The following summer took us to Bermuda, where we were booked to appear for four weeks at *The Talk of the Town* at the Bermudiana Hotel in Hamilton, Bermuda's capital city. As the plane landed, I knew that I was going to love this country, with its chain of 180 coral islands and islets, 65 miles off the coast of North Carolina. We were met by a member of the hotel staff, who drove us down spotlessly clean streets that were lined with pastel pink and white houses – just like icing sugar. Nearly all of them seemed to have private swimming pools and picture-postcard gardens where oleanders, flamboyants and spectacular sub-tropical plants grew in abundance. Then we passed pink and white-sanded creeks and harbours, edged by an unbelievably turquoise blue sea. Once in the hotel, we were accommodated in a beautiful suite with excellent views of the harbour.

We had been forewarned that the hotel manager, Pierre Rollenger, would sit in on the first rehearsal of every new set and ask entertainers to take out any material that he personally did not like – so we were prepared. We found out later that he had been warned about us! Apparently, one of the Cunard ships used to dock in Hamilton every week and two rather jaundiced staff-members of this ship had told Pierre that we were very difficult, temperamental and demanding entertainers and that he would certainly not like us. Nevertheless, in spite of these negative reports on both sides, our first meeting with Pierre was very amicable. He announced that he would like to watch us go through our band call with bandleader Sid Haddon and asked us to give him a preview of our whole performance. He sat watching our act with notebook and pen at the ready. I was quite nervous about what he was going to say and so I kept glancing at him while we were performing but the only time I saw him write was during my table-top clog routine. When we had finished, Pierre told us that he had enjoyed everything with the exception of my clog-dancing and Roy's burlesque of Such a Night – this time in the style of Elvis Presley; he didn't consider either of these two items to be suitable.

However, Colin was determined that they should be included. "If we take these numbers out," he said diplomatically, "I think that the main part of Roy and Jackie's act will be lost. How about keeping them in the performance tonight and then, if the audience doesn't give a positive response, we'll take them out for the rest of the four weeks."

Pierre agreed but warned us with the words, "We have a very influential, severe critic here tonight and if he gives you a poor write-up, the locals will stay away. I have my doubts about the clog-dance and the burlesque, but if you're willing to take the risk, we'll keep them in."

That night, our audience at *The Talk of the Town* was made up of locals and American tourists. From the minute we walked on stage, we had them all in the palms of our hands and we were a tremendous success. We had to perform encore after encore, as they just wouldn't let us leave the stage. Pierre's smile grew wider and wider and Colin's prediction that the clog- dance and the burlesque would bring the greatest rounds of applause was proved to be correct, as the shouts for more were quite deafening.

When we finally left the stage, Pierre greeted us enthusiastically, grinning from ear to ear. "I had an idea at the rehearsal that you might be good but I have to admit that I've never seen anyone work an audience like you two. You were the best act I have ever watched." This was praise indeed from a man who was notorious for being known as a pain to all performers.

And what about the harsh critic we had been warned about? Well, the next morning, he opened his glowing review in the *Bermuda Sun* with the words:

They held an audience of mainly Americans in the palms of their hands, jinked them around like dice and then rolled them out for a jackpot of TWO STANDING OVATIONS. That was the experience of the Toaduffs at the Bermudiana's 'Talk of the Town'.

And the critic Ivan Clifford, wrote thus in The Bermuda Mid Ocean News:

Hats off to the Toaduffs. They seem to have the ability to bring the audience into the act without even asking them to participate. Hand clapping, foot tapping, laughter, nostalgia – they're all there if you look around the nightclub tables. This is Real Entertainment. After Jackie does his famous clog dance on top of a small table (If it had been in a movie, you would swear the film had been speeded up), Roy brings the house down with his hilariously exaggerated imitation of Elvis Presley singing 'Such a Night'.

He finished his review with the words:

Here is a show no one should miss. Already they ARE the Talk of the Town!

Word about the show spread quickly and advance bookings were the best the management had ever known – so much so that they cancelled the act that had been booked to follow us and we were asked to stay for another four weeks, which ended the season.

We didn't go on stage until 11pm, so we had all day to ourselves; we explored the island and made friends with the locals, all of whom seemed to own beautiful houses and yachts. One day, we were invited to join an elderly lady who went by the name of Annette Conklib Bolton but who was known as Toni. She was only in her early sixties but looked much older and seemed quite frail. It was obvious that she was a heavy drinker. It was her much younger boyfriend, Scotty, who introduced us to her. He was a handsome, well-dressed man about 30 years old, who had been Toni's constant companion since the death of her very wealthy husband in 1967.

Toni and Scotty lived at Spithead Lodge, the former home of Eugene O'Neill and the house in which Oona O'Neill was born; Oona, of course, became the wife of Charlie Chaplin in 1943. The owner of Spithead Lodge just before Mrs. Bolton had been Noel Coward and much of his furniture, including his piano, was still in the house. In fact, Noel's music-room had not been touched since the day he left and something of his presence remained in it. There were several photographs of Noel and his friends, and his open guest-book contained many very famous signatures. We were delighted to be given an open invitation to call into Spithead Lodge any time we were in the area and we were always made to feel very welcome.

Our eight weeks in Bermuda simply flew by and we were so successful that Pierre asked us if we would like to return the following year for the whole season. We agreed and made a request that we might be allowed to perform our act in The Moongate Room, which was much larger and with a big stage.

Pierre expressed his doubts about this. "I don't think that would be a very good idea," he said. "The Moongate Room is something of a white elephant and the only time it ever gets full is on New Year's Eve."

We pointed out that every night people had to be turned away at The Talk of the Town, so Pierre somewhat reluctantly agreed, with the words, "All right, but when you've done one week at The Moongate, you'll be wishing you were back in The Talk."

"We'll risk it," said Colin. "We can always change the venue if it doesn't work." He went on to suggest that Pierre might install new lighting to add more atmosphere and also that we should open with a grand Charity Gala for the Bermuda Civic Ballet.

And so it was that we opened the following year in The Moongate Room to a capacity audience, with the Governor of Bermuda and his wife, Sir Edwin and Lady Leather, as guests of honour. Auntie Bertha flew in from Boston; Carl Jones, the operating manager of the Pacific Far East Line, flew in from San Francisco with his wife Rita. In fact, Carl mixed up the dates and they arrived two weeks too early; undeterred, they went home and flew out again to catch our opening night. Scotty and Mrs. Bolton attended, together with our extremely talented English friend, Jane Bainbridge, who was the local radio disc jockey. The evening was a tremendous success.

Pierre had made a deal with us that we could invite twelve friends to fly out to visit us at any time during the season and stay at the hotel full board - all free of charge. Those same friends still talk about it to this day and declare that it was the best time of their lives. Jane made them feel very special, as she always gave them a personal plug on her popular daily radio show. They were invited to the parties and barbecues hosted by people we had befriended in Bermuda, including sumptuous banquets at Spithead Lodge, where champagne flowed like water. Quite recently, I was speaking to Joyce Blaydon, who was our P.R. at the hotel; she reminded me of the time we took her to Spithead Lodge, where she remembered seeing a bathtub full of bottles of champagne, covered with ice and water.

"Do you recall when you covered the bath with tinfoil to keep the water cold?" she reminisced.

"No. Did it work?" I asked.

"I'm not sure," she replied, "but I didn't hear anyone complaining!"

During that season, Colin, Roy and I were twice invited to spend time at Government House with Sir Edward Leather. His daughter, Hope, loved our show and often brought her young friends to see it.

And so, yes, we did play to packed houses at The Moongate Room – every night! My only regret was that Pierre did not see us perform there, as he had resigned before our arrival and we never saw him again. He had been replaced with an Italian general manager, Louis Caviexel, who liked us, even though he could hardly believe the privileges we had managed to negotiate, including percentages!

Our happy time in Bermuda that summer was marred by just one sad incident. Joyce Bainbridge rang us one evening to tell us that Mrs. Toni Bolton had been found dead, floating face down in the harbour, just in front of her house. Apparently, she and Scotty had driven into Hamilton for lunch, where they had consumed a fair amount of alcohol. Scotty had then gone to the cinema, while Toni had driven home alone and then decided to take a swim from her private deck in the harbour. Her next-door neighbour discovered the body and alerted the police. When Scotty arrived home, he was shocked to find Spithead Lodge surrounded by police. They ordered him to collect his belongings quickly and told him that he would not be allowed inside again. Of course, rumours started to circulate like wildfire. Was it suicide? Was it misadventure? Was it murder? Everyone had a theory. However, at the inquest, the coroner's verdict was death by misadventure, with no evidence of foul play. We were later informed that Scotty had featured heavily in Toni's will, as she had no blood relatives, but unfortunately she had not signed it. What became of him later we never found out. What we did know was that he had truly adored her in the few years they had been together.

25

Que Sera Sera

After our season in Bermuda, we flew on to Miami Beach to appear at the Singapore Resort Hotel, which was owned by Bernie Burke, an acquaintance of ours. We had first met Bernie when we were working on a cruise ship and we renewed the friendship in Bermuda. He was interested to learn that we had arranged a meeting with a well-known agent, Charlie Rapp, who booked acts on the Borsh circuit in the Catskills just outside New York. As we had a few days to spare before the meeting, Bernie asked us to fly to Florida first and to appear at his popular nightclub. He was sure that our future lay in the USA and promised to help us secure those all-important green cards.

Our act at the Singapore Resort Hotel was extremely well received, prompting Gus Dana, the famous Miami show critic to write in T*he Sun Reporter*:

The Singapore crowd gave Roy and Jackie Toaduff not one but six standing ovations and would not let them off the stage - and they deserved it too. They have a rare unity on stage, aided by the deliberate use of only one mike, which forces them to stay together even when they are gliding around the stage. Bernie hopes to have them back for a season.

We then went on to New York, only to discover everyone in tears when we entered Charlie Rapp's office. They had just received the news that Charlie had died – not the best of times for us to be negotiating with him! Before his death, however, he had booked us into two clubs in New York – *Kutsher's Monticello* and *The Pines* in South Fallsburg.

The audiences in both of these clubs loved our act, with crowds of lady fans hammering at our dressing-room doors to congratulate us. The security guard at The Pines told us that, in the many years he had worked there, he had seen only one other entertainer who had drawn similar applause – Eddie Cantor in his hey day.

It was unfortunate, therefore, that no one from Charlie's office had been in either of these clubs to see us performing. However, as we sailed home on the *QE2*, we did have the satisfaction of knowing that we could hold those big American audiences in those extra-large cabaret rooms in the palms of our hands and that, given the chance, we could certainly be successful in America.

Once in England, we travelled to Sheffield to open a new West End shopping precinct and then we were off to London to fulfil two consecutive engagements. The first was at the Great Room in Grosvenor House, where we worked with the famous Sidney Lipton and his orchestra. He assured us that we would wow the audience the following night, when we were to appear at the Dorchester to entertain at the Variety Ladies' Guild Ball, at the request of their secretary, Doris Green.

We were to perform for forty-five minutes, with London's *Talk of the Town* girls opening for us. At the last minute, the Ball's committee brought in the popular Dickie Henderson to follow us. We later found out the reason for this - although they had heard rave reviews about our act, none of the committee members had actually seen us perform and they were not sure whether we would be strong enough to be the top act when entertaining a London audience. Dickie was their safeguard, just in case.

It turned out to be a truly extraordinary evening. The great impresario, Sir Bernard Delfont and his wife, who was the former musical comedy star Carole Lynn, hosted the top table. Also at this table were the guest of honour, Dame Vera Lynn, her husband Harry Lewis, their daughter Virginia, and the legendary Maudie Edwards, who was the hostess for the evening. Show business professionals occupied almost all the other tables.

The show opened with the girls of the Talk of the Town dancing an exciting can-can routine and then it was our turn. We both felt on top form that night and the warm applause that greeted our entrance boosted our spirits still further; when we sang our opening number, *Gee but it's Good to be Here,* we well and truly meant it. As we walked round singing to every corner of the room, the audience kept bursting into spontaneous applause. It was the perfect venue for us, with excellent acoustics and a superb orchestra. I noticed that Sir Bernard, his wife and Vera Lynn were applauding every number enthusiastically.

At the end of our performance and a couple of encores, the members of the audience, led by Sir Bernard, were up on their feet cheering loudly. Dickie Henderson, as he later admitted to us, found it difficult to win over the audience for we were a very hard act to follow that night. As we came off stage, the maître d' at the Dorchester greeted us with the words, "You've made it – you were fantastic." He then added, "Sir Bernard would like you to join him at his table. I have to tell you that in all the years I have known the great man, he has never invited anyone to his table before."

When we reached the table, Sir Bernard extended his hand and said, "Gentlemen, you were superb. Wherever have you been hiding?"

Lady Delfont was just as complimentary, commenting on our voices, our clarity of delivery and our outfits. Vera Lynn enthused over Roy's *Love is All I Have to Give* and our rendition of *Dance in the Old-fashioned Way.* She was sitting between Sir Bernard and me and suggested that she and I exchanged seats so that he could talk business with us.

Sir Bernard told us that, if Tommy Steele had not been appearing in the long-running *Hans Christian Anderson* at the London Palladium, he would have put us on that prestigious stage immediately. He explained that he and his wife had to leave early as they had an important engagement with Prince Philip the next evening but he added, "Look, take my card and my personal phone number. Call me tomorrow at noon. I want to have a serious talk with you."

As Vera Lynn was leaving, she reiterated how impressed Sir Bernard had been. In fact, there were so many compliments from people that we were well and truly in a daze. I remember John Inman's words, "You two are perfect performers. You are one of the most professional acts I have ever seen."

The bandleader said, "Don't forget who played for you tonight! You are going to make it big time and when you appear at the *Talk of the Town*, I hope that you'll reserve a table in the front row for me."

Our friends Albert and Betty Kemp, who were also there to see us, were in tears because they were so happy with our success.

That night, I could hardly sleep because I was so excited at the prospect of our forthcoming conversation with Sir Bernard. Colin made the call at noon and Sir Bernard was still as enthusiastic. He asked Colin to send information about where we had been working, together with press cuttings about our act. We posted everything to him immediately.

We were pleased with *The Stage* review of our performance. Beneath a photograph of the two of us in action on the stage, the critic had written:

Roy and Jackie Toaduff were an immaculate act in appearance and performance. The Dorchester audience just would not let them go.

After the Dorchester, we appeared in Wilmslow at the Rex Cinema, where a fashion show and cabaret were being compèred by Stuart Hall and Pete Murray. About a week later, we were listening to Pete's BBC radio show as usual, when we were both surprised and delighted to hear him compliment us on air and say that we should definitely be included in the Royal Variety Performance that year. For the next few hours, our telephone line was red-hot with friends and fans constantly ringing to ask if we had heard the broadcast.

In the meantime, we were still waiting to hear from the Delfont office but a month passed and no one contacted us. The Dorchester bandleader rang to ask whether Delfont had engaged us and couldn't believe that we had heard nothing at all. "You should really have followed up the telephone call before now," he advised. "You see, these people are so busy and have so many things on their minds that your photos and press cuttings could easily have been left on a shelf to gather dust. You have to pester these people, as they soon forget. You must ring them without delay."

In a way, to do this went against the grain, as we were not pushy and we were always so inundated with work offers that we had never had to go cap-in-hand to anyone. However, on this occasion, Colin did ring but could not get through to Sir Bernard. There was a polite message telling us that all our information had been filed but that they had nothing to offer us at that time. They would contact us if anything suitable came up. To this day, we are still waiting for that telephone call!

As fate would have it, we went from strength to strength in our work on the high seas. By now, The Stage was describing us as the most successful entertainers on the ships and all the shipping companies were constantly trying to secure our services.

I sometimes wonder what might have become of us if the Delfont office had taken us on. Would we have become a household name through the medium of television? We'll never know. Nevertheless, I have no regrets whatsoever about the path our lives took in the following years. We continued to work on world-famous ships and to meet fabulous people. We became the personal friends of many great stars and I was involved in one or two loving relationships into the bargain!

26

Ginger Proposes Marriage

We were working on a world cruise aboard the *SS Rotterdam,* when I met up again with Ginger Rogers. Holland-American Lines had employed her to give two performances of her Las Vegas show on our ship.

She apparently arrived in true Hollywood fashion, with a mountain of luggage and an entourage of several people. In addition to her hairdresser, her dresser, her secretary, two male dancers and a sound and lighting expert, Ginger had also brought musical director Hal Borne, who had been the rehearsal pianist for all her films with Fred Astaire. Completing the party was her friend, the lovely Violet Ruden, a Christian Science practitioner.

The day after her arrival, I was relaxing by the swimming pool when a young man came to sit in the next chair to mine. We started chatting and, as I had not seen him on board before, I asked him if he had just joined the ship.

"Yes," he said, "I boarded yesterday.   I'm Ginger Rogers' hairdresser."

"Is she all right to work for?" I asked.

"Oh, yes," he replied. "She's wonderful. I've been with her for years."

I went on to tell him that I had seen her in Mame in London, when our friend Barry Kent had been her leading man. "Next time you see her, remind her that we had a very long conversation one very rainy evening at the stage door of the Drury Lane Theatre while she was waiting for her taxi. Tell her that I did come to see the show again, as she asked, but sadly I did not manage to see her backstage. There's no way in which she would remember me, of course, but tell her that I can't wait to see her show on board." I then went on to tell the hairdresser about our act, adding, "I'd love Ginger to come and see us performing."

The next morning, I was in the coffee lounge with Roy and Colin, when who should walk in but Ginger, surrounded by her retinue; they sat about four tables away from us. Her hairdresser happened to be facing us, so I waved and mimed to him, asking if he had told Ginger about me.   I think he must have forgotten about our conversation because I saw him lean over to Ginger and engage her in conversation. After a couple of minutes, she stood up and said in a loud voice, "Who was it who saw me at Drury Lane? Ah, yes," she smiled when she spotted me. "I remember you. Come over and join us."

It was obvious from her opening remarks when I sat down that she really had remembered me and very soon we were chatting like long lost friends. She asked who was at the table with me and when I told her about Roy and Colin, she beckoned to them to come and join us. This was the beginning of a firm friendship among the four of us and one that was to last until her death

I have read many rather unkind articles about Ginger – that she was mean and a Prima Donna in every sense of the word. However, she was extremely kind to us and we found her very down-to-earth. She was perhaps a little eccentric but I found that quality in her most endearing.   Ginger was devoted to the Christian Science faith and constantly quoted Mary Baker Eddy. She was certainly Fred Astaire's most famous dancing partner but her greatest achievement in her own eyes was winning the Best Actress Oscar for her role in *Kitty Foyle*. Another of her talents which is perhaps not as well known was her considerable flair as an artist and sculptor.

Ginger and I were in each other's company almost all the time and one day she asked me about my early background and my family. When I mentioned my mother, Ginger asked, "Is she still alive?"

"Very much so," I replied, "and I just wish she was here now to see me talking to you like this."

"Give me her address, Jackie," said Ginger. "I really would like to write to her." She immediately began writing the following words:
Dear Sarah,
I am here on board this cruise ship having the most wonderful time with your precious son Jackie. Jackie is just adorable and how I have loved being on board ship with him. He tells me of you and how he used to come home tapping, having seen a movie with Mr. Astaire and me. It pleased me so much that he loved the films I was in ...

The letter continued and ended with the words:

It's nice to have a few minutes to say hello to you, dear Sarah.
Blessings,
Ginger Rogers

When my mother received the letter, she was astonished to think that this world-famous star had taken the trouble to write to her about me and I think it delighted her. I now have that letter as a reminder of my time aboard with Ginger.

Her show on the ship was outstandingly good and she seemed genuinely pleased that I had enjoyed it so much. A couple of nights later, it was our show's performance and Ginger had asked her friend Violet and her secretary Roberta to check us out at the first house – just to find out whether she should take a seat at the front or the back of the room! As it happened, Violet was ecstatic about our act and urged Ginger to make sure that she had a front seat.

During the performance, Ginger showed her enthusiasm and approval by applauding loudly and whistling. (She was, incidentally, a great whistler – an art perfected by hailing cabs, especially in Paris and New York.) After the show, she came backstage and hugged us with excitement. Hal Borne, who had also been in the audience, told us that we were naturals for Las Vegas.

One evening, Ginger, Violet and I were sitting in the ballroom, listening to the music. Ginger said that she would love to dance and asked me if I would partner her. I'd been longing to do this, of course, but hadn't had the courage to ask her.

"Come on then, Jackie – but no fancy steps, mind."

I think I was more nervous dancing with Ginger that I had been with Princess Margaret all those years ago. The orchestra was playing It Had to Be You and as we danced, we both sang the song very quietly. At the end of the number, the orchestra played it again and we stayed on the floor. I whispered to Ginger, "Everybody in this room is looking at me,"

Quick as a flash, Ginger replied laughingly, "They might just be looking at me, honey."

The two weeks we spent together were so fantastic that I was downhearted when it was time for Ginger and her party to disembark. We had already exchanged addresses and telephone numbers and before she left the ship, she made me promise to keep in touch. She told me that she had a spare room at The Thunderbirds Country Club in Palm Springs and that we would always be welcome there.

Roy, Colin and I were also leaving the ship – just for one day, as some friends had invited us to join them. I explained to Ginger that I had to leave her to join the other two and our L.A. friends who were waiting at the dockside. However, she insisted that I wait with her until her luggage had been checked by customs. Then, she linked her arm through mine and we walked down the gangway, laughing together. She was wearing a large picture hat and an expensive designer outfit. I felt like singing *If They Could See Me Now* and was quite disappointed that none of our friends had the presence of mind to take a photograph of the two of us. Then Ginger kissed and hugged me, much to the amazement of my friends, as they stared wide-eyed in wonder.

Ginger and I corresponded regularly. She wrote from New York, Buenos Aries, Los Angeles, Palm Springs and Oregon among other places, and all her letters contained such endearments as *My Darling* and *My Dearest*. We also met quite frequently and she telephoned on a regular basis. I remember one amusing incident when she rang early one morning when we were at home in The Chantry and asked to speak to me.

"Who's calling, may I ask?" inquired our receptionist.

"Ginger Rogers."

The girl thought it was a joke and replied, "Oh, yes? Well, Fred Astaire's still in bed! Shall I call him or can the call wait? Now, what's your real name, love?"

"Ginger Rogers," came back the reply in icy tones.

"Oh, bloody hell, I believe you are! Hold on. I'll get him for you – Jackie, I mean."

Ginger happened to live just a stone's throw from our friend Ruby Keeler and, on the numerous occasions we visited Palm Springs, we seemed to spend a lot of time walking from one house to the other. Ruby hated it when we went to Ginger's house and vice versa. If truth be known, each of these ladies was a little jealous of any time we spent with the other and often vied for our attention.

On one occasion, when Roy and I were staying with Ruby for a week, Ginger telephoned to invite us to dinner and asked us to invite Ruby too. Ruby quickly 'remembered' that she had made plans for us every day except Wednesday (which she knew was Ginger's

Christian Science Church night). She also knew that Ginger, a devout member of this church, never missed a church meeting. Ginger then came up with the idea that we could all enjoy an early dinner at her favourite Mexican restaurant and then she could go on to church. She asked me if I would like to accompany her to church and I quite readily agreed. Ruby was growing more and more furious and tried her best to make us cancel the meal. When this failed, she rang Ginger to tell her that she couldn't possibly leave her Sonny Boy or her niece Patti Porada or even her maid Mary Agnes at home and go out without them!

"That's no problem. Bring them along too," replied Ginger. "The more, the merrier. Perhaps you would all like to come to my church too."

"No thank you," replied Ruby rather curtly. "We have our own church."

It was arranged that we should all meet Ginger at the restaurant but at the last minute, Ginger insisted that I should travel with her in her traffic-stopping green and white Cadillac.

Before I left for Ginger's house, Ruby, an inveterate smoker, said quite casually, "I don't think Ginger smokes, does she?"

"No, she hates smoke," I replied, "and she doesn't approve of alcohol either, so do me a favour, Ruby, and don't smoke during the meal, please."

Of course, I might have been speaking to a brick wall for all the notice Ruby took of my request. No sooner had we all sat down, with me placed strategically between these two stars, than Ruby lit up a cigarette, stretched across me and drawled, "Ginger, you don't mind if I smoke, do you?" Ginger just smiled politely. Then, to annoy Ginger even further, Ruby, who rarely drank alcohol, summoned the waitress to our table. "I'd like a double scotch, please," she said and added for devilment, "and one for my friend Jackie here."

"Not for me, thank you," I quickly replied, out of respect for Ginger. And for this, I received a sharp kick under the table from Ruby and the word "coward" whispered into my ear.

As I wasn't familiar with Mexican food, I chose the same dish as Ginger – chilli con carne and a large coca-cola. Ginger urged me to hurry with the meal as she didn't want us to be late so I had to down the hot dish in record time. Then Ginger took my arm and announced to the table, "Sorry, my dears, but Jackie and I must dash. Are you sure you don't want to come with us?"

"No thank you," replied Ruby quickly, "Roy and I are going dancing. We're all set for a FUN night out."

As we walked to Ginger's car, I chuckled to myself, believing, quite mistakenly as it happened, that Ruby had thought on her feet and that the mention of a fun night out was just to provoke Ginger. I hadn't been in the car very long when the beans from the chilli con carne and the coca-cola began to have an adverse effect on my stomach, which swelled alarmingly as it started to fill with wind. I felt as though it was going to explode there and then. What increased my embarrassment was the fact that the journey to the church seemed to take forever. I was praying that I would not disgrace myself, particularly when the car travelled for another half-hour over very bumpy roads. Ginger had no idea of the agony I was going through and chatted merrily.

"Is there a toilet in the church, Ginger?" I asked desperately as we finally emerged from the car.

"Yes, just inside the main entrance."

"You go into church. I'll be with you shortly," I said. With that, I dashed into the toilet and passed the loudest burst of wind I have ever experienced. I felt that everyone in the church must have heard the noise!

When I finally took my seat next to her, Ginger whispered, "I'm sure that you must feel better after that, honey." It was clear that everyone had heard me!

All in all, that night was quite a memorable one. I have some treasured photographs of us all taken in the restaurant. These are the only pictures of Ruby and Ginger together, apart from when they both appeared in the film *42nd Street* in 1933.

Another vivid memory I have was when Ginger invited Ruby to dine at her house, together with Roy, Colin, myself and some other guests. She and Roberta had gone to great lengths to make this an unforgettable meal. I remember the setting well – a beautifully laid table with roses as centrepiece, set out on the patio beside her swimming pool. Ginger had written and arranged the place cards – Roy on one side of her and me on the other. Before the meal, alcohol was replaced by exotic fruit drinks and the conversation flowed easily among the guests.

While Ginger was in the kitchen and the others were chatting on the patio, Violet, Ginger's Christian Science practitioner, took me to one side and said that she would like to speak to me privately. Once we were alone, Violet took my hands and said quietly and unexpectedly, "Jackie, why don't you ask Ginger to marry you?"

I could hardly believe my ears. "Oh, Violet," I replied laughingly, "what a thing to ask!"

"I'm serious, Jackie. I know for a fact that Ginger loves you. I have been her friend for a very long time and I've never seen her as happy as when she is with you."

"Violet," I protested, "Ginger is an international star and who am I? Jackie Toaduff, an ex-coal miner from the north of England."

"That's of no importance," said Violet. "Ginger adores you. You must have realised that."

"But, Violet, there's a big age gap between us," I went on.

"Age doesn't matter. You and Ginger together will be eternally young, I know."

At this point, Ginger appeared on the scene and told us that dinner was ready. The meal, which had been prepared and served by the star herself, was superb.

After coffee had been served, Roberta announced that Ginger would like to run one of her movies and thereupon brought out a large screen, so that we could watch it by the light of the moon. The title of the film was *It Had to Be You*, in which Ginger had starred with Cornel Wilde. It was about a girl who was forever changing her mind as she walked down the aisle to get married. At the end of the first of the two reels, Ruby with a bitchiness which she seemed to reserve only for Ginger, yawned loudly and said, "Oh, good. Does this mean we go home now?" But, of course, we all stayed to watch the second reel.

At the end of the evening, Violet again quietly took me to one side and urged me to ask for Ginger's hand in marriage but I just smiled.

A few days later, when we were all together, Violet persisted in her quest to get me to propose but I closed my eyes and gently shook my head. Ginger caught me doing this and said, "Do you mind letting me in on what's going on between you two, Jackie?"

"It's nothing," I laughed. "I think that Violet's going a little strange in the head."

"Not my Violet," rejoined Ginger. "Now, come on. What's it all about?"

"Well, if you must know, Ginger, she thinks that you and I should get married."

Without batting an eyelid, Ginger smiled and said enthusiastically. "Of course we should. Why not? Why not? Yes, do let's get married. Marry me, Jackie. Ginger *Toaduff* – that sounds perfect."

To me the name sounded so funny that it made me laugh uncontrollably but Colin was quick to remark. "Ginger *Toaduff* isn't as strange as Ginger *Ayres,*" (actor Lew Ayres was the second of Ginger's five husbands), "and what about Ginger *Pepper* (her first husband had been Jack Culpepper) – it's only a name, you know."

I could quite easily have been Ginger's sixth husband but I tactfully turned down her proposal. Admittedly, we were very happy in each other's company but we were worlds apart and I knew enough about her to realise that living with her permanently would certainly not be a bed of roses.

After that incident, Ginger decided that she wanted Roy and me to form an act with her and requested that we should sing all the songs in her key. We did not take her up on her offer and when we later related this to Jack Gilford's wife, Madeline, she laughingly informed us that we had done the right thing. She was well acquainted with Ginger and knew that the star would insist on wearing dresses with very wide sleeves. This would mean that at the end of every number she would stand between us, raising her arms, so that we would be blocked out completely while she basked in all the applause.

Nevertheless, Ginger remained a very close friend and we shared many amusing times. One such incident was when she was rehearsing *Anything Goes* with Sid Caesar in New York. She knew that we were crossing the Atlantic on the *QE2* and suggested that when we arrived in New York, we made our way to the theatre to watch her rehearse and then we could go out to lunch together.

On that particular crossing, Lynda Gloria, the French star of Les Folies Bergères, was with us. On the evening before we docked in New York, Lynda told us that she had received a telephone call from Mrs. Bobbie Conroy, a tall, very attractive ex-Bluebell Girl and wife of our boss, Terry Conroy. Bobbie was meeting Lynda at the dockside and wanted us all to take lunch with her at Sardis. Of course, Roy, Colin and I had already arranged to meet Ginger and had to decline the invitation. Bobbie and Lynda had been friends of ours for years and could not believe that we had turned them down. The morning we docked, they both came to my cabin and said that they would not take no for an answer.

"Sorry, my darlings," I apologised. "We definitely won't be coming to Sardis with you. We have a date with Ginger Rogers."

"Don't lie to us, Jackie," they replied in unison. "Look, it's our treat," went on Bobbie, "and if you don't come with us, we'll be mortally offended and we'll never speak to you again."

For the last time, Roy and I insisted that we were telling the truth, but Bobbie and Lynda retorted, "Balls, all balls!" and stormed off.

We then went to watch Ginger's rehearsal and at the end, she said, "Do you mind if we don't go to a restaurant? I don't think I'm dressed for a public appearance. I know of a delicatessen that will send in the most delicious sandwiches for us, if you agree."

"Oh dear," I said, looking dejected. "Roy has never been to Sardis and I was hoping that we might go there."

"Roy's never been there?" asked an amazed Ginger. "Then, of course we'll go. Roberta, will you book a table for us, please?"

Without more ado, Ginger, Roy, Colin and I were soon on our way to the famous restaurant and as we walked through the door, the first people we saw were Bobbie and Lynda. I cannot begin to describe the looks on their faces when the head waiter greeted Ginger effusively and ushered us to our table. On the way, we passed Bobbie and Lynda and I couldn't resist slapping Bobbie on the back and saying, "Hi, girls."

When we reached our table, Ginger lost no time in reprimanding me. "Jackie, did you pat that young lady on the back just now?"

"Yes, they're old friends of ours. They wouldn't believe that we were meeting you today."

She insisted that I should bring Lynda and Bobbie over to meet her and so I walked smugly to their table and said, "Now then, who was lying? Is that or is that not the one and only Ginger Rogers?"

"She looka like a clown," replied Lynda sullenly in her heavy French accent. "She wears too mucha mascara."

Bobbie agreed. "And I don't like what she is wearing either," she added for good measure.

"She's just come straight out of rehearsals," I explained. "Now would you like to come over and meet her?"

Bobbie looked furious and said in quite a loud voice, "NO, WE WOULDN'T. NOW FUCK OFF."

I couldn't believe her outburst and didn't know how to get out of the situation. Fortunately, Lynda saw my discomfort and came to my rescue. "Come on, Bobbie," she said. "I think I should like to meet the lady."

When I introduced them, Ginger immediately started to converse with them in French.

"Hold on a minute," I protested. "Speak in English. From the looks on your faces, I think that you might be talking about me."

"That's right," replied Ginger, "and right now we're continuing to talk about you, not to you!" And the three of them giggled uncontrollably.

Needless to say, by the end of their conversation, Ginger's charm had won the hearts of Lynda and Bobbie and from that time they became her fans.

Some years later, in 1987, we were on another world cruise on the *SS Rotterdam* when we docked at Singapore. Colin, Roy and I decided to have lunch in the orchid-filled garden restaurant of the Raffles Hotel. As we walked in, the first person I set eyes on was Ginger, looking every inch the glamorous star, again in a magnificent picture hat. She excitedly told us that she would be with us for the next fortnight as she was travelling back to Los Angeles on our ship. She had not told us that she would be coming on board as a celebrity guest as she had wanted to surprise us. She explained that she was regarding the voyage as a holiday as she had only one interview on board; the rest of the time, she was just required to be seen around on the ship. On this occasion, there was no grand entourage – only Roberta and a family friend, producer Paul Becker, whom we had previously met in Los Angeles.

On the ship, I noticed that Ginger was limping but when I asked her if she was having problems with her legs, she replied that there was nothing wrong.

"But, Ginger," I said, "you look as though you're in pain."

"Jackie," she quickly replied, "there's no such thing as pain. We are all God's perfect creations. Now please don't mention it again."

She obviously was in great pain but her Christian Science faith would not let her admit it. Others on board noticed her pronounced limp, but even so, she insisted on dancing with me whenever she could. She and I often joined Gene Barry and his wife Betty in the ship's coffee shop. Gene, of film, TV and Broadway fame, was most entertaining as he had so many show business stories to tell.

After Singapore, our next stop was Hong Kong, where I lost no time in visiting my favourite tailor there.   Stephen Lo, whose excellent shop was in the basement of the Sheraton Hotel in Kowloon, had made several suits, jackets and shirts for us in the past and he charged me very little, as I always recommended him to passengers who admired our clothes.   On every visit, Stephen insisted on taking us out to restaurants and expensive nightclubs.

While I was at Stephen's, Ginger had been looking for me so that we could go out together.   Colin, knowing how much I liked shopping in Hong Kong, told her that I could be away for hours! He offered to show her some of the sights he knew so well and she agreed. They sailed on the Star Ferry (second class) to Hong Kong Island, where Colin photographed her on a rickshaw and then they went on to enjoy lunch at the Floating Restaurant in Aberdeen Harbour.   After that, Colin took her for her first ride ever on a double-decker tram – which was quite a novelty for her.   She thoroughly enjoyed that day, especially as she had not travelled like an 'ordinary' person for years.

The next day, she came with me to meet Stephen at his shop where she ordered no fewer than thirty different coloured silk blouses to be made in her favourite style. She also ordered a blazer and many other items, all of which Stephen promised to deliver personally to Palm Springs.

One evening, Ginger took all of us to the Spring Deer in Kowloon, a wonderful Chinese restaurant recommended by Stephen. We were the only foreigners in the packed room and the feverish noise of high-pitched voices coming from every quarter added to the enjoyment. It was there, I recall, that Ginger patiently taught me how to use chopsticks.

After Hong Kong, we sailed to Los Angeles, where we had to bid farewell to Ginger as we had arranged to spend a few days with our friend, Opal Wise, who wanted us to stay in her penthouse apartment in Marina Del Rey. It was during our stay there that Gene Barry and his wife invited Opal, Colin, Roy and me to an excellent dinner at his home in Beverly Hills.

Because of our very busy schedule, I did not see Ginger again until 1993, when I was attending the American Cinema Awards at the Beverley Wilshire Hotel in Los Angeles. On this occasion, I was escorting a new friend, the Oscar-winning film actress, Margaret O'Brien. How shocked Margaret and I were to see what had happened to Ginger! She was now in a wheelchair and had gained a tremendous amount of weight. In the past, she had always kept herself fit and active – not only with her dancing but also by playing tennis strenuously, swimming daily and cycling on a regular basis. I must add that Ginger was at the same time an incurable chocoholic, who also loved ice-cream, ice-cream sodas and Kentucky Fried Chicken, so now that she was wheelchair-bound, it was understandable that she should have piled on the weight. Nevertheless, she still looked glamorous and when I joined her table for a little while, I felt quite proud to be in the company of both Ginger and June Haver, who had starred with Betty Grable in *The Dolly Sisters*.

At the table that Margaret and I had been allocated, we were seated with Kirk Douglas, Esther Williams, Maureen O'Sullivan and Johnny Sheffield. Maureen and Johnny had played Jane and Boy in the Johnny Weismuller Tarzan films.

My final meeting with Ginger was in December 1994 at *The Night of Two Hundred Stars* at the Dominion Theatre and later at the Hyde Park Hilton where, along with Sir Anthony Hopkins, Sir John Mills and Anthony Quinn, she was being honoured for Distinguished Achievement in Films. As far as I know, this was her last appearance in public. On this occasion, she was accompanied by the ever-faithful Roberta. By now, Ginger was no longer the glamorous, charismatic star I had once known; she looked very tired and in great pain – even though she still insisted on believing that there was no such thing as pain. I was uncontrollably sad when I saw her being hoisted on to the stage in her wheel chair. I wondered why on earth they had not let her keep her dignity and allowed her to be wheeled on from the wings.

Just four months later, on the 25th April 1995, Ginger died at her home at the Rancho Mirage in Palm Springs. Roberta telephoned to break the news to us before the media announced her death to the world. For years, friends had begged her to seek medical attention but she refused because of her religious convictions. I personally had always felt that she had needed nothing more than a hip-replacement.

So now, this talented, dazzling star had died. She, who had danced cheek to cheek with Fred Astaire, who had enjoyed close relationships with Cary Grant, George Gershwin, James Stewart and Howard Hughes in addition to her five husbands, had actually danced with me too. And not only that - I shall always cherish the thought that the great Ginger Rogers had loved me sufficiently to consider me as possible husband number six.

The way she wore her hats
The way she sipped her tea,
The memories of all that
They can't take that away from me,
No, they can't take that away from me.

27

My Good Friend,
Margaret O'Brien

I have often been asked who was the nicest or the friendliest of all the stars I have met. This is a difficult to answer because most of the big stars were very pleasant; in fact, I always found that the more famous the star, the more pleasant he or she was.

However, certain names stand out as being particularly friendly and the gifted actress Margaret O'Brien is well up on my list. In my opinion, she was without doubt the most talented child star since Shirley Temple. Margaret made her screen debut at the age of four, when she appeared with Judy Garland and Mickey Rooney in *Babes on Broadway*, and in 1942, aged just five, she signed with MGM and went on to appear in a string of first-class movies, including *Little Women, Jane Eyre,* and The *Secret Garden*. It has been well documented how fans wept at her performance when she stole scenes from Judy Garland in *Meet me in St. Louis* – indeed, she received a special Oscar for her outstanding contribution to that film, as she was only seven years old.

It has to be said that nobody in the film business could cry like Margaret! Once, when a famous director asked her to cry in a scene, she asked him quite innocently, "Do you want the tears to stop half-way down my face or all the way down?"

She and I were once chatting about how she and June Allyson were known as the 'town cryers' because they both seemed to have to shed tears in all of their films. I mentioned that I had read that, in order for her to weep uncontrollably on set, someone just had to tell her that her pet dog had died.

"Oh, no," she replied. "My mother would never have allowed that."

The truth was, she explained to me, that if she was told that June Allyson was on another sound stage, crying more effectively than herself, she could really turn on the water-works to full effect. She also admitted that, in *The Canterville Ghost*, she cried effusively because she had been told that her co-star, Charles Laughton, seemed to be stealing the scene from her.

Since the 1960s, Margaret has been less involved in films but she has remained very busy with work in the theatre and on TV; in fact, I saw her quite recently in a cameo role in *Murder She Wrote*.

She and I have shared many wonderful times together not only on world-cruises, but also in England and in California, where she lives. I have escorted her to several Hollywood events, where she always made sure that I was introduced to as many celebrity guests as possible. She and her agent, Marvin Page, once threw a party for Roy, Colin and me in a house that Marilyn Monroe used to rent. Here we met Donald O'Connor, Roddy McDowell, Cornell Wilde, Robert Cummings, Virginia O'Brien (no relation of Margaret) and many other American film and TV stars. I sometimes think that at that time Margaret was as star struck as I was. When I asked her if she had a favourite actor or actress, she replied without hesitation, "Vivienne Leigh", particularly for her performance in *Waterloo Bridge*. When Margaret was in the studio waiting to appear on set, she used to watch this film repeatedly. She desperately wanted Vivienne's autograph and during one her visits to London as a child, it was arranged for her to watch a stage performance of Caesar and Cleopatra, where Vivienne and Laurence Olivier were playing the leading parts. Margaret thought that Laurence was a brilliant actor and was flattered when she saw him peeping at her from behind the curtain – but all she wanted was to meet Vivienne. Backstage, after the performance, Vivienne signed an autograph for her and Olivier joined them and asked if she would like his autograph too.

"No thank you," replied young Margaret. "I just want Miss Leigh's."

On one occasion, after I had known her for some time, I was asked to escort her to *The Night of Two Hundred Stars* at the Dominion Theatre in London. We were given a suite for four nights at The Hyde Park Hilton. This memorable show was compèred by Tyne Daly, fresh from her starring role in *Gypsy*. Shirley Bassey opened and was followed by an outstandingly talented cast, including Michael Bolton, David Cassidy, Petula Clark, The Four Tops, and Elaine Page, just to mention a few. Hollywood 'Legends' had been invited to this charity event, which had been organised to help Great Ormond Street Hospital. Some members of the public had paid as much as £250 each just for the privilege of being able to see some of the great stars close at hand.

I was particularly honoured as I was not only to escort Margaret, who looked incredibly beautiful that night, but also Virginia Mayo, whose escort was not able to attend the event. We were ushered to our seats in the stalls and I was surprised to find *The Golden Girls'* Bea Arthur sitting in the seat next to mine. She told me that her escort should have been Christopher Biggins, who unfortunately was working on a film for television that evening. He had sent a young stand-in, a BA steward, to be her companion, but she whispered to me that they didn't have much in common. Soon, Bea and I were chatting like long lost friends and she declared that she was not going to leave me – so now I had not one but three glamorous stars to accompany! Margaret saw the funny side of this situation and teased me unmercifully about my attracting women like a magnet.

After the show, the four of us piled into a limousine to be driven to the Hilton for the dinner dance. The only uncomfortable moment was when Bea noticed that Virginia was wearing a full-length mink coat. She was horrified and was about to get out of the car when I reminded her that we were holding up a line of cars.

"OK," she said, "but keep me as far away from that coat as possible."

That evening was an exciting one for me, even though the delightfully humorous Bea, whom I should like to have known better, could not manage to secure a seat at our dining-table. Virginia Mayo spotted Robert Powell, whom she had recently seen playing the part of Jesus and she was so impressed that she asked me to introduce him to her – which I gladly did.

During our stay in London, Margaret and I were enjoying breakfast at the hotel when who should walk in but Zorba the Greek himself, Anthony Quinn. I almost choked on my toast when he approached our table and asked if he could join us. He and Margaret had worked together in the film Heller in Pink Tights and they chatted for ages. Then he turned to me and asked if I was Margaret's husband. Much of his conversation then centred on his new wife and their baby son and the joy they both gave him.

After our London trip, Margaret travelled back with me to Derbyshire to stay at the Chantry. As with all our American visitors, we made sure that she came with us to the Peak District, which is practically on our doorstep. Of course, Margaret loved it but one place she will never forget was Hathersage, where we took her first to view the parish church, in whose cemetery Robin Hood's lieutenant, Little John, is reputedly buried. I was quite excited about taking her to the next place of interest in Hathersage – the Old Vicarage, which is mentioned in Charlotte Bronte's *Jane Eyre* and where Jane actually wrote some of the novel. Margaret was delighted to have the opportunity to see this house, now a bed and breakfast establishment, particularly as I told her that it would be easy for us to have a look inside.

I rang the doorbell. There was no answer. I rang again and the door was opened by a woman who asked, "Are you looking for bed and breakfast?"

"No," I explained, "I have with me Margaret O'Brien, the famous Hollywood star, who appeared in the film Jane Eyre. She is most interested in the connection with this house and the Bronte sisters. I wonder if we might just step inside for a moment, please?"

"No, you can't," the woman answered sharply.

I thought that she was joking so I laughed and said, "We only want to step over the threshold so that Margaret can tell her Hollywood friends that she has actually been inside the house."

"Didn't you hear me correctly?" shouted the woman. "I said YOU CAN'T COME IN!" She then slammed the door in our faces.

I was completely taken aback, as I'm sure that we didn't look like shady characters; Margaret was beautifully dressed and I felt presentable in a good suit and tie. I was embarrassed too as, only minutes before, Margaret had been commenting on how polite and friendly the British were. Then we turned and looked at each other and burst out laughing.

"It doesn't matter. She's probably never heard of me," said Margaret graciously.

""Well, Margaret," I replied, "I doubt that she's ever heard of Charlotte Bronte or Jane Eyre either!"

Margaret has stayed at the Chantry on quite a few occasions, including a visit at Christmas and she always describes the hotel to her friends as being like a small castle. Unfortunately, she now has a fear of flying, and will not travel anywhere by plane. However, we do chat to each other on the phone from time to time and she calls us every New Year's Eve without fail. Yes, Margaret O'Brien has indeed been a good friend for years.

28

Romance at Sea

It was on another world cruise on the *SS Rotterdam* that I enjoyed a shipboard romance with Margaret Whiting, one of America's most distinguished and enduring singers. She was the daughter of the acclaimed songwriter Richard Whiting, whose many hits included *Hurray for Hollywood, The Good Ship Lollipop* (for Shirley Temple) *Louise* (for Maurice Chevalier), *Beyond the Blue Horizon* and *Till We Meet Again*, to name but a few. Margaret, godchild of the great Sophie Tucker, had been brought up like a princess, in a house that was filled with music. Throughout Margaret's childhood, stars, musicians and composers, like Jerome Kern, Ira Gershwin, Frank Loesser and Johnny Mercer gathered at that house, composing round her father's piano.

By the time I met her, Margaret was famous in her own right and had recorded hundreds of songs, receiving Gold Disc awards for songs like *Moonlight in Vermont* and *It might as well be Spring.* Her singing voice impressed me greatly but it was her laughter and infectious sense of humour that drew us together. Like so many others, she found it hard to believe that I had been a miner for eleven years and she loved my stories about Dash, my pit pony. I remember how, one evening, she became quite giddy with mirth when I grabbed a towel trolley outside the dining-room and bent double over it while pushing it along; this was to demonstrate how I used to push coal tubs in the mine.

Later that night, I invited her to join me in a drink at the Lido Bar, even though there had been a warning that the ship was heading into a storm. Already, furniture was beginning to slide about and crew members were starting to secure all furniture that moved and fix ropes for passengers to hold on to as they walked. Everyone except Margaret and I seemed to be hell-bent on returning to their cabins but we were determined to have a nightcap.

When we reached the bar, the barman warned, "It's going to be very rough, Jackie. We've been ordered to close the bar immediately but I'll pour your drinks for you just before we do, if you like."

At that moment, there was a tremendous bang and everything in the bar came crashing down. "Don't bother," I called out. "Come on, Margaret. We'll go to my cabin. I have plenty of drinks there."

As we were already slightly drunk, we had a difficult time navigating the stairs, and, rocking and rolling from side to side, we laughed uncontrollably.

"Don't you ever get sea-sick?" asked Margaret.

"No, never," I boasted. "I was in the worst storm in recorded history when we were on the QE2 and I wasn't affected in the slightest. It's a case of mind over matter."

By this time, Margaret was finding it hard to stand up straight and, while trying to grab a rope, she fell forwards, almost her full length.

"Margaret, we've not far to go," I said. "You're not going to be sick, are you? The storm's really bad now."

"Mind over matter, Jackie," she laughed. "Talk about *Stormy Weather*!"
"Didn't you record that?" I shouted.

"What?" she called. "Oh, Stormy Weather. I honestly can't remember. Did I?"

At that point we both fell.

When we reached my cabin, we rolled inside. I gave her a kiss and told her to sit on my bed while I searched for a bottle of champagne. At that moment, the ship rose and sank. I fell and bumped my head. I stood up and the ship rolled again and again. I was beginning to feel very ill. Then Margaret fell to the floor and so I pulled her up and on to the bed.

"Where were we?" she laughed and then she saw my face. "Oh, Jackie, you look ashen."

"I'm fine. I was just about to make love to you."

"That's right – but first I need the bathroom."

With that, we both stumbled into the bathroom and were sick simultaneously. We spent the rest of the night throwing up, then apologising and laughing. Margaret reminded me of a bleary-eyed Buster Keaton and she thought that I looked as if I had been on a two-week binge. So that, alas, put an end to our romantic evening – for that night at least.

After she left the ship, we kept in touch and when we were in California, she arranged for us to perform there. The theatre was very down-market and, in normal circumstances, Roy and I would have avoided performing there – but Margaret had worked hard and gone to great expense to line up some excellent musicians so we couldn't let her down. She herself introduced us to the audience, which mainly consisted of the many fans and friends we had made on the cruise ships. After a successful evening, several of us went on to a trendy disco to finish the night in style. Later, driving me home down Sunset Boulevard, Margaret suddenly turned to me and said, "Jackie, why don't you marry me? You could have a green card then and get work here."

But I did not take her up on her offer as we already had lots of work lined up for us on the ships. We thoroughly enjoyed travelling to exotic locations, working as little or as much as we chose. Added to this, Cunard had just come up with an offer that was too exciting to turn down. As there were so many repeat passengers on the *QE2,* the company wanted us to direct and star in a production show, with outstandingly beautiful showgirls. We requested that Irving Davies should be brought in as our choreographer, and the great Peter Knight was engaged to work on all the musical arrangements. Preparations for this show, *Hooray for Hollywood,* started at rehearsal rooms in London and, within a few days, Terry Conroy of Cunard, rang to inform us that the shipping company now wanted two production shows with us. With limited time to work on both, we called the second show Hello Broadway and we were assured that we could have anything we wanted. Money was no object as far as costumes and music were concerned. Those two shows were so successful that we were asked to put on a third show, which we called *Rhythm of Life.* Thousands of pounds were lavished on these shows and, incidentally, on Roy and me too, as we still had our own song and dance act. In fact, life was so good during that period that I wouldn't have changed it for anyone or anything.

29

Almost Left Behind!

The *QE2* was docked in Cherbourg one day when Rita Morris, a fellow entertainer and friend, wanted to buy some perfume and asked me to accompany her to the Duty Free shop, which was housed in the customs shed. Passengers were informed that only those who were disembarking here could leave the ship, as the stopover was very short. However, as Roy, Colin and I were regular entertainers on this liner, the rules were relaxed for us. We had already arranged to go ashore to say goodbye to Lynda Gloria, who was taking the boat train to her home in Paris, so I readily agreed to call at the Duty free with Rita.

I went round to her cabin, only to find her gazing in disgust at something in the bottom of her wardrobe.

"Just look," she said. "These Y-fronts must belong to Alan Stewart and he's obviously been using them as a shoe rag."

I suddenly had the idea of playing a practical joke on Lynda, who was always teasing me. "Rita, could you give me an envelope? I'll put the pants in and hand them to Lynda, telling her that she's left them in her cabin."

Roy and Colin thought it was a stupid idea but Rita and I found it amusing. When we found Lynda on the train, she was engaged in conversation with a very elegant Frenchwoman. Her face lit up when she saw us. I handed her the envelope but she was reluctant to take it, as she was sure that she had packed all her belongings.

I persisted and hinted that it might be a present from me. Thereupon, she smiled with delight but when she opened the envelope and pulled out the pants, she screamed at me, "Jackie Toaduff, you're a horrible creature."

Rita and I were laughing at the joke when Lynda suddenly dropped a bombshell. "Well, my darlings, I think I'm going to have the last laugh. I can see that your ship is sailing!"

Panic-stricken, the four of us rushed to the dockside, only to watch the *QE2* gliding away. Captain Lawrence Portet, who was on the bridge, spotted us through his binoculars and immediately sent a message that a tender would pick us up and transport us to the ship. When we reached the *QE2*, a rope ladder was dropped and we were ordered to climb it.

"Lady up first and then you three," was the command.

I have to admit that this was the most frightening experience of my life as I hate heights and, as I looked up the fourteen storeys of the ship, it seemed as high as the Empire State Building.

"Don't look down," we were instructed. "Keep looking up."

We were finally pulled aboard, shaken to the core, only to be met by the furious cruise director, Brian Price. "Come on, Rita." he shouted. "You have a show tonight. And you three bastards, I could willingly have left you in France. Now, go and see the Captain. I hope he fines you."

Luckily, the captain did not take action and I vowed never to miss a ship again. But, within a very short time, I almost did!

Lulu Kirk Edwards, an extremely wealthy relative of the Reynolds Tobacco dynasty, was probably one of the *QE2*'s most frequent passengers. She always insisted on having the same stateroom – cabin 1030. Indeed, because she almost lived on the ship, this cabin contained some of her own furniture and had the best-stocked bar on board. She held an open house in her stateroom every Sunday morning for the captain and his senior officers and other invited guests. Roy, Colin and I were always invited too, and there we met many prominent people, as Lulu's eccentricity seemed to attract all the rich and famous.

One Sunday morning, after I had been interviewing Ruby Keeler, Lulu asked me to bring Ruby along with me to her open house.

On that same voyage, the Malaysian King and Queen, His Royal Highness the Sultan of Selangor and Her Royal Highness the Tengku Ampuan of Selangor were travelling with HRH Prince Sulaiman Shah, his Chief of Protocol and a retinue of courtiers. The young Prince and Chief of Protocol were always to be seen around the ship and we had often been invited to join the two of them for drinks in the bar. However, I had never seen his parents – until that Sunday morning when I escorted Ruby to Lulu's cabin.

As we reached Lulu's open door, a very ordinary-looking couple arrived at the same time. This small, rather portly pair were about to enter in front of us but Ruby was finding it difficult to walk, even with her stick   As far as I was concerned, Ruby was a celebrity and this man and woman were certainly not going to walk into the cabin before she did.

"Excuse me," I said rather brusquely to the couple, "Do you mind?"

Ruby and I walked in and were immediately collared by Lulu.

"Ruby," she enthused, "I loved your interview this morning. It's an honour to have you here. And, Jackie, it's always a pleasure to see you."

She turned then to greet the next guests and when I heard her say, "Your Majesties," I swung round, only to see her taking the deepest curtsey to the couple to whom I had been quite rude.

"Oh, God, Ruby," I whispered. "What have I done?"

"Apologise to them, now," advised Ruby.

Taking a deep breath, I began to tell them how sorry I was when the King said, "No apologies are necessary. I would gladly stand aside for that lady any day."

I ventured a weak joke. "Then you're not going to have me beheaded?" I asked.

The King chortled with laughter. "Of course not. And to prove I'm not offended, I shall invite you and your friends to a party at the Palace when our family disembark at Selangor."

His equerry jotted down our names and cabin numbers and sure enough, we all received the promised invitations.

When we reached Selangor, the Royal Family disembarked by a special gangway and we were among the 150 invited guests who followed, walking down the longest red carpet I have ever seen. As far as the eye could see, this carpet was flanked on either side by a guard of honour of lovely girls, dressed in beautiful brocade dresses and carrying golden tree branches so as to make an archway for us. At the end of the carpet, we found a fleet of limousines waiting to drive us to the magnificent Royal Palace.

Once inside, guests were allowed to roam around freely, even taking photographs if they so desired. The King and Queen, who were now looking far more grand than they had on that Sunday morning, posed for photographs with everyone..

When the Prince saw me, he said, "Jackie, I want you to sit with me during lunch – and what a gourmet feast it turned out to be. While we ate, three different groups of musicians played for us and girls in exotic costumes and elaborate head-dresses performed graceful dances.

"I'm truly impressed," I said to the Prince, "and to think that you live here in all this splendour every day."

"Oh, I don't live here," he explained. "The Palace is only used on special occasions and for visiting dignitaries. Jackie, why don't you stay behind when the others go back to the ship? I'll show you where I live."

And so it was that the Prince invited the captain's secretary, Lynn Waring and me to look around first his father's Palace and then one belonging to another family member. He proudly showed us some of his treasures, including the most impressive collection of model aeroplanes I have ever seen.

I suddenly realised that time was passing and asked the Prince how far we were away from the dockside, as our ship was due to set sail shortly.

"Don't worry about that," he replied. "You must let me entertain you both this evening. I'll fly you in my private plane to Singapore, your next port of call."

Lynn's eyes lit up but I had to refuse the invitation as I was performing on the ship that evening. The Prince was sad but arranged for us to be transported back to the *QE2* at great speed in a 4-wheel drive car, bearing the Royal Standard flag and we were escorted by a motorcade. We rushed through those Malaysian streets, with all the people saluting us as we passed.

"Now we know what it's like to be a royal," smiled Lynn.

When we reached the docks, that red carpet was still there. Hundreds of passengers were at the ship's rails to watch it leave and they all saw Lynn and me jump from the car at top speed. The gangway had gone and the only way of boarding the ship was through the hatch at the end of the red carpet. Everyone cheered and applauded us as we raced down the carpet and reached the hatch just seconds before it was closed. All the time we had been speeding along, first in the car and then along the carpet, I had been nervously thinking of a good enough excuse in case we missed the ship.

"Well, you see, it was the Prince's fault..." I could hear myself explaining.

30

Name Dropping

We always felt that we were enjoying a privileged lifestyle on the cruise ships, travelling first-class all over the world. The entertaining was never too demanding, apart from when we worked on the Royal Viking liners, when David de Havilland, their cruise director at the time, insisted that all artists should take part in the different shows he produced. This meant that every few days we were called on to learn the whole score for a potted version of a Broadway show, regardless of the part each person was playing. It was quite hard work learning for example every song from *My Fair Lady*, followed by all the lyrics of *Fiddler on the Roof* a few days later. Nevertheless, the experience was fun. I particularly recall the occasion when I was cast as the eleven-year-old Patrick in *Mame*. I had to wear short trousers and a schoolboy's cap and adopt a young boy's voice. My Auntie Mame was played by Pearl Carr, whose husband, Teddy Johnson, was also in each production. It seemed quite strange to us that I was about ten years older than the girl who played my nanny, but the lighting and make-up were so effective that the audience accepted everything.

Life was certainly fun in those days and during my twenty years on the cruise ships, I met so many famous people that my story would not be complete if I did not mention my encounters with some of them

It was during the time when we were working on the one of the Royal Viking liners that I met the famous author Irving Stone and his wife Jean. They became friends and fans, with Irving giving Roy and myself copies of two of his books. In mine, *The Agony and the Ecstasy,* he wrote:

> *To Roy and Jackie,*
> *Two of the finest professionals I have ever seen on stage*
> *Warmly,*
> *Irving Stone at sea*

Another author whom we befriended on that line was Cole Lesley, Noel Coward's secretary for many years. Roy and I received two of the first copies of Cole's book *The Life of Noel Coward* – straight from the printers. Cole was on the ship with Noel's best friend, Grahame Payne, together with Merle Oberon and her husband, actor Robert Woldens. Merle, who has often been described as one of the most beautiful women of her generation, was certainly living up to that glamorous image when we met her. After she had seen our show, she and her travelling companions came to our dressing-room to congratulate us and to invite us to drink champagne with them. It was a convivial evening and both Roy and I were flattered to be told how much Noel would have enjoyed our act. After that evening, Merle became our constant companion on the ship and invited us to her home on Malibu Beach.

One day, while we were chatting, I mentioned that we worked mainly on the *QE2*.

"Oh, not that horrible ship!" she exclaimed.

Puzzled, I asked, "When did you sail on her, Merle?"

"I haven't been on the *QE2* and I never will," she replied. "Some friends of mine sailed on her from New York and hated every minute on board."

"Well, Merle," I said, "I don't agree with them and I'd like you to see this grand ship for yourself. I'd love to prove to you just how wrong you are. She will be docking alongside our liner in Naples in a few days. If you haven't made any other plans, I'll try to arrange a visit for all of us to go on board."

Merle and Robert agreed and so I cabled Peter Jackson, the captain of the *QE2* at that time and we were given permission to board. Needless to say, from the minute Merle set foot on the famous liner, she fell in love with it and soon after that, she became a celebrity lecturer on it. She later wrote to thank me for introducing her to the shipping company.

We were entertaining on the cruise ship The Cunard Princess, when Opal Wise, one of the passengers and a longstanding friend, invited me to lunch in St Thomas, one of the Virgin Islands. During our conversation, Ginger's name came up and, unbeknown to us, two men at a nearby table had been listening to our comments. As they were leaving, they stopped by our table and apologised for eavesdropping, explaining that they were friends of Ginger Rogers.

"She's stayed at my house here on the island on several occasions," said one of them. "Sorry we have to dash now but, if you are still here next Friday, we'd love you to come to lunch and have a longer chat."

"Unfortunately, Opal flies home to California tomorrow," I replied, "and Friday is my last day on the island before I fly home to England."

"That's no problem," he said. "We'll pick you up at the dockside."

And so, on the Friday, I was driven up to a breathtakingly beautiful house on a hillside; in fact, it looked more like a castle than a house, with an American flag proudly flying above its roof.

After we had swapped several Ginger stories, the owner of the house asked, "Did you notice the gatehouse as you drove in?"

When I told him that I had seen it, He asked me if I had ever heard of Veronica Lake.

"Oh, yes. *The girl with the peek-a-boo hairstyle,*" I quoted. "I especially liked her in those films she made with Alan Ladd."

He then went on to tell me a few sad stories about the latter part of Veronica's life. "She rented that gatehouse from me but she spent more time in this house," he concluded. "In fact, you happen to be sitting on her ashes."

"What!" I gasped, springing up from the chair where I had been sitting and, sure enough, there was a box.

"Why are they here?" I inquired.

"We're holding them until it's decided where they are to be scattered. Veronica loved Magens Bay here on the island and, on several occasions, she had been heard to say that she would like her remains to be disposed of there. However, some of her relatives want her to be flown back to America and so she remains here for the time being."

I eyed the casket and thought to myself, "Talk about sitting in the hot seat!"

In my youth, my favourite recording stars were undoubtedly *The Andrews Sisters,* Patty, Maxene and LaVerne, whose records sold over ninety million. I remember playing their records over and over again and, if they made guest appearances in any of the films I saw, I would make several visits to the cinema just to watch the scenes where they sang. I saved every penny I could just to see them in person when they appeared at the London Palladium in the early 1950s. Although I wasn't able to go backstage to meet them, I wrote to them and received a signed photograph.

Unfortunately, the eldest sister, LaVerne, died of cancer at an early age; after this, the other two sisters branched out as solo performers. I first met Maxene when we were both performing on the *QE2.* Offstage, she was a very friendly and jolly person but on the stage she lacked confidence and always seemed nervous. Colin was quite shocked when she confided in him that she felt intimidated by Roy and me. She had watched our show the night before she had to perform and felt that it was far superior to her act. Perhaps the trouble was that her act had not been very well planned, as it wasn't until she had sung a couple of the Andrew Sisters' well-known hits that the audience began to take any real interest.

Patty, on the other hand, was confidence personified. She and her husband, the pianist Wally Weschler, had created a spectacular act. From the moment they stepped on stage, Patty was in full command and held her audiences spellbound. It was almost as if the three sisters were actually singing. I first heard her in a Los Angeles theatre on an occasion when I was escorting Ruby Keeler to a Film Award presentation. After Patty's spectacular performance that night, I was so much in awe of her that all I could manage to say to her when we were introduced was, "You were great."

Some time later, when we all happened to be working together on one of the *SS Rotterdam*'s world cruises, I became friendly with Patty and Wally. We spent many happy hours together and have kept in touch ever since. Our first Christmas cards every year come from them – always with a handwritten letter telling us what they have been doing and looking forward to visiting us if they come to England.

The Metropolitan opera star Patrice Munsell also entertained on the liners with us at various times. On one memorable occasion, Patrice, who had sung with Pavorotti and appeared in a couple of films, including the title role in The Great Nellie Melba, arrived to perform on the *Sagafjord* - minus her luggage! All her cases had been left behind in New York. It was fortunate that, like us, she always carried her musical arrangements in her hand luggage. She improvised by buying some colourful scarves on the ship and enlisted my help in utilising them. I suggested that she could borrow some of my jackets and my white tuxedo. Even without her own costumes, she was able to present a very glamorous image onstage. She was a great favourite with the audience and when she laughingly told them of her predicament, she publicly credited me with being the owner of her stylish wardrobe. One thing is for sure – she looked far better in my clothes than I did!

One day, I was standing in queue at Barclays bank on the *QE2* when who should join the line but Rod Stewart and Britt Eckland.

"Hi," greeted Rod. "We enjoyed your show last night."

"We liked it a lot," added Britt. "As a matter of fact, we saw it twice."

"Well, once and a half," corrected Rod. "Two nights ago, we were returning to our suite when we passed the ballroom where you were performing. The show was in full swing and looked so good that we sat and watched it until the end. We liked it so much that we came again last night and we were the two who started your standing ovation. It was an excellent show. Congratulations."

Another couple, Robert Wagner and Natalie Wood, once married then divorced, also enjoyed our performance so much that they invited us to join them for drinks. While we were together, they argued with each other constantly and I had a feeling that even the 'divorced' relationship was rather rocky. How surprised I was, therefore, to learn a short time after our meeting that they had remarried!

The star of the film *Patton*, who refused the chance to collect an Oscar for Best Actor, was George C. Scott, a very tall, imposing-looking man. Whenever I spoke to him on board, I always addressed him as *Mr. Scott,* as he bore himself so royally, even though he always asked me to call him George.

It was at a cocktail party that I addressed him formally for the last time. When I insisted on calling him Mr. Scott, He placed his huge hands on my shoulders and said in a very deep voice, "Young man, if you call me that again, I'll have no option but to pick you up and drop you overboard."

"All right, George, I get the message," I replied. "I daren't risk it because I can't swim very well!"

One day, as Roy, Colin and I waiting to board the *QE2* in Honolulu, in readiness for another world cruise, we caught sight of the veteran film actor, Ben Lyon, coming down the gangplank with his wife, Marion Nixon.   He was perhaps most famous for his starring role with Jean Harlow in *Hell's Angels.*

We chatted for a few minutes and he said, "I think I know who you are – the famous Toaduffs! We've heard so much about you from our friends, Irving Stone and his wife, who are eagerly awaiting your arrival on the ship. They're arranging a cocktail party for you so that we can all get to know each other. Marion and I going ashore for the day now but we'll see you at the party, if not before. By the way, if you have nothing better to do at 11 o'clock tomorrow morning, I'd love you to come and hear my talk in the theatre. I'll be speaking about my long-running radio show, *Life with the Lyons* and about my career in movies. I'll also be talking about how, when I was a talent director at 20th Century Fox, I discovered Marilyn Monroe. I think you'll find it interesting."

"We wouldn't miss it for the world," we replied.

Next morning, Roy was up early, looking forward to Ben's talk. I was a little slower getting ready and arranged to meet Roy in the theatre.

A short while later, I made my way to the venue, only to be met by a sad-faced Roy. "We won't be seeing Ben after all," he said. "He died in the night of a heart attack – and his cabin was next to ours!"

During an Atlantic crossing on the *QE2*, Hermione Gingold came to our dressing-room to chat to us one night. I reminded her of the time we had appeared together on the television show *Guess my Story* and she laughed heartily when I mentioned how I had offered her a Woodbine cigarette, athough I am quite sure that she had forgotten all about the incident. She and Colin had a long chat about Maurice Chevalier, with whom she had starred in the film *Gigi*.

During one of our trips, another star of *Gigi,* the French actor Louis Jordan and his beautiful wife Kiki sat at the table next to ours in the dining-room. How they delighted in teasing us! Almost every night, at least two or three passengers – usually older women – would find an excuse to stop by our table, ostensibly to speak to Roy or me but really to get a closer look at the very handsome Louis.

Kiki often used to see them approaching. "Look out, Jackie," she would joke. "Another ravishing beauty is coming to get you."

After each woman left, Louis would tease, "What a heart-throb you are, Jackie. You know how to attract all the best-looking girls!"

On one occasion, Louis challenged me to a game of table-tennis. I quickly declined as I was a hopeless player but Colin, who was quite good at the game, offered to take my place, only to be trounced by the French star.

One day, Louis was telling me how his neighbour in Los Angeles, Michael Caine, had often cooked wonderful Yorkshire pudding and roast beef Sunday lunches for them. How surprised he was when he heard me reply, "Well, Louis, you'll never believe this but we've cooked for Michael on many occasions at our hotel. He, his daughter Nikki and his ex-wife, the actress Patricia Haynes used to be our next-door neighbours in Derbyshire."

When Vincent Price, master of all those horror movies joined the *QE2* on one of our cruises, his wife, the Shakespearean actress Coral Browne arrived with a stomach bug and spent most of her time on board in bed.

We found that Vincent, who had regularly played the frightening villain in films such as The House of Wax, was just the opposite in real life. He was very friendly and with a highly-developed sense of humour. One day, when I asked how Coral was feeling, he replied, "Oh, she's still in bed and can't even think about food. I've just been to see her. The room was in total darkness when I entered, apart from a small light in the bathroom. 'Who's there?' she called out. 'It's your beloved husband,' I replied, 'and I've brought you a present.' 'Oh, thank you, darling. What is it?' 'It's a copy of the *QE2* Cookbook.' 'Oh, fuck off, you idiot,' she laughed. Although she was famous for playing sophisticated upper-crust parts on stage, Coral was apparently well known in the business for her choice vocabulary when the occasion called for it!

Three ladies who were perfect table companions were the world-famous concert pianist Dame Moura Lympany, Lady Penelope Sitwell and Mary Roblee Henry, who was travel editor for Vogue magazine and wife of the French diplomat, Paul Henry. When we first became acquainted with these three women, who were travelling together, I was afraid that they might be rather dull and difficult to make conversation with. How wrong I was! Roy, Colin and I loved being in their company and Lady Penelope even persuaded Colin to dance with her – quite an achievement, as Colin is no dancer.

Dame Moura was a close friend of the Conservative leader, Edward Heath and she told us how the press had seized on their friendship and linked their names romantically, even though they were just platonic companions. She confided that she was never sure which outfits to wear for her concerts, explaining that Edward had once criticised her for donning a black gown in a concert she gave for him. She then asked our advice about what she should wear for the two concerts she was to give on board.

She had a repertoire of over forty concertos and when she told us what she had chosen to play on the ship, Roy, a great lover of classical musical, gently warned her not to make the same mistake as other classical musicians who had played on board.

"You must remember that you are on a cruise ship, not in a concert hall," he advised her. "We've seen so many artists lose their audiences because their choice of music has been too highbrow."

Moura was very grateful for Roy's suggestion and played the more popular classics at her recitals, both of which were a resounding success.

Another memorable table companion was the wife of John Mills, Mary Hayley Bell. Mary was quite a character and offended two American women by criticising the USA over some current issue. The women insisted that Lady Mary should be moved from our table. Laughingly, she changed tables and was heard to remark later that I was the only person she missed at the table, as she loved my sense of humour.

We also became great friends with John Craven and his wife Madeline and with the great bandleader Joe Loss and his wife Mildred, who was one of my favourite dance partners. One night, John and I were enjoying a few drinks and listening to Joe Loss's music when Joe's band started to play a Jolson medley. Simultaneously, John and I decided to sing. Joe heard us and insisted that we came up on to the stage to sing. Everybody said that they loved our duet but it was an act never to be repeated. Joe's regular singers all kept their jobs!

Sally Ann Howes, the musical comedy star came to see us on one of the nights when we received several standing ovations. "I loved the show," she said. "You sang all my favourite songs. The only trouble was that I became very tired with all the standing up and sitting down I had to do."

Indeed, it was amazing just how many celebrities who saw us on stage went out of their way to compliment us. Can you imagine how proud Roy was when Oscar Hammerstein's wife, Dorothy, wrote to us after seeing our Broadway Show, mentioning that she had never heard *Ol' Man River* sung better – and Oscar, if you remember, was the writer of that song.

It was on the Greek liner, *The Danaie*, where I met the Hollywood actress, Barbara Stanwyck. She was enjoying a Black Sea cruise with the columnist Shirley Edar. I stepped into a lift and, behind me, I heard the unmistakable voice of the famous star. I turned round and said nervously, "Hello. I can't believe I'm lucky enough to be standing next to you. I've seen all your films…"

"Name six of them!" interrupted Shirley.

Without any hesitation, I began to reel them off.

"Oh, please don't go on," laughed Barbara. "I believe you."

We all got out of the lift on the same floor and while we were chatting, I told them that I was entertaining on the liner. They asked me to let them know when I was next appearing so that they could come and see our show.

It so happened that our table in the dining room was quite close to theirs and so a few days later I walked up to them while they were enjoying lunch and said, "Tonight's the night."

"Yes," smiled Barbara. "We know. We'll be there but I must warn you that we'll be sitting near the exit as I have a back problem and so we'll probably have to leave before the end."

They came that night and they sat through the whole show – back pain or no back pain! The next morning, they spotted us on deck.

"Hello, Roy; hello, Jackie," they called out as they made their way towards us. "We thought your show was marvellous and we'll certainly come and see you again – with seats near the front next time."

Barbara told us that, the night before our show, she and Shirley had been special guests of the captain at a Gala Greek dinner, where the crew had performed a Greek Folk show.

"We were so bored," she admitted, "but we couldn't move away for fear of offending the captain. To tell you the truth, that's why we asked for seats at the back of your show – just in case yours was boring as well."

After that, we met them daily and during one of our chats, I asked Barbara when she was going to write her autobiography..

"Never!" she declared. "If I wrote my story, I would have to tell the truth – and too many people would be hurt."

While we were in Odessa in the Ukraine, Roy and I joined Barbara and Shirley in booking tickets for the famous Russian Circus. When we arrived, we were separated from the two women. We thought that this was because Barbara and Shirley, as celebrities, would be given special seats. But no – we were the ones who were given the privileged ringside seats. As Roy and I were entertainers on board, we were classed as workers and honoured. The two women were ushered up some stairs and had to sit on stone seats, far behind us. Halfway through the show, Barbara and Shirley walked out and lodged strong complaints – not about their uncomfortable seats but about the cruelty that the horses had to endure.

A few days later, the star and her friend left the ship and one of the cruise company directors came to see us. "Thank you for all these excellent shows you are putting on," he said. "You certainly impressed Barbara Stanwyck. She made several complaints about our ship but, according to the remarks in the Comments form, she was highly delighted with your act. It was about the only part of the cruise she enjoyed."

He later let me have a Photostat copy of her comments but with all the complaints blanked out.

Larry Hagman, that nasty J.R. Ewing from *Dallas*, was possibly one of the friendliest stars we ever met on the cruise ships. He was quite eccentric in many ways. When he walked on deck, he was always immaculately dressed and wore a Stetson. On meeting a group of passengers, he would frequently nod to them and doff this hat in such a way that 100-dollar bills would fall from it like confetti. Of course, the passengers always dashed to pick them up – only to find that they were not authentic, for a grinning J.R.'s face had replaced the President's head.

I witnessed another of his eccentricities one Sunday morning when I was walking past the theatre bar. Larry was sitting at the bar with his wife, who was engaged in conversation with an elderly couple.

"Morning, Larry," I called out.

He gave me a big smile and gestured me to join them all for a drink.

"Are you still enjoying your trip?" I asked him.

Larry nodded and gave me the thumbs up sign.

His mother, the great Mary Martin, had recently been involved in a car accident with the film actress Janet Gaynor. "How's your mother?" I asked politely.

Again, he just nodded and put up his thumbs, not uttering a word.

We clinked glasses and after I had wished him good health, he smiled and nodded.
"When do you leave the ship?" I asked.

With that, Larry reached over and tapped his wife on the shoulder.

"Oh, hello," she smiled. "Have you asked Larry a question? He NEVER speaks on a Sunday, you know, so you'll have to ask me and, if I can't answer it, he'll write his reply on paper for you. He always rests his voice on this day each week."

I enjoyed many a chat with him on days other than Sundays, but we were constantly interrupted by passengers who wanted autographs. He had endless patience, answering questions and posing for photographs, and when I asked him if he ever tired of constantly being in the spotlight, he replied, "No, Jackie. I'm making the most of my popularity while it lasts. Stardom can be very short-lived and people quickly forget you if you are off the screen for too long. Most viewers won't have a clue who I am in a year or two."

The South African heart surgeon, Christian Barnard, who made medical history when he carried out the first heart transplant operation, was a regular cruise passenger. We became quite friendly and he often confessed to me that secretly he was a frustrated singer. He told me that he often had a strong desire to join Roy and me when we were on the stage.

Late one night, after he had imbibed a drink or two in the nightclub, he went over to the trio who were playing and told them that he'd like to sing. Within a minute or two, he realised that he wasn't making a very good job of it and, when he spotted me sitting there listening to him, he called out, "Jackie, come up here and help me."

There were not many people in the bar, so we sang *Sari Moray*, a South African folk song and included some of the words in the native language. The passengers in the bar shouted for more so I turned to Christian and said, "Come on, Doctor. Now let's sing one we all know and without more ado, we belted out, quite appropriately, *Heart of my Heart*.

Those two tough guys of the screen, James Cagney and Pat O'Brien, were sailing on the *QE2* from New York to England to make the film *Ragtime*. Travelling with them were their wives of fifty years and a manager, Mrs. Marge Zimmerman.

James had recently recovered from a stroke and he and his party, remained in their adjoining staterooms, eating all their meals there and rarely venturing out. One evening, Mrs. Zimmerman rang to ask the night steward to bring a drink to help her to sleep.

"It's rather early to be going to bed, isn't it, madam?" asked the steward very politely.

"I suppose so," she replied, "but there's really nothing better to do here, is there?"

"Why don't you go down and watch the *Roy and Jackie Toaduff Show?*" he suggested. "They're very popular entertainers on board and I'm sure you'd like them."

She agreed to give us a try and later that night we were quite excited when the steward rang us to tell us that Cagney's manager had loved our show and that she wanted Cagney and O'Brien to meet us. She then spoke to us, telling us how delighted she was that the show was to be repeated the next evening and asked us to reserve seats for their party.

We felt that performing before these two Hollywood Greats was almost like a Command Performance and I was quite nervous about singing and dancing *Yankee Doodle Dandy,* in honour of Cagney. I needn't have worried, however, as the cruise staff who were watching told me that the great man had applauded enthusiastically during this number. We were hoping that they might come backstage after the show but, in fact, they made a speedy exit as we were taking bows.

We were surprised, therefore, the next morning when Mrs. Zimmerman rang to tell us that James and Pat would like to meet us immediately, if we could spare the time. Of course we went along to their cabins and really enjoyed chatting with them. During the course of the conversation, they invited us to dine with them in the Queen's Grill.

"Oh, we'd love to," I said, "but it's a rule on ship that no staff or entertainers are allowed to eat there."

"Just leave that to us," replied James.

I double-checked with the maître d' before we went down, as we didn't want to be turned away at the door. He reassured me that all the arrangements had been made.

The meal was a great success, with the conversation flowing easily. The main topic, of course, was films. I mentioned to James that, although I had thoroughly enjoyed his performance in Yankee Doodle Dandy, in which he won a well-deserved Oscar for his portrayal of George M. Cohan, my personal favourite was his role in *Love Me or Leave Me*. At the mention of this, his eyes moistened and he said that this was the only film he'd worked on which had not required one word of the script to be altered. He was very sad that Doris Day had not received an Oscar for Best Actress in that film.

They all spoke about the film they were on their way to England to make. Although Ragtime was set in New York at the turn of the century, it would be cheaper to shoot it in England than Hollywood.

At one point during the meal, Pat turned to James, saying, "Tell me, Jimmy, did you die a coward in *Angels with Dirty Faces*?"

With that, the two of them began acting out a scene from that film, especially for us – a party piece they had obviously presented on numerous other occasions because they were word perfect.

Just before the end of this memorable meal, we noticed that the ship's photographer was going from table to table taking shots of the passengers. When he reached our table, Mrs. Zimmerman said, "No photos, please."

Pat interrupted with the words, "Oh, Marge, just this once. I'm sure that Jackie and Roy would like us all to be photographed together."

The photo was taken – the only one of them on that ship – and is one that we display with great pride in the Chantry.

Before they disembarked, Mrs. Zimmerman took me on one side. "Look, Jackie," she said. "I want you to give me some photographs of yourself. A musical is in the process of being written about James and you could be considered for playing the part of the man himself."

I didn't think for one moment that I stood a chance of being selected but her remarks certainly boosted my ego; incidentally, I don't believe that this musical ever materialised.

Unfortunately, I was never able to meet one of my idols, the inimitable Fred Astaire, but I did become friends with his lovely daughter Ava and her talented artist husband, Richard McKenzie. One night, after a performance of our *Hollywood* show, it was such a beautiful moon that I decided to walk on deck before going to bed. Quite a number of passengers were also enjoying the fresh sea breeze that night and it was there that I spoke to Richard for the first time.

"Didn't I see you in the show tonight?" he asked when we came face to face.

When I nodded, he continued, "It was wonderful. I particularly liked the Fred-Ginger segment."

273

"I like that part too, "I agreed. "You see, Ginger Rogers is a friend of mine."

"I know Ginger too," he replied and then astounded me by saying that he was Fred's son-in-law. "Look, my wife's on board and I know she'd love to meet you. Could you and Roy join us for a drink in the midships bar at mid-day tomorrow?"

When we met Ava, both Roy and I were bowled over by her class and charm and, after that first get-together, we met every day and night for the rest of the voyage.

One night, we were all enjoying the music in the Q4 nightclub, when I invited Ava to dance with me.

"I'd rather not, if you don't mind, Jackie," she replied. "I can't dance. Sadly, I've inherited none of my father's skill."
However, I wasn't going to take no for an answer as I was determined to dance with the famous Fred Astaire's daughter. "I remember seeing a photograph of you dancing with your father," I told her, "so come on, Ava."

She agreed and laughed nervously as we moved on to the small dance floor. As I took Fred's most feminine and fragrant daughter in my arms, she whispered, "I really am the world's worse dancer, Jackie."

I felt that she was like a precious, fragile china doll in my arms. In spite of her protestations, Ava certainly was not the world's worst dancer but I'm sure that she will not mind if I mention that she has not quite inherited Fred's expertise on the dance floor.

I have kept in close contact with Ava and Richard since that cruise and have stayed with them at their beautiful home in Southern Ireland. There I discovered that, although dancing was not one of her talents, she had and still has many more to compensate. Not only is she a creative gardener, a fisherwoman, a cordon bleu cook and an expert photographer, she is also the successful author of *At Home in Ireland: Cooking and Entertaining with Ava Astaire McKenzie*.

We last met when she hosted a star-studded tribute to her father at the London Palladium and we are hoping that they will stay with us at our hotel in the not too distant future.

In the course of our many years at sea, we met hundreds more stars, celebrities and interesting people and, although it has not been possible in the scope of this book to mention them, we still spend many a contented hour reminiscing about different passengers who helped to enrich our lives during that period.

And it wasn't just the passengers who have made our time on the sea so memorable. I also miss the happy times I shared with fellow artists on the various cruises. Samantha Jones, Lynda Gloria, Bobby Crush, Bert Weedon, Bernie Clifton, Alan Stewart and Judie Abbott were regular entertainers on the ships and they all did their fair share of helping to fill our lives with joy.

31

Everything's Coming up Roses

Thus, our idyllic life cruising round the world went on and on, and it never entered my head that it would all have to end one day. However, one night, when we were relaxing in our stateroom after an exceptionally well-received performance, Roy dropped a bombshell.

"I've had enough," he announced. "I feel as though I've been on a merry-go-round for far too long and now it's time to get off. We're away from England so often and I really miss my family. It's time for me to go home and stay there."

I was well and truly taken aback by this but I did not protest too much as I thought that it might be just a passing phase of homesickness from which he would quickly recover. But no! A few days later, when Cunard asked us to extend our contract and sail into Nova Scotia, Roy refused point-blank. I tried my hardest to persuade him to change his mind, but to no avail. He suggested that I might go solo but we had been a double act for so many years that I could not consider this.

"No, Roy, "I told him, "Colin, you and I are like the three musketeers. One without the other two would never be the same."

And so it came about that we retired from show business, although I was very reluctant at the time, as I have to admit that I loved our lives on the high seas.

After our retirement, we turned down several tempting offers to headline the odd show. However – and this is quite ironic, considering that we had never achieved national fame during our working lives - we were invited to appear on television on two occasions. The first was when Michael Barrymore's wife, Cheryl, offered to give us the top spot on the award-winning television show *Barrymore,* which at the time was attracting 11 million viewers every Saturday night. Of course, we were sceptical at first, as both Roy and I were out of practice and we knew that Michael enjoyed making fun of his guests on this show, with his merciless leg-pulling. We didn't want to be laughing-stocks and so we refused twice but finally, Cheryl managed to persuade us that this would not be the case.

"Michael really wants you to appear, with twenty minutes in the top-spot," she said. "You can't turn it down. There's not a pro in the business who wouldn't give a right arm for this opportunity. You can choose your own material, as long as you agree to perform a number with Michael. He wants you and he, together with 50 specially selected clog-dancers to end the programme with a great clog-dancing finale. The show will be recorded and we can cut out anything you're unhappy with."

We eventually agreed and the show was a tremendous success. Afterwards we were inundated with telephone calls from viewers and celebrities and were constantly stopped in the street. We were even contacted by agents, who had presumed that we were dead! They offered us work but we were not to be tempted.

A few months later, a BBC2 crew filmed us in our garden at the Chantry. We spoke about our past life in show business and sang *Everything's Coming up Roses*. After this show was televised, we were again approached by agents but we turned down all their offers.

Looking back, I now realise that Roy's decision was for the best as we have thoroughly enjoyed our new career as full-time hoteliers. Colin's business acumen has ensured that our lives have been comfortable while Roy has found a new passion in growing roses and transforming our grounds into a wonderful garden that has won numerous prestigious prizes. And I, of course, have been in my element as mine host, for our small hotel attracts so many interesting people and show business friends. In fact, we couldn't be happier these days, dividing our time between our home in Derbyshire and our beautiful sea-view apartment overlooking the Mediterranean on the Costa del Sol.

I know that fortune has smiled on me throughout life and my only regret has been that my mother, Sarah, died without ever admitting to me that she was proud of my determination to struggle out of the darkness of the pit and achieve success in the world of entertainment. My sister Norma, however, assures me that although my mother found it difficult to praise me to my face, she was actually delighted with how my life turned out and often boasted about me to the point of embarrassment. I'm pleased about that.

Life hasn't always been a bed of roses, but if I could live my life over and know what I know now I wouldn't want to change much. I've had an extraordinary life and have been blessed with good health and great friends with no regrets. I feel at times I have to pinch myself to think of the journey I've had from running around in bare feet in the back streets of Stanley, Co Durham, to Royal Palaces, Hollywood homes and magnificent mansions the world over. I've wined and dined, danced and romanced with Royalty and the rich and famous and befriended people whom I admired as a lad never dreaming they would become my friends.

Life is always interesting, I never get bored even doing nothing. I sit back and reminisce of my life's roundabout that goes so fast and of the many things I've taken for granted. I think of the very special people, some who are no longer with me in person but remain in my heart forever, especially our manager, Colin Edwardes, who died 5 years ago but whose presence I feel every day and Nora Sutton, who encouraged me to keep writing this book and corrected my spelling and grammar. Tragically Nora died just recently of a brain tumour. Ruby Keeler and Ginger Rogers were special and not a day goes by without some memory of them flashes through my mind.

Life goes on and exciting things keep happening, this week for instance I've been teaching some of my more intricate clog dancing steps to Simon Rice, formerly a distinguished soloist with The Royal Ballet, for him to pass on to a class of young, up and coming, Billy Elliott's, and I've been asked via Simon to teach a class of his young students at the Royal Ballet School at White Lodge in Richmond Park, Surrey (which I believe was the birth place of the Duke of Windsor).

Ava Astaire's daughter recently spent her birthday with us (and was nearly trampelled to death by a startled horse in the middle of the village!) We had Joe Louis Barrow Jr stay for a couple of nights, a real gentleman if ever I met one; he is of course the son of the famous Joe Louis, Heavy Weight Boxing Champion of the World 1937 to 1949.

Laughter they say is the best medicine. I'm glad to say I inherited my Mothers sense of humour; she loved to make people laugh as I do and I'm always listening for new jokes. Having as neighbours funny men, Bobby Dennis, a real mad hatter, who even at the age of 82 still has audiences rolling in the aisles and Bernie Clifton, the multi-talented comedian entertainer, perhaps best known for his antics on his wild ostrich. The other day Bernie invited Bobby and ourselves to his farmhouse for breakfast. He cooked the full English with all the trimmings himself which took nearly 3 hours and resulted in the best breakfast I've ever eaten because of all the laughter. There's never a dull moment with the likes of them around, better than a Bottle of Medicine I say.

Last year Roy and I took a trip around the world visiting places we like the best and to meet up again with friends we have kept in touch with over the years. We also enjoyed a nostalgic farewell reunion trip on the *QE2* before it left our shores forever. We met some of the beautiful girls who worked with us in our shows on the great ship. It was a pleasure to see them all again after all these years, now all of them happily married and still looking glamorous, again laughing with tears of laughter at some of the antics we got up to.

Next week my old pal, John McGee, who worked with me all those years ago in the coalmines, is coming to visit for a few days.

He helps me keep my feet firmly on the ground and not get carried away by all the high life and privileges that I've enjoyed throughout my life; it was he of course who helped change my life forever by insisting I enter that talent show, in Blackpool, all those years ago. Thanks John.

In the entrance of our hotel we have a collection of photographs of Roy and myself with movie star friends, among them a photograph of me dancing with Princess Margaret. A customer told Stuart Hammond, my friend and manager of the Chantry, that she had just returned from London and whilst she was there visited Kensington Palace. She said that she had paid to view HRH private quarters, and in her living room was that very picture of me with the Princess.

I found it hard to believe that she would have that framed and in her room, so I phoned Kensington Palace to check on the story. After describing it, they were delighted that I was able to inform them who I was and of the venue where the picture was taken, Cecil Sharp House, Regents Park Road, London. They also invited me to be their guest at the palace so I spent a lovely, interesting day there and they also gave me a nice enlargement of that special photo. I was very saddened with the death of the Princess, who had been so warm and kindly to me each time we met. It hurt me to read the unkind things some of her, so called, friends said of her after she had gone. However, the Princess and the Miner, I like to think, were true friends.

I am pleased to say that I have been lucky enough to visit every region of the world and I'm often asked which is my favourite place on earth. It's a difficult question for me to answer because I love it all but I know I'm happy wherever I am, and I'm happiest at whatever place I'm in at the moment. I love my life and look forward to every new day. I'd like to sum up now with the words of The Gerry Herman song from the musical show La Cage Aux Folles "The Best of Times Is Now, As For Tomorrow, Well Who Knows, Who Knows, Who Knows."